ISBN 0-87666-298-X

Library of Congress
Catalogue Card No. 55–6489

© 1967

Copyright 1960, © 1964
Copyright, 1955, © 1957, by
T.F.H. PUBLICATIONS, INC.
Lithographed in the United States

VOLKER vom ZOLLGRENZSCHUTZ-HAUS, SchH. III
German Youth Sieger: 1958
German Sieger: 1959 and 1960
World Sieger

"Nobly, fascinatingly beautiful,
wrapped in the glory of his
many victories . . ."

NEW REVISED EDITION

•

this is the

GERMAN
SHEPHERD

by

CAPT. WM. GOLDBECKER

and

ERNEST H. HART

•

REVISIONS BY
ERNEST H. HART

ILLUSTRATED BY ERNEST H. HART

Distributed in the U.S.A. by T.F.H. Publications, Inc., 211 West Sylvania Avenue, P.O. Box 27, Neptune City, N.J. 07753; in England by T.F.H. (Gt. Britain) Ltd., 13 Nutley Lane, Reigate, Surrey; in Canada to the book store and library trade by Clarke, Irwin & Company, Clarwin House, 791 St. Clair Avenue West, Toronto 10, Ontario; in Canada to the pet trade by Rolf C. Hagen Ltd., 3225 Sartelon Street, Montreal 382, Quebec; in Southeast Asia by Y.W. Ong, 9 Lorong 36 Geylang, Singapore 14; in Australia and the south Pacific by Pet Imports Pty. Ltd., P.O. Box 149, Brookvale 2100, N.S.W., Australia. Published by T.F.H. Publications Inc. Ltd., The British Crown Colony of Hong Kong.

*. . . for the mate shall stand
beside the man and aid him
in his endeavor.*

**to
our
wives**

CONTENTS

Photo Credits

C.M. Cooke & Son, England, Three Lions, Inc., William Brown, Stephen Klein, Herr Münch, Joan Ludwig, Rudy Reinker, Lundquist, Dr. Alexander Mehlman, Charles Kaman, and Ernest H. and Katharine Hart.

The cover painting is a portrait of Condor v. Sixtberg, SchH. II, AD. done by his owner, E. H. Hart.

FOREWORD

Writing this book has not been an easy task. You who read it and, we hope, enjoy and benefit from it, can have no idea of the tremendous accumulation of data amassed, read, sifted, and selected. Nor can you conceive of the immense amount of correspondence required to trace particular facts that had been hidden behind the veil of time, both at home and abroad. Hours, days, weeks, months of discussion, study, and critical appraisal to separate the wheat from the chaff and true fact from mere opinion.

Perhaps the hardest task of all was to be completely objective, for over the years we, too, had accumulated our own opinions and foibles in regard to the many facets of Shepherd dog breeding, behavior, and keeping. It was difficult, in many instances, to resist coloring or embellishing fact from experience, yet experience in knowing hands has its own value and has been employed where it paralleled fact.

We appreciate the fact that man has never before placed so much trust in learning as in our time. In this book we have attempted to convey to you certain aspects of this particular specialty that we and others have learned and which you will now learn in its reading. Yet we would be other than honest if we did not express here our firm conviction that abilities based on special gifts are not especially accessible to everyone by study alone. We believe that this book will help clarify many things and aid you in attaining a greater sureness in the application of fundamental truths. But we also believe that, though knowledge is basically necessary, the talent for improving—the breeding of consistently top stock—comes under the category of special gifts, belonging in some measure to the arts as well as the sciences and as such, cannot, in the strict sense, be alone acquired by learning.

We have attempted to anticipate your every need, your every question in regard to the breed of your choice, and present the answers in a fashion which you will understand and enjoy reading. We hope that we have made a positive contribution to the meager and often controversial literature dedicated to our breed. We know that some of you will disagree with certain precepts and concepts within these covers which run contrary to your own experience or belief. That is as it should be, for no man is perfect, no book written by man is the complete and end answer, and intelligent argument is ever the basis for new thought, theory, and improvement.

To those of you who have graciously allowed us the privilege of reproducing requested photographs of particular dogs, we offer thanks. Thanks also to our friends in Germany who have given us valuable information and photographs not available here, to Dr. Allan H. Hart for his aid in the chapter on diseases, and to all those learned people listed in our bibliography from whom we have selected and borrowed the results of years of research and accumulated knowledge, to give to you.

No, writing this book has not been an easy task, but we are sure that neither has it been a fruitless one. We have learned much in its writing, and we sincerely hope that you will learn much in its reading.

The work is done, the book is written. Now all that is left is to present it to you and say: This is all we know, this is everything we could find . . . This Is the German Shepherd.

CAPTAIN WILLIAM GOLDBECKER
ERNEST H. HART

Orange, Conn.

Time has passed since this book and the above foreword were written, time rich with experience and new horizons. Several dog generations have also gone by bringing important new animals and their hereditary background into focus, dogs from whom will come the breeding, show and working Shepherds of tomorrow.

There is so much that is new, in canine medicine, genetics, science and other knowledge, and all of it must be reported or I would not feel that I was keeping faith with all of you who trust in this book for objective truth and integrity.

Some of this which you will read for the first time in this revised edition was written in Germany, the fatherland of the breed and the continual source of great dogs and breeding knowledge, some was scripted in other parts of the world through which I passed. And wherever I journeyed I saw German Shepherd dogs, popular in all countries and often working at the side of man, fulfilling their ancient heritage.

In Spain, where I came to rest for a while, I pondered over my gathered data and finished these revisions when I returned to America, where perspective rounded out the picture of a great breed of which we can be proud to be a significant part. What I have added, subtracted or changed here on these pages I think important. I think you, too, will find it so.

Many of the photos of German dogs I myself took at the last several Sieger shows. Others were supplied me through friends in Germany and the Verein für Deutsche Schäferhunde. I want to take this opportunity to thank those friends, people to whom the breeding and training of German Shepherd dogs is not just a hobby, but is a way of life.

ERNEST H. HART

Massachusetts
1966

CHAPTER 1

THE BEGINNING

During almost impossible to grasp eons of time, approximately forty million years, the species canine had been developing on a plastic, forming earth. Long before a curious creature that was to become man crept from the sheltering tree limbs to the floor of the world to seek the path of social consciousness, *Miacis*, a small, climbing, tree-dwelling, carnivorous mammal, that was the common ancestor of both bear and dog, stalked his prey in the verdant forests far beyond prehistory.

Blindly groping with slow, fumbling, unskilled fingers, nature needed thirty million years more to crudely mold the evolutionary clay of this forming species into *Cynodictis*, a creature not yet a dog but moving closer than any mammal before it to the species canine. It would be a mere ten million years more before *Tomarctus*, the prototype dog, would make his appearance on the stage of specie origin and the drama of the true dog would begin to unfold.

Time passed into oblivion as the yeasty stirring of evolving life on earth continued. Nature tested, discarded, kept and fashioned toward specialization. During million-year-long winters continental glaciers came down from the north four times, and four times withdrew again. And those times of intense cold brought drastic changes to the animal life of the planet, eliminating species that could not cope with a shifting environment. Those that survived responded to each new wave of warmth as the terrible ice receded, by multiplying rapidly and, in many instances, increasing in size.

During this same era the mammal, Man, was steadily moving away from his simian beginning toward humanness. Soon, a relative measure of time considering the millenniums that had gone before, the paths of man and dog would converge and they would stand together for over one hundred thousand years and up to the present day.

The tale of those long gone centuries, pieced together from rock stratas by men of science, vision and patience, records the emergence of the prototype dog mentioned earlier, the short-legged predator, *Tomarctus*, who lived fifteen million years ago and was the product of random selection from the same mammalian stock that eventually also produced bears, cats, raccoons, wolves, hyenas and seals. *Tomarctus*, developed to the fullness of his type, was probably the ancestor of the wolf, coyote, jackal, fox and like canine creatures. Also in a direct line of prehistoric descent from *Tomarctus*, and representing the most important cleavage in canine geneology, there appeared during the Miocene era the four prototype

Tomarctus, the prehistoric, short-legged predator who was the prototype dog and whose plastic germplasm produced varied mammalian stock including the species canine.

canine families from which all the known dog breeds evolved. This important quartet consisted of *Canis Familiaris Metris-Optimae*, progenitor of the herding dog breeds, *Canis Familiaris Intermedius*, from which came hunting, hauling and some toy breeds, *Canis Familiaris Leineri*, filial basis of the sight or gaze hounds and terriers, and *Canis Familiaris Inostranzewi*, hereditary basis of the powerful mastiff-type canines and some of the water dogs.

These categories are necessarily broad in concept for many of the popular dog breeds of today are the result of the interlacing and crossing of the genetic qualities of breeds that stemmed originally and purely from the four basic canine types. We are, of course, most interested in Canis Familiaris Metris-Optimae, the fountainhead of the herding breeds, for it was from this line came the ancient Persian Sheepdog whose heredity shaped into crude form all the sheepherding breeds throughout the world, including those that took form in Germany.

The selection that eventually resulted in the segregation of utilitarian canine types was, of course, the product of man's mentality in his changing world. Early in the history of ancient man he and the dog adopted each other. This partnership between man and dog is a natural one, and the reasons for its beginning are as valid today as they were then. Primitive man found in the dog a beast which could be controlled, whose feral instincts could be fashioned to conform to his needs—an animal whose natural talents complemented his own. It was fleet where man was slow; it had a highly developed scenting ability and its auditory sense was many times sharper than man's. The dog found and ran down game for man to kill and eat. It helped fight off the ever-present marauding beasts of prey. In return, man protected his dog from the larger carnivores, gave him shelter and food, and tended to his injuries.

And so a pact was formed between man and dog, a partnership that was to endure from the misty beginnings of time down to the present day. For in the dog man had found more than a hunter; he had found a friend, a companion, and a guardian.

As man progressed out of ignorance into understanding, the time came when his role of hunter no longer suited him. In his wanderings he had found fair land on which he wished to stay and build permanent shelter. But always, to keep the bellies of his family filled, he must travel in the wake of the wild herds. To end this precarious existence, he learned to trap and capture the vagrant food beasts, eliminating the constant need to hunt and ending the deadly periods of starvation that came when the herds disappeared. So began the pastoral age of man; and with this change in man's environment, a new use was born for his dog.

Here we find the real beginning of a specialized breed. An animal evolved which could adapt itself to the herding and protection of its master's flocks, and the earliest Shepherd breed was born. Within these early dogs mutations occurred and, when these sudden changes in heredity made the dog more adaptable to its work, man selected for them. By this natural process all the varied breeds of dogs came into being.

That shepherds and hounds were the earliest specialized breeds known to man is a definite fact. We cannot, however, be any more specific than that; for the truth is that the evolution of the herding dogs which eventually came into focus in Germany as the German Shepherd dog is hidden in the years.

Centuries ago there developed in Germany, as in all countries where grazing animals were herded, several types of Shepherd dog. In the southern mountain regions, where the terrain is irregular and the flocks wander up and down hill in search of fodder, a comparatively heavy dog, compact and sturdy, was evolved. On the northern plains, where the herds travel faster and farther, a small, lithe, long-trotting Shepherd came into being. A long-coated composite of the two strains was produced in central Germany. The conformation of these various dogs differed to suit the changes in terrain, and thus distinct types were formed by environment. Coat length and texture varied widely, from short to wire and long coats. Color was also very varied and included white, cream, brindle, blue, sable, and solid black, as well as the color combinations familiar today. These old colors and coat qualities occasionally appear in modern litters regardless of how carefully we breed. There were four qualities, however, which these basic types possessed in common: ruggedness, intelligence, general soundness, and the ability to do their specialized job well.

At this point in the evolution of our breed advancing civilization took a hand in its fashioning. The fingers of commerce reached into the rural areas for the wool, meat, and milk of the herds. New means of transportation made the world a smaller place. Men came together to discuss herds and weather, crops and prices, and finally, to boast about their dogs. The natural evolutionary processes which had formed a specific breed were then to be aided by some crude attempts at selective breeding. As the herding ability and intelligence of a dog was recognized, his fame would spread throughout the community. Other herders would breed their bitches to him and select from the litter those most resembling their sire, hoping that these puppies would inherit the characteristics that had made the father valuable. When a bitch attained similar fame, her pups were eagerly sought after for the same reasons. Groups were formed, bound together by an interest in dogs and a desire to improve the working ability of their stock. Correspondence with other, similar groups in different parts of the country was carried on, stock was exchanged, records of breeding kept, and gradually, greater structural uniformity was attained.

A particular basic type was found to be the best for the specific work which the Shepherd had been bred for. Again selection took place, this time for type. The several physical types native to the country blended into a rough major type which could work equally well under all conditions. When this goal had been achieved, a herder could select a young, unproven dog from this blended type with the assurance that it would, within reason, mature into a good working Shepherd.

It was in this early stage of the German Shepherd dog's development that one man took the roughly fashioned clay that had become a breed and molded it into the magnificent animal we know today. That man was Rittmeister (Cavalry Captain) Max Emil Friedrich von Stephanitz. It was at the end of the last century, in 1889, that von Stephanitz, later known as "the father of the breed," began his crusade to standardize the Shepherd. It was due to his efforts that the popularity of this little known breed eventually spread beyond its native borders and into all corners of the world.

Together with Artur Meyer, von Stephanitz founded the *Verein für Deutsche Schäferhunde, S.V.* (German Shepherd Dog Club). He became the first president and, in an incredibly short period of time, accomplished a unification of form and a standardization of type which has varied little in essentials to the present day. It is safe to say that this amazing accomplishment could only have been made under some rather unusual circumstances. Von Stephanitz was typical of a class leader prevalent in Germany at that time. To understand completely how one man could have dominated such a large field and have dictated policy to all Shepherd breeders of that day, one must understand a bit of the background of Germany of the time.

Chancellor Bismarck had recently unified the German-speaking peoples by force of military arms. The Hohenzollern monarchy was in the ascendancy under Prussian imperialistic dominance. Militarism was the prime moving factor in German politics at home and abroad. To the great mass of quiet, industrious German people, a uniform had become the badge of authority. They had become used to regimentation and were quick to respond to the voice of authority. Rittmeister Max von Stephanitz made himself the voice of authority for the *Verein für Deutsche Schäferhunde*. The Shepherd breeders obeyed his dictatorial commands in matters pertaining to the breed without question, since this was the pattern to which they had become accustomed. Thus the *Verein* became the guiding hand of the breed, and that hand was the extension of the will of von Stephanitz. Under these circumstances, he was able to shape the breed to his own specifications in an amazingly short period.

The Rittmeister's love for the breed, coupled with a genius for organization, gave rapid growth to the club, and before long his rigid control over the destiny of the German Shepherd dog was absolute. He drew up a standard based on mental stability and utility. Beauty, in itself, was not stressed, but was a natural by-product of this standard. He outlined a program of inbreeding and careful selection that would further enhance and concentrate the great working qualities of the breed. He was judge, breeding master, and breed inspector. Under his unyielding leadership, the *Verein* became the largest breed club in Germany, with more than thirty thousand members and hundreds of allied clubs. It was, in fact, the largest organization devoted to a single breed in the world.

The captain's motto was "Utility and intelligence." To him beauty was secondary, and a dog was worthless in his eyes if it lacked in any slight degree the intelligence, temperament, and structural efficiency that would make it a good servant of man. He realized that an animal of the Shepherd's intelligence, with its highly sensitive nervous system, could degenerate quickly into the extremes of mental instability if bred toward beauty alone and away from its natural skills. He wanted neither cowards nor canine criminals in the ranks of the breed. He demanded strong, sound, dependable animals fit for their role as useful working friends and companions of man.

Von Stephanitz appreciated the fact that his country was becoming increasingly industrial and that the pastoral era in Germany was over. And he knew that this might well result in the decline of the breed he loved so well. So, by unfailing perseverance, and in the face of early refusal and ridicule, he eventually persuaded the authorities to use the German Shepherd dog in various branches of government service.

Throughout his life "the father of the breed" worked mightily in the cause of the Shepherd. He wrote hundreds of pamphlets touching on all phases of the breed. His crowning literary achievement was the mammoth work entitled *The German Shepherd Dog in Word and Picture*—a volume that has been translated into many languages and was for many years the "Bible" of German Shepherd fanciers. Today, with our wider knowledge of genetics, medicine, and animal husbandry, the value of much of this work has been nullified. But we cannot fail to recognize the great value of that which is left.

Herr von Stephanitz died on April 22, 1936, after a lingering illness. He had seen the successful accomplishment of a life's work. The German Shepherd dog as he had visualized it was a breed without peer, and had been accepted as such throughout the world. This dedication of a lifetime in the service of a breed is probably unique in the annals of dogdom.

Horand von Grafrath S.Z. 1
(Hektor Linksrhein)

E.H.HART

CHAPTER 2

THE EARLY BASIC STRAINS

The *Verein für Deutsche Schäferhunde, S.V.*, which was to become the life work of Rittmeister von Stephanitz, came into being suddenly, one might almost say by chance, on April 3, 1899. On this day von Stephanitz and his friend Artur Meyer were in Karlsruhe in western Germany, attending one of the first all-breed shows ever held. As they walked about, critical but dispassionate observers, their attention was caught by a medium-sized yellow-and-gray wolflike dog standing quietly next to his handler. Both men had long been interested in the native Shepherd dogs and had admired their outstanding herding performances in Württemberg, Thuringia, and Saxony, where they had seen the dogs work. But neither had seen before so perfect an example of the best of the Shepherd breed. They examined the animal with mounting excitement. The dog was of the primal canine type, uncorrupted by the influence of man. He was supple and powerful, and evidently possessed great endurance, steadiness, and intelligence. On questioning the handler, they were told that this dog was not a show dog. He was a working sheepherder, and like all of his breed, was born with this ability, requiring no training other than direction and finish to become proficient. This inborn desire and ability to serve mankind belied the animal's wolfish appearance. The dog's name was Hektor Linksrhein.

Von Stephanitz and his friend saw in this animal an answer to their secret desires. Here was the breed which, in their estimation, represented the true native working dog. A breed unspoiled, awaiting the touch of a master's hands to mold the basic clay of its being into enduring beauty.

Then and there, with no previous preparation and with little discussion, they formed the *Verein für Deutsche Schäferhunde, S.V.* Von Stephanitz bought Hektor Linksrhein for his Grafrath Kennels and renamed him Horand von Grafrath. Thus Horand became the first registered German Shepherd Dog, S.Z. 1, and the foundation of a great breed.

In passing, it might be well to mention the fact that another society had been formed eight years earlier to further the development of the native herding dogs. It was called the "Phylax" Society, and was an abortive gesture that swiftly succumbed to its own inertia. It did have value, though, in that it made the breeders conscious of the worth of their stock and more careful in their breeding ventures. The short-lived society also endowed the Shepherd fanciers with an idea of type, so that when Hektor Linksrhein appeared on the scene, his value was appreciated and he was bred to many bitches. He was successively owned by several breeders before von Stephanitz bought him and rechristened him Horand von Grafrath.

By this time you are probably wondering just what this paragon of dogs, Horand von Grafrath, really looked like. His photos certainly do not do him justice. Perhaps the closest we can get to a full appreciation of Horand is by seeing him through the eyes of Captain von Stephanitz, though we must remember that the good captain saw more in this dog than would probably meet our eyes. To his owner he was not just a dog, he was the symbol of a great breed to come. Also, we must not compare him with the finished products of today, but rather evaluate him against the animals of his time.

These are the words von Stephanitz used in describing this basic male. "Horand embodied for the enthusiasts of that time the fulfilment of their fondest dreams. He was big for that period, between 24″ and 24½″, even for the present day a good medium size, with powerful frame, beautiful lines, and a nobly formed head. Clean and sinewy in build, the entire dog was one live wire. His character was on a par with his exterior qualities; marvelous in his obedient fidelity to his master, and above all else, the straightforward nature of a gentleman with a boundless zest for living. Although untrained in puppyhood, nevertheless obedient to the slightest nod when at his master's side; but when left to himself, the maddest rascal, the wildest ruffian and incorrigible provoker of strife. Never idle, always on the go; well disposed to harmless people, but no cringer, mad about children and always in love. What could not have been the accomplishments of such a dog if we, at that time, had only had military or police

Horst v. Boll
(sire)
Munko v. Boll
(dam)
Hella v. Boll

Big, powerful, square, Horst was used more frequently than any other stud dog of his era.

service training? His faults were the failings of his upbringing, never of his stock. He suffered from a superfluity of unemployed energy, for he was in Heaven when someone was occupied with him and was then the most tractable of dogs."

This was the dog destined to shape a breed. It was not an easy undertaking. Consider the variations of type, coat, temperament, and color that existed in the breed of that day. The Thuringian and Frankonian dogs were coarse, wiry, small and stocky, wolf-gray in color, and with prick ears. The dogs of Württemberg were big-boned, large in structure, powerful behind, and swift in gait. Generally, they were phlegmatic and sported lopped or only semierect ears. Von Stephanitz and his associates searched far and wide for dogs, and especially bitches, in which the strains had been blended enough to produce type similar to Horand's. When such bitches were found and it was ascertained that they could produce the wanted type, they were treasured and carefully inbred. One such bitch, Freya von Grafrath, S.Z. 7, was bred to Horand four times.

Under the Rittmeister's critical eye and firm guidance, each litter was ruthlessly culled at birth, and final selection took place at an age when mentality, temperament, and structure could be definitely analyzed. Judicious inbreeding to a selected few and more rigid selection of their offspring then took place. Soon the heterogeneous mass of herding dogs began to shape toward a standard type. Thus, with one male as the fountainhead, a river of utility and beauty gushed forth whose tributaries were destined to flow to all parts of the world.

Horand sired a great many dogs, as you can readily imagine, but the most important of his get was Hektor von Schwaben. Hektor, in turn, sired Beowulf, Heinz von Starkenburg, and Pilot III. Beowulf and Pilot III were brothers out of Thekla I von der Krone, who was by Horand. These three sons of Hektor von Schwaben were the great triumvirate which bore the fruit of the master breeder's seed. Beowulf's particular value was in the bitches he produced, and from him came the line to Geri von Oberklamm and thence to Cito Bergerslust and Attilos Argos. Pilot III, through his grandson Graf Eberhard von Hohen-Esp, was the foundation of the von Boll and Kriminalpolizei strains, with branches to Reidekenburg and Eichenpark, Harras von der Juch, and Mohr Secretainerie. The third and most important dog was Heinz von Starkenburg.

On November 1, 1903, a litter was born to Bella von Starkenburg, sired by Heinz, in which there was a black male puppy. As this pup grew, it became evident that here was a mutant, and he was recognized as such by von Stephanitz and his colleagues. This dog, Roland von Starkenburg, became a model for the breed, for in this one animal a vast genetic improvement had taken place, and he proved to be the only stud of his time

ROLAND von STARKENBURG
Sieger 1906-1907

The black mutant whose genetic qualities did so much to shape the breed. Note, in his pedigree study, the intense inbreeding that gave Roland his marked prepotency.

Heinz v. Starkenburg	Hektor v. Schwaben	Horand v. Grafrath
		Mores Plieningen
	Lucie v. Starkenburg	Pollux
		Prima
Bella v. Starkenburg	Beowulf	Hektor v. Schwaben
		Thekla I v.d. Krone
	Lucie v. Starkenburg	Pollux
		Prima

Tell v. Kriminalpolizei
(sire)

Luchs v. Kalsmunt-Wetzlar
(dam)

Herta v.d. Kriminalpolizei

Considered the best German Shepherd of his day.

who could produce the type von Stephanitz was breeding toward from available bitches. There is no Shepherd dog living today whose breeding does not trace back to Roland.

Roland's pedigree accompanies his portrait and is worthy of study. It is a classic example of the necessary inbreeding involved to purify genetic structure in shaping a breed toward a particular goal.

Roland's best male offspring, Hettel Uckermark, was crowned Sieger in 1909. When bred to Bella von der Leine, Hettel produced Alex von Westfalenheim, who in turn, by Bianka von Riedekenburg (Hettel-Roland-Dewet-Krone breeding), sired the unforgettable International Grand Champion and 1920 Sieger, Erich von Grafenwerth. Meanwhile, other strains had come into being from the same basic stock, the most important being the von Boll, Kriminalpolizei, and Riedekenburg. Study of the basic family lineage chart indicates how each of the older strains branched off from the root stock. Remember, though, that the chart is concerned only with male lines. Since the breeding basis was necessarily extremely narrow at that time, one can assume that the bitches used would cause an intermingling of root inheritance.

But let us get back to Erich von Grafenwerth, for he is of immeasurable importance to modern-day breeders. He was the basic male from whom descended a host of great dogs which led directly to the young hopefuls you have in your kennels today. It is important, then, that we analyze Erich as carefully as hindsight and the records allow.

Structurally he was a grand specimen of the breed. He was noble in appearance, swift and sure in gait. Credit for his structural excellencies cannot be entirely given to his sire, Alex. Both the male lines in the second generation of his pedigree are stopped by Hettel Uckermark, and of im-

19

BASIC SIRE LINES FROM HORAND von GRAFRATH, S.V. I

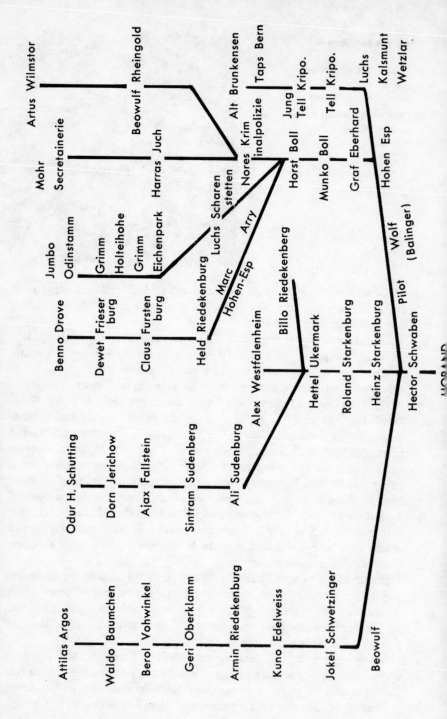

measurable importance is the tail-female line to Flora Berkemeyer, mother and pillar of the Riedekenburg line. This lovely bitch was also a fortuitous mutant whose impact upon the genetic make-up of her line is felt to this day. She gave a beauty of form, an essence of refinement and quality that was mirrored in her grandson Erich.

Erich's double grandsire, Hettel Uckermark, was a dog of stable, sane temperament, yet Erich himself was faulty in this respect, possessing a temperament complex which came through his sire, Alex, and his great-grandsire, Roland. The beautiful Flora was not temperamentally sure, either. This slight unsureness of Erich's led to stricter jurisdiction in temperament tests at shows and breeding surveys and eventually resulted in an S.V. warning against breeding to Alex, and also the importation of Erich to the United States. Erich also possessed a slight wave in his coat which he passed on to his descendants. To this day a wavy coat is alluded to by the older and knowledgeable breeders as an "Erich" coat. Erich was undoubtedly the greatest sire of his era, a dominant stud whose genetic influence was destined to affect generations to come.

Many fine dogs came into the limelight during the 1920's as the branches of the basic stock widened. The value of some is questionable, but most can be found, buried far back, in the pedigrees of the dogs of today. Many of these German-bred dogs began to migrate at that time, finding their way to America and England.

To mention all the early dogs and bitches, cataloguing their merits and faults, would take immense research, many volumes, and be of no great value to us today. In consideration, therefore, of time and space require-ments, we will merely set down a résumé of the attributes of the basic stock.

We find that the major early strains were: Starkenburg (through Roland) —of good pigmentation and finish, but somewhat lacking in mental sure-ness; Uckermark—big, but of good length and with heavy bones (particu-larly through Hettel) and of good, sure temperament; Kriminalpolizei (particularly the young Kriminalpolizei strain)—weak nerves, faded pig-mentation and bad dentition. Regardless of their shortcomings, the animals of this strain were big and handsome and caught the eye. (Nores v.d. Kriminalpolizei was typical of the young Kriminal stock. He passed on all the faults of the strain plus oversize and a tendency toward short tails which he inherited from his mother, Lori v. Brenztal.) Riedekenburg— heavy through Roland, but of good quality and refinement (through Flora), of varied temperament, from good to slight unsureness, Von Boll— a tendency for bigness and squareness but of fine mentality.

A study of the above paragraph gives us a definite indication of what was to follow. The Shepherd, through inbreeding and line-breeding on the

Flora Berkemeyer
(sire)
Harras v. Lippestrand
(dam)
Cilla Distelbruch
Mother of the Riedekenburg strain. Through the "A," "B" and "D" litters Riedekenburg she established her vital worth.

only available lines, concentrated the tallness and squareness. By 1925 the breed as a whole had become too leggy, too high and square, and lacking in the balance and flow of movement which was the structural ideal of von Stephanitz and the German master breeders. Lack of steady temperament was noticed in many instances, and faults of dentition were on the increase. The Rittmeister and his colleagues were not happy about the situation and decided that a drastic step must be taken. They felt entirely ready to take it. Such was the situation in Germany at the beginning of 1925.

Quite naturally, as the breed developed in Germany, the fame of the German Shepherd spread to England and the United States. By the early twenties the breed had many advocates in both countries, and its popularity was on the increase. England seemed to lean heavily toward the older working stock and imported a good many fine animals of the Blasienberg strain. It soon became evident that the fanciers in America,

Ch. Erich v. Grafenwerth
(sire)
Alex v. Westfalenheim
(dam)
Bianka v. Riedekenburg
Sieger 1920—International Grand Champion "Destined to influence generations to come . . ."

Harras v. Glockenbrink
(sire)
Erich v. Glockenbrink
(dam)
Frieda v. Glockenbrink
Excellent in conformation, but
. . . "The Rittmeister regretted
. . ." Sire of Alex v. Ebers-
nacken (Alex-Dachs-Pfeffer)

with few exceptions, desired the finest show stock Germany had produced. They had the necessary money to purchase these animals, and they did. Unfortunately, along with these great dogs they imported were many whom the S.V. had condemned or warned against for the faults which they transmitted.

Specimens of the breed had been brought to this country as early as 1904, but had made no great impression upon the ranks of American dog fanciers. This was still the case in 1913 when Benjamin H. Throop of Pennsylvania, and Miss Anne Tracy of New York, organized the German Shepherd Dog Club of America. The first Shepherd of any importance to come to America was Apollo von Hunenstein, imported in 1914, a dog who had been a top winner on the Continent. In Germany he had been bred to Flora Berkemeyer, a breeding which resulted in the "D" litter— Riedekenburg. He was criticized by German judges as being bitchy and because this fault, plus light pigmentation, was transmitted to his get. However, it is quite possible that this criticism stemmed from a lack of appreciation of a refinement and quality not recognized in those days. Other Americans interested in the breed during this time were: Peter A. B. Widener, of Joselle Kennels; Thomas F. Ryan; Mr. and Mrs. Halstead Yates; Mr. John Gans, whose Hoheluft Kennels were marked for fame; Mrs. Alvin Untermeyer and Mrs. Elliot Dexter, both of whom became important factors in Shepherd affairs on the West Coast.

Then came World War I, and emotionalism swept the German Shepherd dog into eclipse. Anything German became anathema in America to such an extent that books of German writers were burned, German music banned, and the German Shepherd dog, which was just becoming popular, was forgotten. But in many ways the war actually helped to develop a new appreciation of the breed in this country. The German Army had made good use of the canine population during the long and bloody war years, and the Shepherd dog had taken his place as a war dog without peer. Tales were told by returning U.S. fighting men of the prowess of these animals, stories no doubt colored by mankind's gift for exaggeration, particularly where our canine friends are concerned. Some of the returning soldiers brought Shepherds with them, and the intelligence and the striking wolflike appearance of these specimens caught the general fancy of the public.

When the war was over, people turned from the recently passed frenzy and despair and sought entertainment in the nostalgic, simple themes of life. Rin-Tin-Tin and Strongheart (Etzel von Oeringen) flashed across the silver screens of America's theaters. The boy and his dog, a combination guaranteed to pluck the heartstrings; the rescue through raging waters or sky-swept flame; the wounded Shepherd leaving his pitiful trail of blood behind as he crawls to the rescue of his loved ones; the boy saying a last tearful good-bye to his dog accused of being a sheep killer as the hard-hearted posse waits with loaded guns, and all the while we know that it's the mutt on the other farm which the villain owns that is killing the cute little lambs; the dirty villain getting his just deserts as the dog attacks in the snow-swept reaches of Hollywood's north woods, saving his mistress from a fate worse than death; and then the final fade-out with the two pals, boy and dog, together again, and all is right with the world. The old *schmaltz* that the movie makers use so well; the audiences loved it and cried for more and, be assured, they got it.

The popularity of the breed these two stalwart canine actors represented shot skyward. Everyone wanted a dog like Rin-Tin-Tin or Strongheart. Puppy factories flourished under the auspices of greedy canine merchants who turned to the Shepherd to meet a demand and reap their harvest in dollars and cents. What they produced should be forgotten, but it cannot, for these nondescript animals of uncertain temperament which they called "German police dogs," and with which they gutted the American market, were responsible, at least temporarily, for the breed's downfall. Of one thing we can be thankful, those myriad monstrosities have disappeared, gone into limbo where they belong, and no trace of them can be found in the modern-day dog. But the gradual disappearance of these nondescripts and the waning of breed popularity did not occur until a later date than that dealt with in this chapter, so we will drop this unpleasant subject for the moment and take it up again in its proper place.

Earnest breeders, meanwhile, were attempting to lay a firm foundation for the breed in all parts of the world. In Switzerland after the war, Mrs. Harrison Eustis, intrigued by the sagacity of the breed, established her famous Fortunate Fields Kennels, where truly important experiments were conducted for the purpose of establishing a definite working strain of

Shepherds. At Fortunate Fields the approach was completely scientific. Dogs and breedings were studied and analyzed. Complete records were kept of the individual's and the strain's adaptability and mental ability to do certain tasks. Exhaustive research and a tremendous amount of money and time eventually produced Shepherds fit for every branch of canine endeavor in which the breed's physical and mental characteristics made it possible for them to serve. The most widely known usefulness to which they were put was as guide dogs for the blind at the famous Seeing Eye in Morristown, New Jersey.

Amazingly enough, Germany, during and after the war, was still producing great specimens of the breed. Of course Germany had been neither invaded nor devastated during the great struggle, but her economy

Erich v. Glockenbrink, Sch.H.
(sire)
Gundo Isentrud
(dam)
Dolli v. Glockenbrink

Sieger 1926-28. An outstanding show dog of his day, he transmitted the faults as well as the virtues of his heritage.

had nevertheless been wrecked by the long, expensive war years, and monetary inflation was a very real threat to the breeding and feeding of fine dogs. By the early twenties the inflation had reached its height. Germany was impoverished, and the American dollar was worth millions of German marks. This unfortunate circumstance abroad was a fortunate turn of events for wealthy American Shepherd enthusiasts, and is undeniably the underlying reason why German breeders sold the great dogs of that day to American purchasers.

Germany, in 1922, introduced a system of regular breed surveys (*Ankorung*), an impartial criticism of each dog, with an accurate, graded description and recommendation concerning breeding for best results. The basic principle of the survey was to present openly a true genetic and surface picture of the dog, uncolored by the owner's opinion, to stabilize a type and eliminate harmful tendencies and characteristics before they became acute. Soon American fanciers, realizing the tremendous value of such data, formed their own breed survey, but in a modified form that more or less defeated its own purpose. What worked in Germany could never work here, due entirely to the characteristic differences of the inhabitants of the two countries. Not only did the S.V. recommend that certain breeding partners not be used with particular studs when genetic tendencies promised disaster, they insisted that certain breedings not be made, and the German breeders conformed to their edict. In America, no individual or group of individuals is considered so infallible that they can dictate procedure to any other individual or group without having an outsized quarrel on its hands. Under the circumstances the breed survey, as practised in America, had its day and then slid silently into oblivion.

By 1925, earnest breeders in this country were importing, or had already imported, the finest animals in Germany. The great Erich von Grafenwerth had reached our shores, Cito Bergerslust, Harras von der Juch, Roland von Riedekenburg, Iso von Doernerhof, Gerri von Oberklamm (of the wonderful gait), Apollo von Hunenstein, Dolf von Dusternbrook, Alf von Tollensettel, Anni von Humboltspark, and a host of other greats and near-greats. Many other dogs imported were animals the Germans wanted to get rid of. One such was Nores von der Kriminalpolizei, sire of the silver-screen star Strongheart. Because of his son, he was frequently bred to, even though his lack of worth as a breeding animal had been recognized in Germany and he had been barred from further use as a stud. He does appear in the pedigrees of many fine dogs, but their excellence comes in spite of Nores, not because of him, and is due to dominant quality in the germ plasm from other sources.

The sad part of the picture, in those days of bustling activity within the breed, was the complete or partial disregard of great dogs whose genetic worth was shadowed by other, more popularized animals. Had some of these dogs been used with greater frequency and their inherited characteristics concentrated, a rich fund of genetic material might still, to a small degree, shape influence in the dogs of today. Dogs such as Gerri von Oberklamm, eclipsed by his famous son, Cito Bergerslust, at Hoheluft Kennels; Alf von Webbelmanslust, a fine son of the great Klodo; Alrich von Jena-Paradies; Caspar von Hain; Armin von Pasewalk, and many other animals of great potential could have given so much to the breed had they been used well and more frequently. In more recent years a parallel existed in the partial disregard shown such dogs as Dewet von der Starrenburg of Giralda Farms, a son of Odin von Stolzenfels and Othilde von der Starrenburg; and Attilas Argos, by Waldo von Baumchen and Freude von Rich-

Odin v. Stolzenfels, Z.Pr.
(sire)
Curt v. Herzog-Hedan
(dam)
Bella v. Jagdschloss Platte

Sieger 1933. A basic and prepotent stud who sired a host of valuable shepherds.

Ch. Dewet v.d. Starrenburg
(sire)
Odin v. Stolzenfels
(dam)
Othilde v. Starrenburg

"Full advantage was not **taken of his breeding value . . .**"

Ferdl v.d. Secretainerie, Sch.H.
(sire)
Odin v. Stolzenfels
(dam)
Tunte v.d. Secretainerie

Holland Sieger 1936, 1938. Prominent sire in American, English and German breeding.

Bodo v. Brahmenau, HGH, Z.Pr.
(sire)
Donar v. Zuchtgut
(dam)
Fanny v. Neuerburg

A prominent German sire. Sieger 1938 (Japan). "A tendency to produce long coats . . .".

rath—an outcross stud of dark pigmentation and fine temperament who was eclipsed by his more glamorous contemporary, the great Pfeffer. There were other dogs of like worth who might well have given us much that was good had they not been almost overlooked at the time.

By the middle twenties many well-known personalities had taken their places in the ranks of the fanciers of the breed. One need only glance through the pages of the *Shepherd Dog Review* of that time to see familiar names, names seen in the show catalogues of today and recognized by the initiate wherever Shepherds are shown. We had breeding surveys, *angekort* certificates, and the parent club and the New England Shepherd Dog Club were in the midst of a heated controversy. There were more shows, bigger entries, a healthy growth of newcomers flocking to the breed, and

a greater knowledge of the breed amongst earnest fanciers, due primarily to knowledge publicly imparted by such men as Rex Cleveland and Elliot S. Humphrey. The latter gentleman was a veritable fount of information concerning the breed. He is the same E. S. Humphrey who was associated with Mrs. Eustis in the remarkable experiment at Fortunate Fields, and who, with Lucien Warner, wrote of that activity in a valuable book entitled *Working Dogs*. Would that we had a man of his caliber today!

The year 1925 drew to a close with expansion and important activity, the breeders of the day not being conscious that they stood on the threshold of change, or that a new era was about to dawn for the German Shepherd dog.

CHAPTER 3

THE NEW ERA—MODERN PRODUCING STRAINS

August 29, 1925! A red-letter day in the history of the breed. It was the date of the Sieger Show of that year and the beginning of a new era for the German Shepherd dog.

Whispers had been heard of a four-day gathering of breeding masters from all over Germany in Ossig. The meeting had been called by the National President of the *Verein für Deutsche Schäferhunde*, Max von Stephanitz, and was unprecedented in the annals of the breed. The group met behind closed doors, and rumor had it that holding this evidently important and secret meeting on the eve of the Sieger Show was no coincidence. There was much speculation and argument about the effect of this gathering upon the coming show.

Hushed expectancy vied with preparatory activity in the Fest-Halle at Frankfurt Am Main, where the Sieger Show was held. An electrical tenseness pervaded the spacious area, from the benches to the large and shady rings. This, the Sieger Show, was the Mecca for all true lovers of the breed. To this shrine of the Shepherd the lucky few from abroad who could manage it made their annual pilgrimage. Here, each year, a new champion was crowned who would be destined to influence the breed for good or evil in the years to come.

The young-dog classes were judged first. Finally the *Gebrauchshund Klasse* (equivalent to our Open Class) was called. The club president, Max von Stephanitz, stepped into the ring to judge this most important of all classes, the class from which the world's Sieger would be chosen. The dogs and their handlers entered the huge ring, forming in catalogue order, an array of great specimens of the breed, champions of other years, champions of adjacent countries, dogs of greatness and near greatness. Each dog was brought to the center of the ring for individual examination. After this they were separately moved away and then toward the judge, then circled around the edges of the immense ring at a slightly faster trot. During all this procedure the dogs' temperament was severely tested. The preliminary judging went on and on until any animal who showed the slightest taint of some basic fault of structure or temperament had been ruthlessly eliminated. By the end of that first day only the cream of the huge class remained.

On the second day of the show those fortunates who had passed the Rittmeister's severe tests began their seemingly endless trotting around the ring, their handlers walking at approximately one hundred and twenty steps a minute. Certain dogs were singled out and their handlers asked to circle faster so the judge could ascertain if some hidden fault which he suspected might be exhibited under the pressure of a faster pace. Handlers were changed often during the day as the dogs continued their steady, ground-eating trot around the ring. Pails of fresh water from which the dogs could refresh themselves were placed in each inside-ring corner. For more than two hours this continued while more elimination took place.

Finally von Stephanitz motioned a fleet gray dog forward into third place. He signaled again, and the dog moved into second place. With a dramatic gesture the judge swept this dog forward to first place in the line, then halted the class as a murmur swelled and swept through the tightly packed throng of ringsiders. The gray dog was led to the center of the ring by his perspiring but triumphant handler, and Klodo von Boxberg had become the new World's Sieger, destined to begin a new era in the history of the breed.

Sg. and Ch. Klodo v. Boxberg
(sire)
Erich v. Grafenwerth
(dam)
Elfe v. Boxberg
. . . and a new era was born!

Klodo was not an unknown dog. He had been Czechoslovakian Sieger in 1923, but he was a different type from that which had previously won in Germany. Former winners had been high, square dogs, but in Klodo, von Stephanitz had selected a dog of lower station, deeper and longer than his competitors, yet short in loin and back and with a far-reaching and fleeting gait. This gray-and-tan son of the premier sire and show dog, Erich von Grafenwerth, and out of Elfe von Boxberg, was within the required height measurement, beautifully proportioned, magnificent in outline and movement, and firm and fearless in character. He was line-bred on Hettel Uckermark and combined the best of the Uckermark and Kriminalpolizei inheritance.

With the elevation of Klodo to the Sieger title, it became apparent why von Stephanitz had called the meeting of the breed wardens before the show. He had realized the danger inherent in the oversized square dogs prevalent at that time and feared that this trait was threatening to become the standard by which the breed would be judged. He brought this distressing fact to the attention of the breed wardens, and it was agreed by them that drastic measures should be taken without delay to check this departure from the basic standard. The dramatic choice of Klodo von Boxberg as Sieger accomplished this end admirably. The new Sieger was so definitely different in type than those that had gone before him, and he was so prepotent in handling down that type to his get, that the year of the 1925 Sieger Show was from then on known to the Shepherd fancy as the line of demarcation between the "old blood" and the "new blood."*

Klodo von Boxberg sired many great dogs and others of near greatness that were valuable in stud or brood pen. He was undoubtedly the best son of his sire, Erich. One of Klodo's best sons was Curt von Herzog Hedan who in turn sired the great Odin von Stolzenfels. Long coats were occasionally produced by both Curt and Odin, especially when bred to Klodo bitches. This characteristic was further concentrated in Curt von Herzog Hedan's dam, through Roland von Park and Liese von Geusnitz. Curt and Odin are prominent in German pedigrees as they are in ours in America.

The other important son of Klodo, to present-day breeders, was Utz von Haus Schütting. There has been great controversy over the merits of Utz. He triumphed in Germany and then was imported to America. From evaluation and descriptions of knowledgeable persons who saw the dog, we can gather that he was not overly large, on the bench was not impressive, and lacked spirit and nobility. But in the ring he became a different dog, beautifully made structurally and wonderfully balanced in motion.

By the end of the year, Klodo had been purchased and brought to America by A. C. Gilbert, of erector fame. The Sieger was at stud at Mr. Gilbert's Maraldene Kennels in Hamden, Connecticut. On the day

* In the excitement caused by Klodo's win, another triumph was swept aside and, even to this day, forgotten by shepherdists. This was the triumph of the breeding practice of Tobias Ott, whose Seffe von Blasienberg was awarded the Siegerin title while her litter brother, Sultan von Blasienberg, was reserve Sieger to Klodo. Both Seffe and Sultan were home-breds. Sultan later became one of the basic studs used in the valuable Fortunate Fields experiment. Even though he was gunshy, a trait which he passed on to his progeny, he was sound in character in all other respects, had a great willingness to please, trainability and type, and was invaluable in the production of basic stock to further the Fortunate Fields program in which working qualities were paramount.

Donna z. Reuer
(sire)
Falko v. Indetal
(dam)
Donna v. Ludwigskai
Dam of Utz v. Haus Schutting.
Through Donna came a tendency
toward paling pigmentation.

that Klodo arrived at the Maraldene Kennels, a boy of fourteen walked eagerly through the high iron gates of the Gilbert estate toward the kennels, his mind filled with the exhilarating eagerness known only to the enthusiastic young. Today he would see Klodo von Boxberg, the Sieger of Germany, the Shepherd said to be the greatest dog of his breed ever known. A big, richly pigmented dog trotted to the boy and wagged his tail in recognition. The boy petted the dog without lessening his stride toward the wire-enclosed runs, and the dog, Alf von Tollensetal, moved along beside him toward where his trainer and a young man stood before an outside run, watching a gray dog float back and forth. The boy stopped beside them, and in the silence stood with rapt attention centered upon the gray Shepherd. No need to tell him that this was the great Klodo. The trainer's proud glance, the keen-eyed watchfulness of the young man, weighing and evaluating every move of the Sieger, the dog himself, filling the eyes and hearts of the observers as a living creature so near to perfection must always do, were the obvious clues to the gray dog's identity. Presently the boy and the young man looked up at each other and smiled. There must be talk now, for the beauty of this dog would not be completed in the being of the individual unless shared with one of like enthusiasm. They spoke; and the words they spoke then and the words they spoke through the years that followed became a thread of like interest

Utz v. Haus Schutting, Z.Pr.
(sire)
Klodo v. Boxberg
(dam)
Donna z. Reuer
The famous German Sieger who
started a controversy that exists
to this day.

loosely thrown around them. Finally, there came a time when these two people, alas no longer a boy or a young man, came together and the thread, stretching back through the years to the magnificent gray dog, was gathered up and woven bit by bit into a book. The book you are reading, *This Is the German Shepherd*, is that book; the authors are the boy and young man of that long-ago day.

In 1925 and 1926 the Shepherd steadily climbed in popularity, until in America there were 21,596 Shepherds registered out of an all-breed total of 59,496. The breed began to decline from this peak in 1926, until in 1934 only 792 Shepherds were registered. This rapid falling off in popularity was the result of puppy factories run by unscrupulous individuals who climbed on the bandwagon of breed popularity; bad publicity; and stupid breeding practices engaged in by breeders who should have known

Vicki v. Bern, Z.Pr. (sire)
Utz v. Haus Schutting (dam)
Olle v. Bern
Dam of Gockel and Dachs v. Bern. "The dog Germany refused to part with . . ."

better. Yet during all those years of the breed's decline in America, Germany kept producing fine stock, and a nucleus of earnest breeders and fanciers in this country continued to breed small numbers of fine animals from the good stock still available.

The animals of greatest importance to us are Klodo and his sons and daughters, particularly Utz and Curt, Curt's son Odin von Stolzenfels, Odin's son, Ferdl von der Secretainerie, and Harras von Glockenbrink, who stemmed directly from Erich von Grafenwerth. These dogs bulk large in the breeding of our modern-day dogs, and are greatly responsible for the faults and virtues which our present Shepherds possess. A study of the family charts will give the reader a clearer view of relationship.

Unfortunately monorchids were allowed to breed in Germany, the

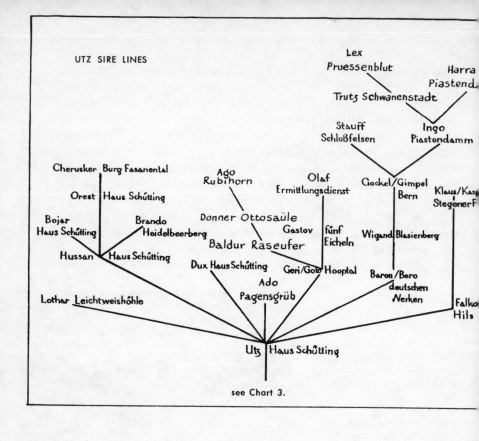

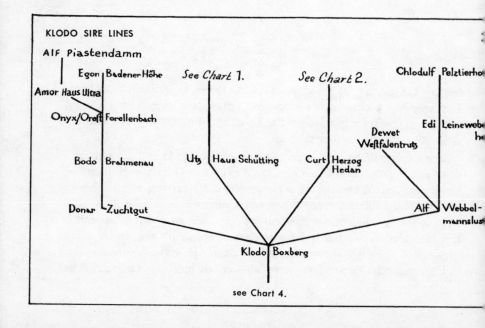

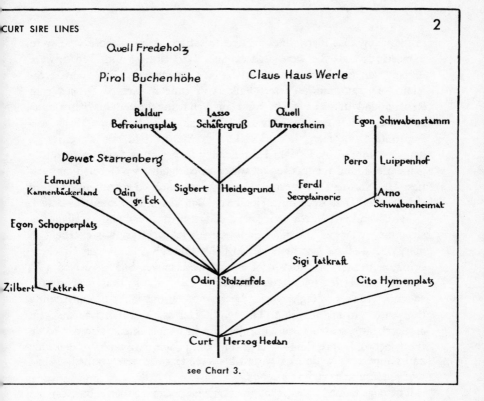

see Chart 3.

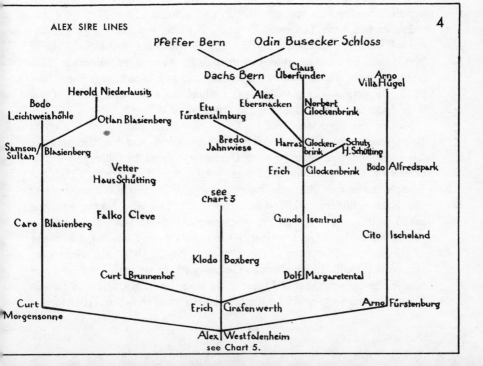

see Chart 5.

result being that many lines carried this trait. Among those who were monorchids and who were used extensively both here and abroad, were Aribert von Saarland, son of Erich von Grafenwerth, Graf von Cleverhamm, Drusus zum Reuerer, Falko von Indetal (sire of Drusus zum Reuerer, and grandsire of Utz von Haus Schütting through his dam Donna zum Reuerer, sister to Drusus). Through Utz then, orchidism was transmitted. In fact, the 1935 German Sieger, Jalk von Pagensgrüb, who was inbred on Utz, had a tendency to pass this fault on to future generations, and for this reason was warned against by German authorities. Utz, through his mother, Donna, also inherited a tendency toward paling color. The lines from Horst von Boll also transmitted this defect.

Ferdl von der Secretainerie was a dog of great finish and excellence in structure, who was not quite tight enough in back, yet was excellent in gait, with a slight lack of power in drive-through. Harras von Glockenbrink, at twenty-two months of age at the Hanover Show received a V, or Excellent, rating under von Stephanitz. Later the Rittmeister regretted awarding Harras so high a rating because of various faults he consistently transmitted to his offspring. The son of Harras, Alex von Ebersnacken, an excellent dog structurally but not firm in temperament, also passed on the defects of his breeding—orchidism, fading color, and faults of dentition and temperament. Both Alex and his sire, Harras, were warned against by the German breeding masters.

The dogs named above, though excellent specimens themselves, carried in a recessive state the faults of their breeding and passed them on to their progeny, who in turn transmitted them ad infinitum.

Pfeffer von Bern, Odin von Busecker Schloss, and Chlodulf von Pelztierhof were the triumvirate whose genetic influence molded the major portion of our modern American-bred dogs. They were dominant studs and were employed in intense inbreeding and line-breeding. A knowledge of their genetic heritage will show us where the faults and merits of our dogs come from, as well as what to expect from their get.

Pfeffer von Bern was sired by Dachs von Bern and out of Clara von Bern. Dachs was sired by Alex von Ebersnacken, and his dam was the fabulous Viki von Bern (a bitch Germany refused to sell regardless of price), by Utz von Haus Schütting. Pfeffer von Bern's dam, Clara von Bern, was sired by Ado von Pagensgrüb, who in turn was sired by Utz von Haus Schütting. Pfeffer was a great individual who did more for the breed in this country than any other single dog. He was purchased as a young dog by John Gans, of Hoheluft Kennels fame, from Franz Schorlin in Hanover, and brought to the United States in 1936. Mr. Gans subsequently brought Pfeffer back to Germany in the spring of 1937 to enter him in the Sieger Show at Munich. He won the Sieger title and Best in Show over the Siegers of all other breeds. His great show career in America

Ch. Pfeffer v. Bern, Z.Pr., M.H.

(sire) Dachs v. Bern   (dam) Clara v. Bern

German Sieger and Double
U.S. Grand Victor
"The one and only . . ."

is known to all true Shepherd enthusiasts. His litter sister, Perchta von Bern, a fine bitch, was also imported by Mr. Gans. Though an excellent bitch, she, more than her brother, indicated the faults in her breeding, though not to the extent that they marred her show career. She had four missing teeth. Pfeffer had an excellent character and great nobility. His head was noble and he was rich in color and truly a male dog. He was excellent in forequarter assembly and possessed fine angulation behind. One could not say that he had faults, but rather that he could have been lower in hock, slightly firmer in back, a trifle shorter in loin, and could have possessed more drive behind. He moved beautifully, with a slight tendency to kick up behind. An over-all evaluation of this superb animal must necessarily be "excellent."

Pfeffer, line-bred on Utz v. Haus Schütting, was dominant in most of his virtues, passing them on freely to his progeny, the best of which were truly superb dogs and great producers. Any animal who can sire such familiar greats as Nox, Noble, Nora, etc., of Ruthland; the exquisite Lady of Ruthland; Vetter of Dornwald; Ajax, Amigo, etc., von Hoheluft; and the many other fine animals that Pfeffer sired, can certainly be named a great producer. Yet it must be remembered that in his children and his children's children the hidden faults of the line still exist.

Thus, through Pfeffer's most illustrious son, the double Grand Victor, Ch. Nox of Ruthland, who was himself a great dog and who sired a host of greats and near greats, we can get all the faults as well as the merits which were known to be passed on by Alex von Ebersnacken, Utz von Haus Schütting, Odin von Stolzenfels, Ferdl von der Secretainerie, and Dachs von Bern. Nox's dam, Carol of Ruthland, who produced a number of great animals when bred to Pfeffer (a breeding several times repeated), was by Ferdl, son of Odin von Stolzenfels. Her mother was Devise von Haus Schütting, a daughter of Dachs von Bern, Pfeffer's sire. In Nox, then through his dam, the line to Dachs, Alex, and Utz was further strengthened.

Through the Pfeffer line we established in America a uniformity of superb type. With the sweet we must also take the bitter, and perhaps this

Gr. Vix. & Ch. Lady of Ruthland (sire)
Ch. Pfeffer v. Bern (dam)
Ch. Frigga v. Kannenbackerland

A picture of unsurpassed beauty. American bred but of imported, German stock.

is as it should be, for without comparison we can have no true evaluation. The bitter in this case was the occasional cropping up of the recessives of the Pfeffer line, generally through Pfeffer's children or grandchildren, mainly occasional long coats, missing dentition, faulty temperament, overlong bodies and loins, and orchidism.

Odin von Busecker Schloss was Pfeffer's half brother, both having been sired by Dachs von Bern. His dam, Gerda von Busecker Schloss, was a fine bitch rated V in Germany. In Berlin, under Dr. Sachs, a renowned authority on the breed, Odin was given a V 1—Excellent and First. This was on September 19, 1936, when Odin was two and a half years old. Dr. Sachs describes him as follows:

"Fully developed. Very good body construction and a far-reaching

Dachs von Bern

sire: Alex v. Ebersnacken
dam: Viki v. Bern

Sire of the great Pfeffer and Odin. His genetic heritage molded type in America.

gait. Appears to me today to be of a dry type of herding dog, but however, somewhat overheavy and therefore does not show in the long gaiting the energy or endurance of a herding dog. One premolar missing."

At Frankfurt, at the world Sieger Show, in the Young Dog Class, he was one of the top seven dogs, described as being "very good in structure, but, for his age, very big and heavy."

Odin was a gray dog, heavy in structure, and light in pigmentation. He was well balanced, but could have used more angulation in the shoulder. His middle-piece was particularly good, deep, well ribbed, and showing great power and muscular transmission. Odin and Pfeffer met in competition in Germany at the Sieger Show, and after extensive gaiting and testing, Pfeffer was declared the Sieger over Odin, on gait and temperament. Odin's temperament was described as "bold and aggressive." He was, in fact, over-aggressive and not readily approachable.

His sire, Dachs von Bern, and Dachs's sire, Alex von Ebersnacken, are described by Odin's breeder and former owner, Herr Alfred Hahn, as "beautiful dogs, but no heroes. . . . Today they would not pass any [temperament or character] examination, would not be approved, or entered in the special book [Koerbook] as most suitable for breeding." He further

Ch. Odin v. Busecker Schloss

A dominant stud force in America, particularly in the Middle West and Pacific Coast.

goes on to state: "This tight Utz line did not agree with the line of Harras von Glockenbrink [Harras was the father of Alex von Ebersnacken] in the trait of good character. Further, there appeared tooth trouble, color fading, and so forth."

Odin, like his half brother Pfeffer, was dominant in passing on his good traits to his progeny rather than his faults, and he was used extensively for line-breeding, almost invariably stamping his excellent middle-piece on the influenced stock. Still, we must remember and evaluate the faults which lurk dormant in his germ plasm.

Chlodulf von Pelztierhof, used extensively on the Pacific Coast, was imported to the U.S. by Anton Korbel in 1936. Chlodulf was a gray dog of good size and possessing heavy bone. He was deep and had a tremendous chest. His back was strong and he was well gaited. He could have used more spring in pastern and was rather heavy all through his structure. Chlodulf was by Edi a. d. Leineweberhofe, and out of Bella von der Hohbrugger-Hohe. He was a foundation sire on the West Coast and sired some excellent offspring to carry on his inheritance. He was especially useful for breeding to small and light-boned bitches. His get generally inherited his size and structural strength and possessed a good deal of nobility. This line also gives us generally a good gait, a slight softness in back, less than the desired ninety-degree angulation in the shoulder assembly, but good balance throughout, good temperament and trainability.

There are any number of fine American-breds now being used as stud dogs or brood matrons which are strongly line-bred on Pfeffer. There are many others whose breeding is based upon a blending of the inheritable qualities of both Pfeffer and Odin. You will find many dogs line-bred on Chlodulf, and others, blending the breeding of Odin and Chlodulf. Still others possess lines of inheritance going back to all three of these foundation studs. Upon consideration, it is therefore slightly short of amazing that so little has been known or written about these three dogs.

It is always a touchy situation when one speaks of the faults of a dog. The general concensus seems to be, "If you can't say something nice about him, don't speak at all." This attitude is one which, through the years, has given us false impressions of important dogs, for only whispered rumors have been allowed by our misguided sense of politeness and they, like all gossip, have become warped as they progressed. If we are sincere breeders, we must have a true picture of the animals whose germ plasm has fashioned our stock. We must know what was behind them and what hidden faults, or virtues, have been handed down through them, to our own stock. Only through a knowledge of the genetic inheritance of our animals can we evaluate expectancy and, by compensation and selection, attempt to overcome unwanted features or strengthen desired characteristics.

Gr. Vic. & Ch. Nox of Ruthland
(sire)
Ch. Pfeffer v. Bern
(dam)
Carol of Ruthland

Double Grand Victor. Top Americanbred producer. He did much to establish breed uniformity in America.

Imports are coming with increasing rapidity to our shores these days. They will be used extensively in America and leave their mark upon our American-breds, becoming a part of the genetic structure of our animals. Dependable information about their ancestry is not easily accessible, yet it is information we must have if we are to use these imports intelligently and, by their use, upgrade our stock above norm. The great import is no different from the great domestic dog. Regardless of how perfect they may seem; both carry masked characteristics, recessives, which are as

The two great imported half brothers who so potently molded the destiny of the German Shepherd dog in America.

Pedigree Studies of
PFEFFER von BERN
German Sieger, 1937, American Champion and Grand Victor, 1937

Dachs v. Bern	Alex v. Ebersnacken	Harras v. Glockenbrink
		Frigga v. Hils
	Viki v. Bern	Utz v. Haus Schütting
		Olle v. Bern
Clara v. Bern	Ado v. Pagensgrüb	Utz v. Haus Schütting
		Pauline Bergerslust
	Freude v. Richrath	Blitz v.d. Juch
		Cilly Edox

CH. ODIN von BUSECKER SCHLOSS

Dachs v. Bern	Alex v. Ebersnacken	Harras v. Glockenbrink
		Frigga v. Hils
	Viki v. Bern	Utz v. Haus Schütting
		Olle v. Bern
Gerda v. Busecker Schloss	Claus v. Busecker Schloss	Samson v. Blasienberg
		Clara v. Buseckertal
	Lore v. Scheuernschloss	Klodo v. Boxberg
		Carin v. Kannenbackerland

Ingo v. Piastendamm,
SchH. II
(sire)
Gockel v. Bern
(dam)
Illa v. Oppeln-Ost
A superb individual and
great sire.

much a part of an animal as his surface perfection. In most instances the animals imported are examples of the best of their lines. When we see them, we view only a small section of the over-all picture of their strain quality. To visualize the complete picture, it would be necessary to scan and evaluate this dog's brothers and sisters, his sire and dam, and be familiar with the animals represented in his pedigree for approximately five generations. This is, of course, almost impossible, yet we must realize that any import possesses genetic factors which he doesn't show and which may be detrimental to the breeding which we propose to make.

Luckily, the faults of the various German lines of breeding are not the object of hush-hush campaigns in Germany. The German breeders consider healthy criticism and open discussion beneficial to the breed. We know, therefore, that one of the strongest sire lines in Germany came through the fine stud and show dog, Rolf von Osnabruckerland. This sire line, coming down in the upper bracket from Weigand von Blasienberg, represented some of the top dogs in Germany. From father to son, in the fifth generation, we have Wiegand von Blasienberg, then Gockel von Bern, Ingo von Piastendamm, Trutz aus der Schwanestadt, Lex Preussenblut, Rolf von Osnabruckerland. Gockel von Bern and his son, Ingo von Piastendamm were great dogs and highly rated in German pedigrees.

Harras v. Piastendamm,
SchH. III
(sire)
Ingo v. Piastendamm
(dam)
Birge v. Haus Mehner
Ingo's great son. Both
sire and son were con-
sidered living breed
ideals by German
authorities.

A study of Ingo's pedigree is interesting in that it shows such close relationship to our own American-bred stock through Pfeffer and Odin.

Ingo v. Piastendamm
{
Gockel v. Bern
{
Wiegand v. Blasienberg
Viki v. Bern
}
Illa v. Oppeln-Ost
{
Alex v. Ebersnacken
Arnhild v. Piastendamm
}
}

Alex von Ebersnacken was the sire and Viki von Bern the dam of Dachs von Bern, who was the sire of both Pfeffer and Odin. Ingo von Piastendamm is line-bred on Utz von Haus Schütting.

This line, through Rolf von Osnabruckerland and similar breeding, produced good temperament, wonderful front assemblies—shoulder, chest, etc.—powerful heads, good movement, but rather long backs and lack of desired rear angulation. When the line is intensely inbred, as it has been at times in the Preussenblut and Osnabruckerland kennels, it will also bring fading pigmentation. In color, representative examples of this breeding are of a reddish tan with black saddle. Much more will be mentioned about this important line later.

Another leading line in Germany that has produced the best is that of Sigbert Heidegrund, who was himself a truly great dog. Sigbert was sired by the great Odin von Stolzenfels, and was out of Dina von Webbelmannslust, an Utz daughter. Sigbert produced all-around excellence. He is most usually represented in our imports through the "Q" litter—Durmersheim, and through his illustrious son, Baldur von Befreiungsplatz. Through this line, including the Baldur sons Arry von der Gassenquelle and Pirol von der Buchenhohe, we get firm, strong backs and good movement, temperament, and hindquarter assemblies. Quell von Fredeholz, who was in this country and produced a good deal of stock here, was a son of Pirol von der Buchenhohe. Quell was considered, both in Germany and here, to be a top dog. In using this strain, we must be careful of too much length in loin and less than the wanted ninety-degree angulation in the shoulder, as this line, particularly through Pirol, carries these faults. In Germany

Trutz a.d. Schwanenstadt,
SchH. III
(sire)
Ingo v. Piastendamm
(dam)
Ruth v. Stolzenfels
A basic stud force in
Preussenblut and Osna-
bruckerland breeding.

Rolf v. Osnabruckerland,
SchH. III
(sire)
Lex Preussenblut
(dam)
Maja v. Osnabrucker-
land
One of Germany's lead-
ing sires. Product of a
genetically dominant line.

Lex Preussenblut,
SchH. III
(sire)
Trutz a.d. Schwanenstadt
(dam)
Esta Preussenblut
A dominant German sire.

Arry von der Gassenquelle was highly regarded as an individual and as a sire who gave to his progeny all the virtues of his breeding.

The Piastendamm line is another of great excellence in Germany. The main line stems from Gockel von Bern through Ingo von Piastendamm and Ingo's son Harras von Piastendamm. Though Gockel possessed too great length of back and loin and this was produced as a dominant in the Schwanenstadt, Preussenblut, and Osnabruckerland line, neither Ingo nor his son Harras exhibited this fault. Both these dogs were considered models for the breed in Germany. Beowulf von Piastendamm was another example of the fine stock produced by this breeding. Beowulf was sold to Japan. A son of Harras, Bingo von Stellerburg, has produced outstanding animals in Germany. Cuno von der Teufelslache, sent to America, was

Stella v. Haus Schutting (sire)
Hussan v. Haus Schutting (dam)
Flora v. Hils
Twice German Siegerin and one of Germany's great producing bitches.

one of his sons; Ingo von Burgunderhort and Jola von Burgunderhort are grandget of Bingo's.

Brando von Heidelbeerberg, sometimes found in American-bred pedigrees, passed on faults of temperament and long coats. Other dogs appearing in German pedigrees and sometimes in American pedigrees who threw long coats, especially when line-bred or inbred upon, were Curt von Herzog Hedan, Bodo von der Brahmenau, and his son Onyx von Forellenbach. Nox of Ruthland carried a recessive for long coats.

Other sires that came to the fore in Germany for the excellence of their get were, Immo von Hasenfang, Siggo von Corneliushof, and Vali and Nestor von Wiegerfelsen. Nestor is the sire of Immo von Hasenfang, who in turn sired a superb animal in Axel von der Deininghauserheide, sire of Sieger Alf v. Nordfelsen. Unless used with discretion, Axel had a tendency to transmit ear weakness, but seems to transmit his fine body structure to his progeny. Vali von Wiegerfelsen was the sire of Atlas von Dinas-Eck, who was a consistent winner at German shows and a fine producer. Structurally he was a strong, balanced dog of great power and a fine mover. He was a bit short in body, with a very slight bounce of back in motion. From the American standpoint, he could have used a bit more angulation. His son, Olex z.d. Sieben-Faulen, sold to Japan, was a superb animal in whose breeding the sire's fault tendencies have been corrected. Siggo von Corneliushof sired Arno von der Pfaffenau, a top German show dog. Arno produced strong heads and generally good strength throughout, with good angulation of the hindquarters. Arras von Nibelungengold, by Bingo von der Stellerburg, was another top show dog of Germany producing high-class pro-

Claus v. Haus Werle, SchH. III
(sire)
Quido v. Durmersheim
(dam)
Bussy v. Haus Detwiller
A great German show dog of marvelous character and intelligence. Brought to America when aged.

geny, rather on the large side but good throughout. One thing most of these German dogs had in common was excellence of temperament, character, intelligence, and trainability.

MODERN BREEDING LINES IN GERMANY

The newest producing families in Germany are based largely on a breeding foundation formed by the older lines already mentioned. But in every era, fresh lines come to the fore giving the Shepherd breed new genetic vitality. Individuals gain such stature that they, in themselves, represent a particular type of inheritance and their names are given as identification to certain, constantly produced, genetic characteristics. Thus, as time passes, old lines can be assessed more thoroughly for their worth, new lines can be tested and utilized if found to be of real value, and new individuals will be found who prepotently transmit virtues fashioned

Illa v. Oppeln-Ost, SchH.
(sire)
Alex v. Ebersnacken
(dam)
Arnheld v. Piastendamm
Dam of Ingo and Lump v.
Piastendamm. A top show
and brood bitch.

Quido v. Durmersheim,
SchH. III
(sire)
Sigbert Heidegrund
(dam)
Gisa v. Durmerscheim
From the famous "Q" litter,
prominent in the breeding
of many of Germany's finest
modern showdogs.

Sigbert Heidergrund,
Z.Pr. MHI.
(sire)
Odin v. Stolzenfels
(dam)
Dino v.d. Webbelmanslust
A superb animal and pre-
potent stud. One of the most
important names in modern
German pedigrees. Sire of
he "Q" liiter Durmersheim.

Pirol v. Buchenhohe,
SchH. II
(sire)
Baldur v. Befreiungsplatz
(dam)
Carmen v.d. Buchenhohe
"From this line comes good
quarters and backs."

Baldur v. Befreiungsplatz,
SchH. III
(sire)
Sigbert Heidegrund
(dam)
Berna z. Saarkante
Important German sire and
showdog. Excellent type and
breeding.

Ch. Quell v. Fredeholz,
SchH. III
(sire)
Pirol v.d. Buchenhohe
(dam)
Nixe v. Fredeholz
The imported, top-winning
American and German
showdog and sire.

Atlas v. Dinas-eck, SchH. III (sire) Vali v. Weigerfelsen (dam) Elka v. Menkenmoor A consistent German "V" dog. His get begin to prove his genetic quality. Owned by an American in Germany.

from combined genetic lines, or that differ from the characteristics that the family line generally produces. Incidently, and I want this to be completely understood, what you read here in reference to any dog or their progeny must not be construed in any way as criticism. It is merely reporting for your edification, and as objectively as possible, all that has been learned about these animals and family lines over a period of years and much travel and data collecting in Germany.

Grim v.d. Fahrmuhle, sire of the famous "A" litter von Elfenhain, and also sire of the top German dog (now in the U.S., where he has garnered both his American and Canadian championships) Frack v.d. Burg Arkenstede, was one of the truly great dogs bred in Germany. His breeding was open, going back quickly to some of the old and great names such as, Sigbert Heidegrund, Ferdl v.d. Secretainerie and Primus v. Maschtor. Through his dam, Fella v.d. Fahrmuhle, also came the valuable working qualities of fine, old sheepherding families. He was a pleasing shade of gray and possessed great beauty and nobility and almost uncanny intelligence. A top "V" dog, Germany allowed him to slip through their fingers to Brazil where he promptly became Brazilian Sieger. This is a family of great vitality, of males that live long and are capable of siring large, healthy litters at an advanced age.

The Sieben-Faulen kennels of Herr Heinz Röper, of Bremen, have produced a great deal of fine stock over the years based mainly on the Preussenblut-Osnabruckerland bloodlines but with judicious innovations which has resulted for this canny breeder in animals of fine conformation and good breeding potential. Vello z.d. Sieben-Faulen, a grand and noble male from this kennel, almost became Sieger of Germany but was eliminated from that high honor because he was slightly oversized. He has proved to be a fine producer as have his get, examples being the top rated showdogs and sires, Jalk v. Fohlenbrunnen (sire of the 1965 Siegerin) and Roon z.d. Sieben-Faulen, the latter a true stallion-type animal. This

49

family line is producing generally good stock, but care must be taken to select for strong pigmentation and to keep size within reasonable bounds. Excellent to fairly good front assemblies are also characteristic of this breeding. Ursus z.d. Sieben-Faulen, produces good fronts but also repeats his own failings of lack of hind angulation and less than the wanted croup. Ursus was also a top German show dog.

Alf v. Nordfelsen is still very highly thought of in Germany. This most celebrated son of Axel v. Deininghauserheide (also sire of Troll and Wotan v. Richterbach and Watzer v. Bad Melle, etc.) gave generally to the best of his progeny, nobility, true, dry working type, excellent temperament and trainability, and a shoulder that lacks the desired angulation together with a lack in forechest, or a forechest that takes a long time to develop. These last were Alf's own faults, too. When first brought out he could make no higher than a "G" rating in the Sieger show but, as the years passed, his front filled and developed and he finally became German Sieger in 1955. The type that comes from Alf is very uniform and, like their sire, balanced and harmonious, with beautiful and natural movement despite any lack in the front assembly. Veus v.d. Starrenburg, Sieger 1961, is a fine example of Alf progeny. This sire line of descent bypasses Klodo v. Boxberg and Utz v. Haus Schütting and goes directly, through Billo v. Riedekenburg, to Hettel Uckermark.

Alf, and now his descendants, were, and still are, generally bred to partners that can improve fronts. The same pattern of breeding was used uncountable times, and with great success, with Alf's sire, Alex v. Deininghauserheide, who was bred profusely to bitches carrying strong "R" litter Osnabruckerland breeding. A son of Alf's, Jonny v.d. Riedperle, is siring top "V," working type animals of excellent balance, such as Alf v. Appenhainer Forst and Barry v. Riedgold. A light eye must be watched for in Jonny progeny. This is true working stock and animals of this family line make excellent guard and police dogs. Alf himself was also sire of the "C" litter Elfenhain from which came much fine and influential German stock (Caret v. Elfenhain, the great brood bitch, etc.).

Colonia Agrippina kennels continue to produce excellent animals of a marked type, generally dark in pigmentation, particularly on the head, a bit short and steep in croup, usually with large ears set on a distinctive head. These animals are generally possessed of good substance and move well. The background basis of this stock is Wiegerfelsen, Osnabrucker-land and Preussenblut, with outcross breeding cautiously used as a balancing agent. Klodo v. Colonia Agrippina, product of an outcross sire, Amor a.d. Chan-Geschlecht (a good sire who is also the father of Ingo v. Haus Elkemann), is typical of the top animals of this strain and is himself proving to be a fine producer.

Grim v.d. Fahrmuhle, SchH. II
(sire) Arry v.d. Gassenquelle, Sch. II   (dam) Fella v.d. Fahrmuhle, HGH.
One of the unheralded great dogs of Germany. Sold to South America he became
Brazilian Sieger. Grim closely approached the ideal.

Condor v. Hohenstamm has produced very well in Germany, his most famous son being the 1962 Sieger, Mutz a.d. Kuckstrasse. He passes on his big, male head (sometimes with a tendency to a slight shortness of muzzle) and his excellent balance and movement. As an individual he lacked somewhat in hind angulation and flare in stifle but, when bred to bitches who had excellent hindquarters themselves and through their forebears, he produced the wanted angulation behind. Pigmentation must be watched as well as feet, and a slight tendency toward over-aggressiveness. Mutz is beginning to prove himself as a sire, particularly of good bitches. The 1964 Siegerin, Blanka v. Kisskamp is a Mutz daughter. His progeny are generally showy and flashy in color and markings, some not quite perfect in front assembly, with often a slightly pinched expression through the eyes. A few exhibit rather high energy. Condor v. Hohenstamm is a grandson of Rolf v. Osnabruckerland and Axel v. Deininghauserheide (there is that famous breeding cross again).

The breeding that produced the famous "K" litter Eremitenklause (Klodo, Kay, etc.), Arras v. Adam-Riesezwinger × Halla a.d. Eremitenklause, has been repeated time and time again and with marked success almost every time. Arras has also sired good stock out of other bitches, but seems to have "nicked" beautifully with Halla. This breeding is open and valuable because it is free of the names found too frequently in German pedigrees. "K" litter studs have proven to be successful sires giving nice type, good backs and excellent temperament to their progeny. From this line also comes good balance, dry working type, good size and nice hindquarters, lack of massiveness in male heads, occasional ear trouble, and that bug-a-boo of almost all modern lines, lack of perfection in shoulder angulation.

Gero v. Katherinentor produces uniformly a definite richness in pigmentation, dark rust color and black. He himself displayed this fine color. He was of middle size, stretched in body, harmonious and with good bone. His progeny have good balance, good gaits, but a tendency to slightness. In motion many display a slight nick or dip behind the withers. Among other fine animals Gero is the sire of the top "V" litter mates, Gero and Gitta v. Haus Irene.

Hein v. Richterbach produces the same rich pigmentation as Gero, and so does Cäsar v.d. Malmannsheide, Dick, his brother from another breeding, and the progeny of many of these dogs. This coloring seems to be the hallmark of animals rich in "R" litter Osnabruckerland breeding. Both Cäsar and Dick are used frequently by sheepmen for the breeding of herding dogs. They are known to give endurance and strength over a long period of time to their progeny. Grief v. Elfenhain, from the famous Elfenhain Kennels of Willi Sufke (Grief is now in the U.S.), also throws this rich coloring. Cäsar, Dick and Grief are all sired by Hein v. Richterbach, a powerful, muscular, medium sized animal of excellent temperament. Hein was a son of Rosel v. Osnabruckerland, "V" sister to Rolf, and is a controversial animal in Germany, though the 1965 Sieger shows a double cross to him. Gero v. Katharinentor, analyzed in the previous

Vello z.d. Sieben-Faulen, SchH. III, F.H.
(sire)
Lex v. Drei-Kinderhaus
(dam)
Grille z.d. Sieben-Faulen
A top "V" dog and great sire, Vello was produced by a canny breeder, Heinz Roper. Considered for Sieger he was eliminated from that exalted spot due to being slightly oversized.

Frack v.d. Burg Arkenstede, SchH. III
(sire)
Grimm v.d. Fahrmuhle,
(dam)
Elke v.d. Burg Arkenstede, A son of the great Grimm, Frack, imported to the U.S. at seven, made his championship in three shows. Also a Canadian Champion, he exemplifies utilitarian beauty.

paragraph, is a son of Hein's son, Cäsar v.d. Malmannsheide. Most of these animals with "R" litter and Hein breeding are capable of getting good front assemblies, but can, in their less desirable offspring, produce too great length in back, long loins, and sometimes a weakness in back due to length. Cäsar seems to sire two types, one light and foxlike, the other large and powerful.

Alf v. Walddorf-Emst, a heavy dog of much substance, and a direct son of Rolf v. Osnabruckerland, produces animals like himself, heavy and imposing, but inclined to "wetness" and, in some instances, spongy bone. One of Alf's litter mates, Audi, was longcoated, so it is quite possible that Alf, too, carries a recessive for long coats. Alf is the sire of the excellent Marko v. Boxhochburg who is, himself, an excellent producer. This line can (as can most any other line) produce a percentage of dysplasia.

The "D" litter vom Elfenhain (Donar, Dux, etc., Dux is in the U.S.) are typical and true working Shepherds. They have gotten very nice type, firm, nice moving working animals of various sizes but generally on the small side. This "D" litter is a repeat breeding due to the success of the "C" litter vom Elfenhain. The sire is Alf v. Nordfelsen and the dam from another famous Elfenhain breeding, the "A" litter. The good dog, Gero v.d. Malzmuhle is a typical Donar son.

Harold v. Haus Tigges progeny has been classified in Germany as being weak in bone, pointed in muzzle and narrow throughout. Yet many top individual animals have come from this breeding, one of whom is the beautiful "V-A" bitch, Gisa v. Rugereid, one of the finest Shepherd females of the day and now in the U.S. The *good* progeny sired by Harold also seem to produce fine stock if bred correctly.

Arno v. Haus Gersie has sired excellent, all-around working dogs of stretched body and good fronts. The "V" litter Busecker Schloss (Valet,

Veit, etc.) are excellent examples of the quality this dog can produce. These sons are, in turn, getting top animals in Germany. The Busecker Schloss animals are noted for their working ability, many of them displaying the HGH award (Sheepherding). Arno and his children usually exhibit good front assemblies. His breeding is outcrossed. The "V" litter Busecker Schloss produces fine stock with good fronts and backs, sometimes a bit long in body and occasionally displaying a slight roachiness in back.

Volker v. Zollgrenzschutz-Haus is the most celebrated individual of a very fine litter. This dog's breeding is open with none of the usual and familiar crossing of bloodlines behind him. His progeny have proven the value of his heritary power. He himself is a living model of what a male Shepherd should be, and some of his best children have that aura of nobility and majesty that is so scarce and so difficult to define. His progeny are habitually of good size, typical Shepherd dog temperament and character, and excellent trainability. They exhibit exceptional balance, angulation and generally good fronts. Some of his get show a slight shortness and dropping off of the croup, and an occasional pup will exhibit a bit of back bounce in movement. Volker's "K" litter produced the Sieger of Japan, Kolex v. Galgenwald. His "C" and "D" litters vom Sixtberg, out of the "V" bitch, Caret v. Elfenhain, produced excellent progeny. The top "V" dog, Condor v. Sixtberg, considered by Herr Wassermann to be Volker's best son, is now in America. Carmen and Centa v. Sixtberg, sisters to Condor, have produced top dogs in Germany, Carmen is dam of the Landesgruppen Sieger and top "V" dog, Condor v. Zollgrenzschutz-Haus ("V-A4," 1965 Sieger Show). One of Volker's best daughters, Della v. Devrienthof, is a top "V" bitch in conformation, twice German sheepherding champion, and first in regional Service Dog competition (Berlin) in 1962; beauty and high utility combined. Della is now also in America sharing the same home with Condor v. Sixtberg. This last named stud,

Axel von der Deininghauserheide, SchH. III, DPH, FH.
(sire)
Immo v. Hasenfang, SchH. III
(dam)
Helma v. Hildegardsheim, SchH. III
Famous show dog, and sire of a host of great German dogs including, Alf v. Nordfelsen, Troll v. Richterbach, Watzer v. Bad Melle, Wotan v. Richterbach, etc.

Alf. v. Nordfelsen, SchH. III (sire)
Axel v.d. Deininghauserheide SchH. III, DPH, FH. (dam)
Carin v. Bombergachen Park SchH. II
German Sieger 1955 and famous progenitor of fine show and working-type Shepherds. His genetic influence is obvious even today.

Condor, transmits his balance, mental and physical, rich pigmentation, excellent angulation, beautiful type and wonderful character. He sires large progeny that sometimes show a slight falling off in the croup, but have, at their best, wonderful heads, feet, and dry but strong and heavy bone. Several other fine sons and daughters of Volker are also in America. Incidentally, this great German dog, Volker, came to America for a visit to stand at stud for a short while in the East so that American breeders would have the rare opportunity of utilizing his great genetic heritage to better their own stock. While he was here his son, Condor v. Sixtberg, took his place at stud in Germany. Strangely enough, the demand for Volker's services were much less than expected, perhaps because he was not ballyhooed as so many other, lesser dogs are. It was, in truth, a sad commentary on the breeding acumen of the fancy in America.

Animals such as Brix v. Grafenkrone (now in America and the new Grand Victor) and the handsome Bar v.d. Starenheimat, are proving the worth of Bar v.d. Weissen Pforte as a sire. Lovely type and temperament, good bone and substance, lacking slightly in shoulder assembly, but dogs of evident quality and value.

Both Gero v. Haus Elkemann and Ingo v. Haus Elkemann, exceptionally beautiful animals, have been bred too extensively. Gero seems to give to his progeny, on the whole, the beautiful hindquarters and unique turn of stifle he himself possesses. Ingo generally passes on his rich color and nice balance, but neither of these studs have, as yet, proven to be consistent producers, nor have they yet produced animals as good as they themselves are.

Zibu and Witz v. Haus Schütting, are both top animals, specimens of the breed who have that certain something that makes them stand above the crowd. Witz has always been knocking at the door at the Sieger shows but never quite made it into the parlor though he has always been given almost as high a rating as the Sieger. Zibu has also been among the "V-A"

Arno vom Haus Gersie, SchH. III

(sire) Edo v. Gehrdener Berg, SchH. III   (dam) Delia v. Walburgitor, SchH. II

A great German stud and show dog, Arno is the sire of the "R" litter von Haus Schutting, and the famous "V" litter, vom Busecker Schloss.

Valet v. Busecker Schloss, SchH. III

(sire) Arno v. Haus Gersie, SchH. III, FH   (dam) Daja v. Bernstein-Strand, SchH. II

From a very old and always important kennel, Valet is a valuable stud in the Fatherland due to his breeding and prepotency. Masculine, excellent front, croup, stretched body.

animals and in 1964 became Sieger. Both these dogs come from Dr. Funk's kennels. Witz, now in Japan, has sired some very fine animals, dogs such as Hanko v.d. Hetschmuhle (V-A and 1965 Sieger). Claus v. Obergrombacher Schloss (V), and Swen v.d. Barnberger Hohle (V), attest to his success as a sire. Witz can produce light pigmentation, a slight roach in back, and sometimes a smaller ear than is cosmetically wanted. Zibu's get greatly mirror their sire's type, though he can also produce too much length, shortness in the neck and some flatness in the croup. Jacko v. Bimohlen (V-A) and Quido v. Haus Schütting (V), are prime examples of the best of Zibu's get. Young Witz stock coming to the fore are Nice v. Hackhauser Weg and the "H" and "G" litters vom Sixtberg in which there are some top animals out of Caret v. Elfenhain. At their best both these dogs are capable of siring superb animals with the wanted, but not often found, front and overall balance.

The dogs mentioned here are those in the forefront of German breeding, the highest examples of the fatherland's richest breeding heritage. Only males have been analyzed due to lack of space and the fact that well known studs influence the breed to a greater extent than do bitches. All these dogs carry and can reproduce many (perhaps almost all) the faults our breed is heir to, but when used with the right breeding partners they are more capable of producing top stock in greater quantity than other studs or breeding lines.

A study of German pedigrees can teach us a great deal about the breeding methods employed with such success by German breeding masters. The stable and basic line stemmed from the "R" litter Osnabrucklerland through the best of the succeeding progeny such as Hein, Alf Walddorf-Emst, Cäsar, "A" litter Elfenhain, etc., and the best stock produced from any of the "R" litter lines. Soon, due to too much massing of the "R" litter Osnabruckerland in pedigrees, many faults began to crop up, so many that they could not be denied, even in the face of the few superb individuals from this same breeding. There subsequently became a great need for outcross breeding, genetic lines completely free of "R" litter influence, and the canny German breeders had evolved such lines and kept them pure for just such an emergency. These new, fresh lines, were utilized as a balance for "R" litter lines and brought rejuvenated vigor and strength to German breeding, eliminating in one stroke (or pushing them down to a recessive role) the prevalent ills.

Axel v.d. Deininghauserheide and his son, Alf v. Nordfelsen, provided one of these needed, fresh lines. Other outcross breeding lines are represented by Arno v. Haus Gersie, Volker v. Zollgrenzschutz-Haus, "K"

Alf v. Waldorf-Emst, SchH. III, FH. (sire) Rolf v. Osnabruckerland, (dam) Elga v. Villosahaus, A son of the famous Rolf, Alf produces his own substance and heavyness, and sometimes a lack of firmness. A litter mate, Audi, carried a long coat.

(and subsequent litters) Eremitenklaus, Bill v. Osterhagen, Grim v.d. Fahrmuhle, Amor a.d. Chan-Geschlecht, etc.

Following are a few classic examples of the balancing of the "R" litter line against fresh lines free of this breeding.

Troll v. Richterbach	Axel v.d. Deininghauserheide	Immo v. Hasenfang / Helma v. Hildergardsheim
	Lende v. Richterbach	Fels v. Vogtlandshof / Rosel v. Osnabruckerland
Condor v. Hohenstamm	Arko v.d. Delog	Rolf v. Osnabruckerland / Amsel v. Garagenhof
	Asta v.d. Jakobsleiter	Axel v.d. Deininghauserheide / Delma v. Ruhrsieg
Frack v.d. Burg Arkenstede	Grimm v.d. Fahrmuhle	Arry v.d. Gassenquelle / Fella v.d. Fahrmuhle
	Elke v.d. Burg Arkenstede	Rolf v. Osnabruckerland / Asta v.d. Burg Arkenstede

As time goes on the balancing of these free lines with "R" litter lines becomes more subtle and precariously involved. As show business people say, *"What do you do for an encore?"* The answer lies in the good, divergent genetic material of outcross breeding that carry little or none of the old lines. A little of this old breeding, of and from the "R" litter, can be of vast benefit. A lot, massing formidably at the tail end of a pedigree on both the sire and dam's side, can be, in some cases, little short of disastrous.

Mention should be made here of a non-profit organization, Fidelco Breeders Foundation, Inc., of which I, Ernest H. Hart, was one of the founders with Charles H. Kaman. Quietly, over the last several years, Fidelco has experimentally bred to produce true working dog tempera-

Hein v. Richterbach, SchH. III, FH.
(sire)
Billo v. Oberviehland,
(dam)
Rosel v. Osnabrucker Land,
A powerful, muscular, impressive dog, richly pigmented and of excellent temperament, Hein is a foundation dog in many German lines.

ment and utility. The program is very like that which was set up by Humphrey and Warner for their invaluable Fortunate Fields experiment. The program deals with scores of German Shepherds, produced by basic, selected stock. These animals are distributed to various families who raise them in a wholesome environment, care for them and, if they are bitches, whelp them when the time comes. The tools used to produce the animals that fit the Fidelco pattern of utility are: exhaustive data compiled through research here and abroad, intensive charting, testing, and breeding experiments, coupled with genetic knowledge and completely objective selection of the animals utilized to perpetuate the program. Fidelco-bred dogs are doing a job for mankind, serving as Police Dogs, guards for industries producing vital government material, and as guide dogs for the blind.

Many vital facts become manifest in such a breeding program when the approach is clinical and there are a great number of animals with which to work. The basic problems that became apparent early in the program were the lack of stability of the required temperament, and the necessary elimination of dogs that exhibited all the wanted mental and

Arras vom Adam - Reisezwinger, SchH. III, FH.
(sire)
Cito v. Coburger Land,
(dam)
Ella a.d. Eremitenklause,
This photo of this "V" German dog was taken at ten years of age. Arras is a fine stud with an open pedigree, the sire of the "K" litter Eremitenklaus, and many other Eremitenklause litters.

Mutz a.d. Kuckstrasse, SchH. III
(sire) Condor v. Hohenstamm, SchH. III   (dam) Mori v. Gieser Waldchen, SchH. II
German Sieger and son of a Sieger, Mutz has proven his worth in the stud. He now
resides in Pakistan.

Condor v. Hohenstamm, SchH. III, FH.
(sire) Arko v.d. Delog, SchH. III   (dam) Asta v.d. Jakobsleiter, SchH. II
Sieger and sire of a Sieger, Condor's worth as a stud force in Germany is attested to
by the excellence of his get.

physical characteristics, due to a high incidence of hip-dysplasia.

Condensed and rather arbitrarily summarized, the conclusions arrived at by Fidelco and proven through research and actual breeding of many animals over a period of many generations, led the program to almost completely discard stock carrying American-bred lines, because of lack of consistently sound, working temperament, and to concentrate on pure German breeding as the genetic background. Inbreeding and close line-breeding of certain strains indicated that a high percentage of dysplasia (subluxation) accompanies the massing of specific lines in the hereditary background. This is particularly true of Osnabruckerland and Preussen-blut breeding ("R" litter Osnabruckerland in particular) and animals rich in "R" litter breeding. Outcross breeding utilizing the fresh, new German lines (and incorporating pure herding breeding), produces animals that most consistently fit the Fidelco working ideal. The percentage of useful stock is now approaching a highly satisfactory average (approximately 80 per cent).

It is evident that the clever German breeders are also aware of the necessity for change. Today you will find many stud advertisements declaring that this or that animal is "free of," Rolf, Hein, Gero and Cäsar bloodlines. Others are also adding the names of Alex, Alf, Arno, Edo, and Claudius (v. Hain) to the list. Top "V" animals such as Donner v. Maiweg, Ursus z.d. Sieben-Faulen, Ilk v. Busecker Schloss, Hiasl v.d. Burg Kendenich, Fax v. Diershein, Axel v. Haus Stutterheim, Elch v.d. Schilfmuhle, and many more are advertised in this manner. Other studs, rich in "R" litter breeding, are advertised as ideal partners for bitches of Arno, Vello, Klodo, Axel, Volker, and other outcross bloodlines.

German judges have lifted the end results of many of the fine outcross lines to great eminence, declaring that, besides their evident beauty of conformation and vigorous working ability, they come from a "fine family."

Dogs whose genetic background is saturated with the familiar names of well known producers of the old familiar lineage are still begetting top stock, but they are also compounding faults and German breeders know that salvation lies in the new lines that are open and free. Wisely blended new vigor appears and the ills that have begun to multiply are greatly reduced.

The broader the breed basis and the greater variety there is to choose from in the gene-pool of the Shepherd breed, the easier it is to select for and attain certain objectives while eliminating, or at least reducing to a minimum, unwanted but persistent characteristics.

Type has changed drastically in our breed since the time of Klodo von Boxberg and the new era. The change has been more gradual, but just as

Atlas v. Elfenhain, SchH. I

(sire) Grim v.d. Fahrmuhle, SchH. II   (dam) Lexa v. Osnabrucker Land, SchH. II

An American Champion, this imported male was an example of the quality inherent in the famous "A" litter v. Elfenhain.

Jalk v. Fohlenbrunnen, SchH. III
(sire) Vello z.d. Sieben - Faulen, SchH. III, FH.
(dam) Gunda v. Fohlenbrunnen, SchH. II
Sired by a famous stud, Jalk, in turn, gives much to his progeny. Early to mature he
was a "V-A" dog when 2½ years of age, and is a very popular stud in Germany.

marked as the change that ushered in the new era. Change is constant and
is a part of progress and of life, but it must be upward toward greater merit
and perfection or it brings us to retrogression. The pattern of heredity
must be clearly seen and understood if progress is to be made in breeding
activity, and that pattern cannot be known unless it is unveiled and the
faults as well as the virtues, dominant and recessive, are revealed and
honestly evaluated. In the light of modern-day knowledge of genetics,
the breeding of fine dogs has not advanced as rapidly as it should have due
to a lack of knowledge of many breeders of the hidden faults in the available
breeding stock. Perhaps we breeders in America will soon outgrow our
adolescence—perhaps the time is near when we will be able to discuss the
faults of our dogs and the reasons for them. We acknowledge that all dogs
have faults, but it is "bad form" to speak openly about them. Let us hope
that the near future will bring an end to such a childish attitude so that
we may progress toward the ideal in sureness and light, where now we
creep in semidarkness.

CHAPTER 4

THE RIDDLE OF INHERITANCE

The "*Why ?*" and "*What ?*" of being have been pondered by man since he first became aware of himself as an entity. He wondered who he was, why he was, and what he was, and he focused the flickering light of these same questions upon all the living creatures around him.

The first interpretations given to natural phenomena by ancient man were, prompted by his ignorance, mythological. But as early as 600 years before Christ the Greek philosopher, Thales, applied scientific thought to the subject and shrewdly concluded that all life originated and came from the water (the Aegean Sea). Aristotle later collected and analyzed all known facts and zoological data up to his time and made the initial attempt, on the basis of comparative anatomy, to classify the animal kingdom.

Down through the centuries other men of splendid and inquiring minds bent their efforts to shed more light upon the study of specie origin. But it remained for one man to find the key to the origin of species and that man was Charles Robert Darwin. He found the answer to the mystery of progressive life in *evolution*, the theory that all life-forms find kinship through a basic and common ancestry, and that divergence occurs to permit variation to fit changing environment.

Darwin's principles of evolution were accepted. Natural selection produced changes in all living things. But how did these changes come about? There seemed to be no rules, nothing that could be considered definite, no design to follow to a logical conclusion. There had to be a pattern of inheritance, but what was it? men of science asked, and how did it work?

Charles Darwin asked these questions, too, but could find no answers. He never knew that his basic laws of evolution and those of heredity were being developed at approximately the same time, for his epic tome, *The Origin of Species*, propounding the theory of evolution, was published in 1859, but it was not until the year 1900 that the laws governing inheritable linkage were given hesitantly to the world.*

Meanwhile superstition and arrogant and baseless theorizing pushed truth to the background as false formulas of inheritance were dictatorially advanced by pseudo-scientists and sham philosophers. The inheritance of acquired characteristics is one of the fallacious theories that was widely

* See "The Dog Breeders' Handbook" by Ernest H. Hart, T.F.H. Publications, Inc.

believed and has its disciples even today. Birthmarking is another false theory which must be discarded in the light of present-day genetical knowledge. The genes which give our dogs all their inheritable material are isolated in the body from any environmental influence. What the host does or has done to him influences them not at all. The so-called "proofs" advanced by the adherents of both these bogus theories were simply isolated coincidences.

Telegony is another of the untrue beliefs about influencing inherited characteristics. This is the theory that the sire of one litter could or would influence the progeny of a future litter out of the same bitch but sired by an entirely different stud. Telegony is, in its essence, comparable to the theory of saturation—which is the belief that if a bitch is bred many times in succession to the same stud, she will become so "saturated" with his "blood" that she will produce only puppies of his type, even when mated to an entirely different stud. By far the strongest and most widely believed was the theory that the blood was the vehicle through which all inheritable material was passed from parents to offspring, from one generation to the next. The taint of that superstition still persists in the phraseology we employ in our breeding terms such as "bloodlines," "percentage of blood," "pure-blooded," "blue-blooded," etc. This "blood" reference in regard to heredity crops up in all places and for all allied references, as witness the politician who cries vehemently, "I am proud that the blood of Paul Revere runs in my veins!" To achieve such a remarkable accomplishment would require transfusion from a long-dead corpse.

The truth was found in spite of such a persistent theory, and in the history of science there is no more dramatic story than that of the discovery of the true method of inheritance. No, the truth was not arrived at in some fine endowed scientific laboratory gleaming with the mysterious implements of research. The scene was instead a small dirt garden in Moravia, which is now a part of Czechoslovakia. Here Johann Gregor Mendel, a Moravian monk, planted and crossed several varieties of common garden peas and quietly recorded the differences that occurred through several generations. Over a period of eight years this remarkable man continued his studies. Then, in 1865, he read a paper he had prepared regarding his experiments to the local Brunn, a society of historians and naturalists. The society subsequently published this paper in its journal, which was obscure and definitely limited in distribution.

Now we come to the amazing part of this story, for Mendel's theory of inheritance, which contained the fundamental laws upon which all modern advances in genetics have been based, gathered dust for thirty-four years, and it seemed that one of the most important scientific discoveries of the

Etu v.d. Furstensalmburg, SchH.
(sire)
Bredo v.d. Jahnwiese
(dam)
Dina v.d. Webbelmanns-lust Holland Sieger 1935. Sire of Anni v.d. Badener-Hohe, producer of the important "E" litter Badener-Hohe.

nineteenth century was to be lost to mankind. Then in 1900, sixteen years after Mendel's death, the paper was rediscovered and his great work given to the world.

In his experiments with the breeding of garden peas, Mendel discovered and identified the units of heredity. He found that when two individual plants which differed in a unit trait were mated, one trait appeared in the offspring and one did not. The trait which was visible he named the "dominant" trait, and the one which was not visible he called the "recessive" trait. He proposed that traits, such as color, are transmitted by means of units in the sex cells and that one of these units must be pure, let us say either black or white, but never a mixture of both. From a black parent which is pure for that trait, only black units are transmitted, and from a white parent, only white units can be passed down. But when one parent is black and one is white, a hybrid occurs which transmits both the black and white units in equal amounts. The hybrid itself will take the color of the dominant parent, yet carry the other color as a recessive. Various combinations of unit crosses were tried by Mendel, and he found that there were six possible ways in which a pair of determiners (Mendel's "units") could combine with a similar pair. The Mendelian chart shows

Achilles v.d. Hollenquelle, SchH. III
(sire)
Ultimo v. Haus Schutting
(dam)
Quitta v. Aufeld
German sire and show dog. Sire of the fine bitch, Maja v. Osnabruckerla 'd.

how this law of Mendel's operates and the expected results. This simple Mendelian law holds true in the actual breeding of all living things—of plants, mice, humans, or German Shepherd dogs.

The beginning of new life in animals arises from the union of a male sperm and a female egg cell during the process of breeding. Each sperm cell has a nucleus containing one set of chromosomes, which are small packages, or units, of inheritable material. Each egg also possesses a nucleus of one set of chromosomes. The new life formed by the union of sperm cell and egg cell then possesses two sets of chromosomes—one from the sperm, one from the egg, or one set from the sire and one set from the dam. For when the sperm cell enters the egg, it does two things—it starts the egg developing and it adds a set of chromosomes to the set already in the egg. Here is the secret of heredity. For in the chromosomes lie the living genes that shape the destiny of the unborn young. Thus we see that the pattern of heredity, physical and mental, is transmitted to our dog from its sire and dam through tiny living cells called genes, which are the connecting links between the puppy and his ancestors.

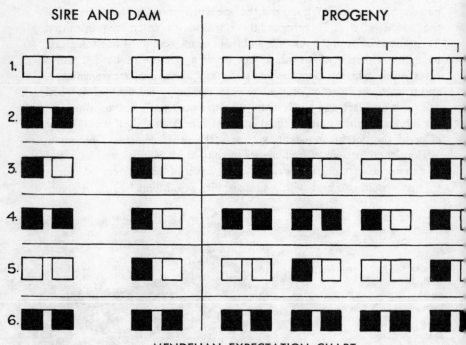

SIRE AND DAM   PROGENY

MENDELIAN EXPECTATION CHART

The six possible ways in which a pair of determiners can unite. Ratios apply to expectancy over large numbers, except in lines no. 1, 2 and 6 where exact expectancy is realized in every litter

Chromosomes in
nucleus of cell

Chromosomes arranged in
pairs, showing partnership

These packets of genes, the chromosomes, resemble long, paired strings of beads. Each pair is alike, the partners formed the same, yet differing from the like partners of the next pair. In the male we find the exception to this rule, for here there is one pair of chromosomes composed of two that are not alike. These are the sex chromosomes, and in the male they are different from those in the female in that the female possesses a like pair while the male does not. If we designate the female chromosomes as X, then the female pair is XX. The male too has an X chromosome, but its partner is a Y chromosome. If the male X chromosome unites with the female X chromosome, then the resulting embryo will be a female. But if the male Y chromosome is carried by the particular sperm that fertilizes the female egg, the resulting progeny will be a male. It is, therefore, a matter of chance as to what sex the offspring will be, since the sperm is capricious and fertilization is random. Including those of sex the dog possesses seventy-eight chromosomes.

The actual embryonic growth of the puppy is a process of division of cells to form more and more new cells and at each cell division of the fertilized egg each of the two sets of chromosomes provided by sire and dam also divide, until all the myriad divisions of cells and chromosomes have reached an amount necessary to form a complete and living entity. Then birth becomes an accomplished fact, and we see before us a living, squealing Shepherd puppy.

What is he like, this puppy? He is what his controlling genes have made him. His sire and dam have contributed one gene of each kind to their puppy, and this gene which they have given him is but one of the two which each parent possesses for a particular characteristic. Since he has drawn these determiners at random, they can be either dominant or recessive genes. His dominant heritage we can see when he develops, but what he possesses in recessive traits is hidden.

There are rules governing dominant and recessive traits useful in summarizing what is known of the subject at the present time. We can be reasonably sure that a dominant trait: (1.) Does not skip a generation.

Harry v. Donaukai, SchH. III

(sire) Falk v. Emsschleuse, SchH. II   (dam) Freia v. Donaukai, SchH. II

A top dog in Germany, Harry is sire of the great "V" litter Zollgrenzschutz-Haus. Imported he became Canadian Grand Victor and Champion, and American Champion. Owned by Arbor Kennels.

Perle v. Zollgrenzschutz - Haus, SchH. II

(sire) Igor v. Tempelblick, SchH. III   (dam) Krafta v. Zollgrenzschutz-Haus, SchH. III

This strong, fleet, "Vorzuglich" bitch was the dam of the famous "V" litter v. Zollgrenzschutz-Haus.

Volker v. Zollgrenzschutz-Haus, SchH. III, CACIB

(sire) Harry v. Donaukai, SchH. III   (dam) Perle v. Zollgrenzschutz-Haus, SchH. II

". . . Finally, what made the decision in his favor is that he comes from a good 'family,' and that he has already proven his qualities in breeding." . . . Dr. W. Funk, after awarding the Sieger title to Volker for the second time. Volker was bred and is owned by Josef Wassermann.

(2.) Will affect a relatively large number of the progeny. (3.) Will be carried only by the affected individuals. (4.) Will minimize the danger of continuing undesirable characteristics in a strain. (5.) Will make the breeding formula of each individual quite certain.

With recessive traits we note that: (1.) The trait may skip one or more generations. (2.) On the average a relatively small percentage of the individuals in the strain carry the trait. (3.) Only those individuals which carry a pair of determiners for the trait, exhibit it. (4.) Individuals carrying only one determiner can be ascertained only by mating. (5.) The trait must come through both sire and dam.

You will hear some breeders say that the bitch contributes 60 per cent or more to the excellence of the puppies. Others swear that the influence of the sire is greater than that of the dam. Actually, the puppy receives 50 per cent of his germ plasm from each, though one parent may be so dominant that it seems that the puppy received most of his inheritable material from that parent. From the fact that the puppy's parents also both received but one set of determiners from each of their parents and in turn have passed on but one of their sets to the puppy, it would seem that one of those sets that the grandparents contributed has been lost and that therefore the puppy has inherited the germ plasm from only two of its grandparents, not four. But chromosomes cross over, and it is possible for the puppy's four grandparents to contribute an equal 25 per cent of all the genes inherited, or various and individual percentages, one grandparent contributing more and another less. It is even possible for the pup to inherit no genes at all from one grandparent and 50 per cent from another.

The genes that have fashioned this puppy of ours are of chemical composition and are living cells securely isolated from any outside influence, a point which we have made before and which bears repeating. Only certain kinds of man-directed radiation, some poisons or other unnatural means can cause change in the genes. No natural means can influence them. Environment can effect an individual but not his germ plasm. For instance, if the puppy's nutritional needs are not fully provided for during his period of growth, his end potential will not be attained; but regardless of his outward appearance, his germ plasm remains inviolate and capable of passing on to the next generation the potential that was denied him by improper feeding.

Breeding fine Shepherds would be a simple procedure if all characteristics were governed by simple Mendelian factors, but alas, this is not so. Single genes are not solely responsible for single characteristics, mental or physical. The complexity of any part of the body and its dependence upon other parts in order to function properly makes it obvious

72

that we must deal with interlocking blocks of controlling genes in a life pattern of chain reaction. Eye color, for instance, is determined by a simple genetic factor, but the ability to see, the complicated mechanism of the eye, the nerves, the blood supply, the retina and iris, even how your Shepherd reacts to what he sees, are all part of the genetic pattern of which eye color is but a segment.

Since they are living cells in themselves, the genes can and do change, or mutate. In fact, it is thought now that many more gene mutations take place than were formerly suspected, but that the great majority are either within the animal, where they cannot be seen, or are so small in general scope that they are overlooked. The dramatic mutations which affect the surface are the ones we notice and select for or against according to whether they direct us toward our goal or away from it. Again, with the vagary inherent in all living things, the mutated gene can change once again back to its original form.

Extreme examples of mutations are the albino Shepherd, pure white and with pink eyes and nose, and the pure black Shepherd. A male and female albino when bred together cannot produce any but albino young. When two pure mutant blacks are bred, they can produce only black young.*

We see then that the Shepherd puppy is the product of his germ plasm, which has been handed down from generation to generation. We know that there are certain rules that generally govern the pattern that the genes form and that a gene which prevents another gene from showing in an individual is said to be a dominant and the repressed gene a recessive. Remember, the animal itself is not dominant or recessive in color or any other characteristic. It is the gene that is dominant or recessive, as judged by results. We find that an animal can contain in each of his body cells a dominant and a recessive gene. When this occurs, the dog is said to be heterozygous. As illustrated in the Mendelian chart, we know that there is an opposite to the heterozygous individual, an animal which possesses two genes of the same kind in its cells—either two dominants or two recessives—and this animal is said to be homozygous. The loss of a gene or the gain of a gene, or the process of change among the genes, is known as mutation, and the animal affected is called a mutant.

* In Shepherds it has been established that several alleles of the albino series are present in the breed. The danger of paling color (which German writers on the breed describe as "a sign of degeneracy") does not come through the dark-eyed, dark-nosed, white dog, since, if bred to dogs homozygous for rich pigmentation, the resulting progeny will be either white or normal colors. The cream, or pale cream, and pale gray Shepherd is the dog that contributes to color paling (Grey-Agouti), as does dilute blue.

Ch. Hugo of Cosalta, C.D.—1939
A son of Utz v. Haus Schutting.

Int. Gr. Ch. Asta v.d. Kaltenweide
Sch.H.—1926
Triple German Siegerin.

Ch. Frigga v. Kannenbackerland—
1936
Dam of Lady of Ruthland.

A GALLERY

of

FAMOUS

GRAND VICTORS

and

VICTRIXES

OF THE PAST

Perchta v. Bern—1937
Little sister to Pfeffer v. Bern.

Ch. Noble of Ruthland—1942
Nox of Ruthland's litter brother.

Every bitch that stands before us, every stud we intend to use, is not just one dog, but two. Every living thing is a Jekyll and Hyde, shadow and substance. The substance is the Shepherd that lives and breathes and moves before us, the animal that we see, the physical manifestation of the interaction of genotypic characters and environment—the "phenotype." The shadow is the Shepherd we don't see, yet this shadow is as much a part of the dog before us as the animal we see. This shadow-Shepherd is the gene-complex, or total collection of its genes—the "genotype." The visual substance is easily evaluated, but the invisible shadow must also be clearly seen and evaluated, for both shadow and substance equally contribute to the generations to come. Without understanding the complete genetic picture of any particular dog, we cannot hope to successfully use that dog to accomplish specific results. In order to understand, we must delve into the genetic background of the animal's ancestry until the shadow becomes as clearly discernible as the substance and we can evaluate the dog's genetic worth as a whole; for this dog that stands before us is but the containing vessel, the custodian of a specific pattern of heredity.

We have tried to present to you a working knowledge of the process of inheritance, picking the most pertinent aspects from the great amount of literature pertaining to this subject. If you wish to delve deeper into this most fascinating of all sciences, you will find in the bibliography books of much greater scope than we could cram into this one chapter. But before we leave the subject, one more important phase must be examined. This is the relationship of animal to man in regard to genetics. Though man is an animal and follows the pattern of genetic inheritance precisely as the lower animals do, we must not fashion a parallel between the two. Animals have only biological heredity, while man is greatly influenced by a very complicated and demanding cultural or social inheritance. In our breeding operations we can select, but man does not, and the mesh of civilization which he has woven around himself does not allow for natural selection except in extreme cases. Though social inheritance is not transmitted through the chromosomes, being an acquired characteristic, it is nevertheless linked with inheritance in that it is absorbed by the reasoning human brain. Here is the great difference between man and animal. Man can reason and invent, the animal cannot. Man conquers environment through imagination, reasoning, and invention; the animal either dies or adapts itself through changes in function and bodily structure.

With the basic concept of heredity that Mendel discovered as a foundation, other scientists went forward to fantastic new discoveries. Genetics became a science of vast importance and surpassing interest. The units of inheritance, the genes, were studied and their behavior catalogued. Mutations were recognized and understood. But the makeup, the chemistry of the gene itself remained a mystery. But not for long. Science, these days, moves with giant steps and a breakthrough was not long in coming.

It was discovered that there was a chemical powder called deoxyribonucleic acid (DNA for ease in identification), and another nucleic acid named RNA (ribonucleic acid), in the chromosomes that were, with protein, the materials of heredity. DNA was found to be a kind of genetic Svengali, with complete domination over all living cells, an absolute dictator of cell formation, function and specialization. DNA is also capable of constantly reproducing itself, the whole concept one of startling uniqueness.

So tiny it requires an enormous electron microscope to become visible, yet so omniscient that it contains within itself a creative diversity to command uncountable billions of forms; this is DNA. It is composed of four nucleotides which produce twenty universal amino acids which, in their turn, create over 100,000 proteins that give shape, form and substance to the infinite diversity of life-forms inhabiting this planet.

The study of genetics still goes on, as men of science delve deeper and deeper into cause and effect. What we know today of inheritance is of immeasurable importance in animal breeding, removing a great deal of the guesswork from our operations. Yet we do not know enough to make the breeding of top stock a cut-and-dried matter, or to reduce it to the realm of pure science, with a definite answer to every problem. Perhaps this is where the fascination lies. Life is spontaneous and many times unstable, so that even with the greater knowledge that the future will no doubt bring, it is possible that the breeding of top animals will still remain a combination or science and art, with a touch of necessary genius and aesthetic innovation, to ever lend fascination to this riddle of inheritance.

Ch. Hexe of Rotundina (sire)
Kaspar v. Hain, Imp. (dam)
Alma of Rotundina

Grand Victrix 1941. This fine female was used as a foundation bitch by Grossland Kennels.

CHAPTER 5

THE ROOTS OF BREEDING

In today's mechanistic world, with its rushing pace and easy pleasures, much of the creative urge in man has been throttled. We who breed dogs are extremely fortunate, for in our work we have a real creative outlet—we are in the position of being able to mold beauty and utility in living flesh and blood. Our tools are the genes of inheritance, and our art, their infinite combination. We have the power to create a work of art that will show the evidence of our touch for generations to come.

Now that we have absorbed some of the basic facts of heredity, we can, with greater understanding, examine the various kinds of breeding which can be used in perpetuating wanted characteristics. We have learned that within the design of the germ plasm great variation occurs. But within the breed itself as a whole, we have an average, or norm, which the great majority of German Shepherds mirror. Draw a straight horizontal line on a piece of paper and label this line, "norm." Above this line draw another and label it, "above norm." This latter line represents the top dogs, the great ones, and the length of this line will be very much shorter than the length of the "norm" line. Below the "norm" line draw still another line, designating this to be, "below norm." These are the animals possessing faults which we do not wish to perpetuate.

Since the time of Horand von Grafrath, S.V. 1, the first registered German Shepherd, the number of breeders who have molded the characteristics of the breed both here and abroad have been legion. So many have bred without a basic knowledge of any of the fundamentals that the stock produced has the detrimental effect of dangerously lowering the norm. Examine the pedigrees of your dogs, and in many instances you will find an example of this—a line incorporated in your pedigree that causes worry to the true student of breeding. The real objective of all breeding is to raise the norm of a given breed and thereby approach always closer to the breed standard.

If we are to achieve the greatest good from any program of breeding, there are four important traits which we must examine. It is essential that these traits should never depart from the norm.

The first is fertility. The lack of this essential in any degree must be guarded against diligently.

The second is vigor. Loss of vigor, or hardiness, and its allied ills, such as lowered resistance to disease, finicky eating, etc., will lead to disaster.

Longevity is the third important trait. An individual of great worth—who represents a fortunate combination of excellent characteristics which he dominantly passes on to his offspring—must be useful for a long time after his or her worth is recognized by the progeny produced.

The fourth is temperament. Here is the sum total of the dog's usefulness to man in the various categories in which he serves. Lack of true Shepherd character nullifies any other advances which you may make in your breeding program.

The norm can be likened to the force of gravity, possessing a powerful pull toward itself, so that regression toward the average is strong, even though you have used in your breeding parents which are both above average. The same holds true for progeny bred from animals below norm, but from these you will get a lesser number which reach the mean average and a greater number which remain below norm. In the case of the better-than-average parents, some of the progeny will stay above the norm line and the majority will regress. Occasionally a dog of superior structure is produced by a poor family, but inevitably this animal is useless as a stud because he will produce all his objectionable family traits and none of the fortuitous characteristics he displays in himself. From a breeding standpoint it is far better to use an average individual from top stock than a top individual from average or below-average stock. It is also true that many times a great show dog produces average progeny while his little-known brother, obscured by the shadow of the great dog's eminence, produces many above-average young. This is not as strange as it sounds when we consider the fact that the individual animal is the custodian of his germ plasm and it is this germ plasm that produces, not the individual. In this instance, due to variation in the germ plasm, the top dog does not possess the happy genetic combinations that his average brother does and so cannot produce stock of comparative value.

Any of the various categories of breeding practice which we will outline can be followed for the betterment of the breed if used intelligently. Regardless of which practice one follows, there generally comes a time when it is necessary to incorporate one or more of the other forms into the breeding program in order to concentrate certain genetic characters, or to introduce new ones which are imperative for over-all balance. Outcross breeding is not recommended as a consistent practice. Rather, it is a valuable adjunct to the other methods when used as a corrective measure. Yet outcross breeding in the German Shepherd dog does not, as would be supposed from definition, produce completely heterozygous young. The root stock of the breed is the same regardless of which breeding partners are used and, as we have previously shown, much of the stock which represents what we term outcross breeding shows common ancestry within a few generations.

Ch. Fenton of Kentwood

This is the top English Shepherd (or Alsatian as they are called in Britain) who made breed history by going Best in Show at the famous Crufts show. Fenton is typical of the best of English Shepherd breeding.

INBREEDING

By breeding father to daughter, half brother to half sister, son to mother, and, by closest inbreeding of all, brother to sister, stability and purity of inherited material is obtained. Specifically, inbreeding concentrates both good features and faults, strengthening dominants and bringing recessives out into the open where they can be seen and evaluated. It supplies the breeder with the only control he can have over prepotency and homozygosity, or the combining and balancing of similar genetic factors. Inbreeding does not produce degeneration, it merely concentrates weaknesses already present so that they can be recognized and eliminated. This applies to both physical and psychical hereditary transmission.

The most important phases of inbreeding are: (1.) To choose as nearly faultless partners as is possible; (2.) To cull, or select, rigidly from the resultant progeny.

Selection is always important regardless of which breeding procedure is used, but in inbreeding it becomes imperative. It is of interest to note that the most successful inbreeding programs have used as a base an animal which was either inbred or line-bred. To the breeder, the inbred animal represents an individual whose breeding formula has been so simplified that certain results can almost always be depended upon.

There are many examples of extreme inbreeding over a period of generations in other animal and plant life. Perhaps the most widely known are the experimental rats bred by Dr. Helen L. King, which are the result of over one hundred generations of direct brother and sister mating. The end result has been bigger, finer rodents than the original pair, and entirely dependable uniformity. Dr. Leon F. Whitney has bred and developed a beautiful strain of tropical fish, *Lebistes reticulatis*, commonly known as "guppies," by consecutive brother to sister breeding for ten generations. Dr. Whitney found that each succeeding generation was a little smaller and less vigorous, but that in the fifth generation a change occurred for the better, and in each generation thereafter size, vigor, and color improved. This pattern should hold true with all life forms developed from the same type of breeding.

It is interesting to note that genetic experiments with plants, vegetables, and animals which we consider lower in the evolutionary scale than our beloved dogs, have shown that when two intensely inbred lines of consecutive brother and sister matings are crossed, the resultant progeny are larger than the original heterozygous stock and possess hybrid vigor such as the mongrel possesses, which enables him to exist even under environmental neglect (heterosis).

Can we Shepherd breeders indulge in such concentrated inbreeding with our stock, as has been attempted successfully by scientists with other genetic material? We don't know, simply because, to our knowledge, it has never been tried. It would be an expensive undertaking to keep two or more lines progressing of direct brother and sister inbreedings; to cull and destroy, always keeping the best pair as breeding partners for the next generation. Lethal faults, hitherto unsuspected in the stock, might become so drastically concentrated as to bring the experiment to a premature conclusion, even if one had the time, money, and energy to attempt it. But such is the inherent character of germ plasm that one direct outcross

Ch. Beckgold's Ingo v. Burgunderhort, Imp.
(sire)
Arno v.d. Pfaffenau
(dam)
Asta v. Nibelungengold
Beauty, power, character and breeding, he has much to give.

Udine v. Beckgold
(sire)
Ch. Ingo v. Burgunderhort
(dam)
Pert v. Hoheluft
Lovely bitch type in an eleven months old pup. With owner, Ernest H. Hart.

will bring complete normality to an inbred line drastically weakened by its own concentrated faults.

Close breeding is at the very roots of the Shepherd breed, as pedigree studies of the early stock will show. In more recent years we have many examples of the several degrees of inbreeding. Following, you will find pedigrees of well-known Shepherds, selected at random, to illustrate the various inbreeding degrees.

Cita v. Da-Rie-Mar-Hill	Pfeffer v. Bern	Dachs v. Bern
		Clara v. Bern
	Perchta v. Bern	Dachs v. Bern
		Clara v. Bern

This bitch Cita, the result of breeding Pfeffer to his sister Perchta, was the granddam of Grand Victor Ch. Valiant of Draham, owned by David I. McCahill.

Father to daughter breeding (Blondy was the dam of Grand Victor Ch. Dorian v. Beckgold):

Blondy v. Hoheluft	Pfeffer v. Bern	Dachs v. Bern
		Clara v. Bern
	Lady of Ruthland	Pfeffer v. Bern
		Frigga v. Kannenbackerland

In Germany inbreeding to any great extent is frowned upon. Breeders in the Fatherland know, from experience, that there are too many latent faults that can be concentrated by inbreeding, faults that can sap the breed's abilities as working dogs and so destroy the very foundation upon which it has been built in Germany. Yet inbreeding was indulged in, particularly by the brothers Dettmar who owned the Preussenblut and Osnabruckerland Kennels and attempted, through in and linebreeding, to concentrate the virtues they produced in some of their great stock. They

81

Ch. Vol. of Longworth (sire)

Ch. Derry of Longworth (dam)

Ch. Ophelia of Greenfair

A product of close line-breeding, Vol is the sire of the sensational Ch. Jory of Edgetowne.

reached the apex of their careers with the famous "R" litter Osnabrucker-land. There is some doubt that Lex Preussenblut is the sire of the "R" litter as registered. A very good source informed the junior writer of this book that, while in heat, Maja jumped the fence and was bred to by Falk v. Osnabruckerland (Falk could not be shown because of a goiter). Maja was then bred several times to Lex and the litter registered in his name as sire. Lex × Maja breedings were made many times but never produced animals of the caliber of the "R" litter.

There are numerous examples of half brother to half sister breeding, which is the least concentrated of the types of inbreeding, since it can give us two free lines. The following pedigrees are examples of this variety of inbreeding, which produced well-known animals:

Jory of Edgetowne (Grand Victor)
- Vol of Long-Worth
  - Derry of Long-Worth
  - Ophelia of Greenfair
- Orpha of Edgetowne
  - Derry of Long-Worth
  - Bonita of Edgetowne

Viking v. Hoheluft
- Nox of Ruthland
  - Pfeffer v. Bern
  - Carol of Ruthland
- Lady of Ruthland
  - Pfeffer v. Bern
  - Frigga v. Kannenbackerland

It is essential that the breeder have a complete understanding of the merits of inbreeding, for by employing it skillfully results can be obtained to equal those found in other animal-breeding fields. We must remember that inbreeding in itself creates neither faults nor virtues, it merely strengthens and fixes them in the resulting animals. If the basic stock used is generally good, possessing but few, and those minor, faults, then inbreeding will concentrate all those virtues which are so valuable in that basic stock. Inbreeding gives us great breeding worth by its unique ability to produce prepotency and unusual similarity of type. It exposes the "skeletons in the closet" by bringing to light hitherto hidden faults, so that they may be selected against. We do not correct faults by inbreeding, therefore, we merely make them recognizable so they can be eliminated. The end result of inbreeding, coupled with rigid selection, is complete stability of the breeding material.

With certain strains inbreeding can be capricious, revealing organic weaknesses never suspected that result in decreased vitality, abnormalities —physical and mental—or lethal or crippling factors. Unfortunately, it is not possible to foretell results when embarking on such a program, even if seemingly robust and healthy breeding partners are used as a base. The best chance of success generally comes from the employment of animals which themselves have been strongly inbred and have not been appreciably weakened by it in any way.

An interesting development frequently found in inbreeding is in the extremes produced. The average progeny from inbreeding is equal to the average from line-breeding or outbreeding, but the extremes are greater than those produced by either of the latter breeding methods. Inbreeding, then, is at once capable of producing the best and the worst, and these degrees can be found present in the same litter.

Here again, in inbreeding, as in most of the elements of animal husbandry, we must avoid thinking in terms of human equations. Whether for good or ill, your Shepherd was man-made, and his destiny and that of his progeny lie in your hands. By selection you improve the strain, culling and killing misfits and monsters. Mankind indulges in no such practice of purification of the race. He mates without any great mental calculation or plan for the future generation. His choice of a mate is both geographically and socially limited in scope. No one plans this mating of his for the future betterment of the breed. Instead, he is blindly led by emotions labeled

Ch. Jory of Edgetowne
(sire)
Ch. Vol of Longworth
(dam)
Orpha of Edgetowne
Grand Victor 1951. A
sensational show career.

Harold v. Haus Tigges, SchH. III
(sire) Hein v. Richterbach, SchH. III   (dam) Elwira v. Ekeiplatz, SchH. III
"V-A" in Germany and an American Champion, Harold was a controversial dog who
nevertheless sired some top stock in Germany. Owned by Erich and Erna Renner
(Bundespolizei Kennels.)

"love," and sometimes by lesser romantics, "desire." Perish the thought
that we should cast mud upon the scented waters of romance, but for our
Shepherds we want something vastly better than the hit-and-miss pro-
position that has been the racial procedure of man.

Another type of inbreeding, which is not practiced as much as it should
be, is "backcrossing." Here we think largely in terms of the male dog, since
the element of time is involved. The process involves finding a superior
breeding male who is so magnificent in type that we want to perpetuate his
qualities and produce, as closely as we can, the prototype of this certain individual. This good male is bred to a fine bitch, and the best female pup
who is similar to her sire in type is bred back again to her sire. Again, the
best female pup is selected and bred back to her sire. This is continued as
long as the male can reproduce, or until weaknesses become apparent (if
they do) that make it impractical to continue. If this excellent male seems
to have acquired his superiority through the genetic influence of his
mother, the first breeding made should possibly be the mating of son to
mother, and the subsequent breeding as described above. In each litter
the bitch retained to backcross to her sire should, of course, greatly mirror
the sire's type.

LINE-BREEDING

Line-breeding is a broader kind of inbreeding that conserves valuable characteristics by concentration and in a general sense gives us some control of type but a lesser control over specific characteristics. It creates "strains," or "families," within the breed which are easily recognized by their similar conformation. This is the breeding method used by most of the larger kennels, with varied success, since it is not extreme and therefore relatively safe. It is also the method the neophyte is generally advised to employ, for the same reasons.

Specifically, line-breeding entails the selection of breeding partners who have, in their pedigrees, one or more common ancestors. These individuals (or individual) occur repeatedly within the first four or five generations, so that it can be assumed their genetic influence molds the type of succeeding generations. It is a fact that in many breeds success has been obtained by line-breeding to outstanding individuals.

The method varies greatly in intensity, so that some dogs may be strongly line-bred, while others only remotely so. Selection is an important factor here, too, for if we line-breed to procure the specific type of a certain fine animal, then we must select in succeeding generations breeding stock which is the prototype of that individual, or our reason for line-breeding is lost.

One of the chief dangers of line-breeding can be contributed by the breeder of the strain. Many times the breeder reaches a point where he selects his breeding partners on pedigree alone, instead of by individual selection and pedigree combined, within the line.

In some instances intense line-breeding, particularly when the individual line-bred to is known to be prepotent, can have all the strength of direct inbreeding. The following pedigree is a revealing example of this type of line-breeding on Pfeffer, disregarding the obvious inbreeding through Lady.

Pfeffer v. Hoheluft ("P" litter-v. Hoheluft)	Nox of Ruthland	Pfeffer v. Bern
		Carol of Ruthland
	Lady of Ruthland	Pfeffer v. Bern
		Frigga v. Kannenbackerland
Lona v. Hoheluft	Ajax v. Hoheluft	Pfeffer v. Bern
		Arla v. Verstamme
	Lady of Ruthland	Pfeffer v. Bern
		Frigga v. Kannenbackerland

Not quite as heavily line-bred as the example above is the following breeding, which shows line-breeding on the "R" litter—von Osnabrucker-land.

Lexa v. Osnabruckerland
- Rolf v. Osnabruckerland
  - Lex Preussenblut
    - Trutz Schwanenstadt
    - Esta Preussenblut
  - Maja v. Osnabruckerland
    - Achilles Hollenquelle
    - Xanda Preussenblut
- Vena v. Osnabruckerland
  - Racker v. Osnabruckerland
    - Lex Preussenblut
    - Maja Osnabruckerland
  - Blanka Fortunastolz
    - Falk Osnabruckerland
    - Asta Siegeswillen

Close line-breeding on the famous "V" litter Zollgrenzschutz-Haus, is seen in the pedigree below. German breeders must receive special permission from the SV to make such breedings and this permission is only granted when the authorities agree that the "family" is strong and with many virtues.

Trassa v. Zollgrenzschutz-Haus
- Tom v.d. Murrenhutte
  - *Volker v. Zollgrenzschutz-Haus
  - Thea v. Freitagsblick
- *Vera v. Zollgrenzschutz-Haus
  - Harry v. Donaukai
  - Perle v. Zollgrenzschutz-Haus

* Vera and Volker are litter mates.

To found a strain which has definite characteristics, within the breed, the following recommendations, based mainly on the work of Humphrey and Warner and Kelley and Whitney, can be used as a guide.

1. Decide what few traits are essential and what faults are intolerable. Vigor, fertility, character, and temperament must be included in these essentials.

2. Develop a scoring system and score selected virtues and faults in accordance with your breeding aim. Particular stress should be put upon scoring for individual traits which need improvement.

3. Line-breed consistently to the best individuals produced which, by the progeny test, show that they will further improve the strain. Inbreeding can be indulged in if the animal used is of exceptional quality and with no outstanding faults. Outcrossings can be made to bring in wanted charac-

Carmen vom Sixtberg, SchH. II, AD.
(sire)
Volker v. Zollgrenzschutz-Haus, SchH. III
(dam)
Caret v. Elfenhain, SchH. I
This top "V" bitch is also a proven producer. Her son, Condor v. Zollgrenzschutz-Haus, Sch. III, was "V-A" 4 at the '65 Sieger show.

teristics if they are missing from the basic stock. Relationship need not be close in the foundation animals, since wide outcrosses will give greater variation and therefore offer a much wider selection of desirable trait combinations.

Every Shepherd used in this breeding program to establish a strain must be rigidly assessed for individual and breeding excellence and the average excellence of its relatives and its progeny.

OUTCROSS BREEDING

Outcross breeding is the choosing of breeding partners whose pedigrees, in the first five or six generations, are free from any common ancestry. With our Shepherds we cannot outcross in the true sense of the term, since the genetic basis of all Shepherds, both here and abroad, is based upon the germ plasm of a few selected individuals. To outcross completely, using the term literally (complete heterozygosity), it would be necessary to use an individual of an alien breed as one of the breeding partners.

For the breeder to exercise any control over the progeny of an outcross mating, one of the partners should be inbred or closely line-bred. The other partner should show, in himself and by the progeny test when bred to other bitches, that he is dominant in the needed compensations which are the reasons for the outcross. Thus, by outcross breeding, we bring new and needed characteristics into a strain, along with greater vigor and, generally, a lack of uniformity in the young. Greater uniformity can be achieved if the outcross is made between animals of similar family type. Here again we have a breeding method which has produced excellent individuals, since it tends to conceal recessive genes and promote individual merit. But it generally leads to a lower breeding worth in the outbred animal by dispersing favorable genetic combinations which have given us strain uniformity.

Outcross breeding can be likened to a jigsaw puzzle. We have a puzzle

Caret vom Elfenhain, SchH. I (sire)
Alf v. Nordfelsen, Sch. III (dam)
Anka v. Elfenhain, SchH. II
One of Germany's greatest producing bitches, this top "V" bitch is the daughter of Germany's fine working-type Sieger Alf, and Anka, from the famous "A" litter vom Elfenhain.

Condor v. Zollgrenzschutz - Haus, SchH. III, AD.

(sire) Condor v. Schnapp, SchH. II   (dam) Carmen v. Sixtberg, SchH. II
Landesgruppen Youth Sieger, Bundessieger, V-A4 at 1965 Sieger Show. A fine show
and working dog, this handsome Shepherd, whose dam is a "V" litter-sister to Condor
vom Sixtberg, is the product of a great producing line. Bred and owned by Josef
Wassermann, Germany.

made up of pieces of various shapes and sizes which, when fitted together, form a certain pattern. This basic puzzle is comparable to our line-bred or inbred strain. But in this puzzle there are a few pieces that we would like to change, and in so doing change the finished puzzle pattern for the better. We outcross by removing some of the pieces and reshaping them to our fancy, remembering that these new shapes also affect the shapes of the adjoining pieces, which must then be slightly altered for perfect fit. When this has been successfully accomplished, the finished pattern has been altered to suit our pleasure—we hope.

It sometimes happens that a line-bred or inbred bitch will be outcross bred to a stud possessed of an open pedigree. It would be assumed by the breeder that the bitch's family type would dominate in the resulting progeny. But occasionally the stud proves himself to be strongly prepotent, and the young instead reflect his individual qualities, not those of the bitch. This can be good or bad, depending on what you are looking for in the resultant litter.

Incidently, when we speak of corrective, or compensation, breeding, we do not mean the breeding of extremes to achieve an intermediate effect. We would not breed an extremely shy bitch to an overaggressive or vicious stud in the hope of getting progeny of good temperament. The offspring of such a mating would show temperament faults of both the extremes. Neither would we breed a long, level-crouped bitch to a stud whose croup is short and drops off sharply. From such a breeding we could expect either level croups or steep croups, but no intermediate possessing the desired croups. Corrective, or compensation, breeding means the breeding of one partner which is lacking, or faulty, in any specific respect, to an animal which is normal or excellent in the particular area where the other partner is found lacking. In the resulting progeny we can expect to find some young which show the desired improvement.

To sum up briefly, we find that *inbreeding* brings us a fixity of type and simplifies the breeding formula. It strengthens desirable dominants and brings hidden and undesirable recessives to the surface where they can be recognized and possibly corrected by *outcross breeding*. When we have thus established definite improvement in type by rigid selection for wanted characteristics, we *line-breed* to create and establish a strain or family line which, in various degrees, incorporates and produces the improvements which have been attained.

In this maze of hidden and obvious genetic stirring, we must not forget the importance of the concrete essence that stands before us. The breeding partners must be examined as individuals in themselves, apart from the story their pedigrees tell us. For as individuals they have been fashioned by, and are the custodians of, their germ plasm, and mirror this fact in their being. Breedings made from paper study only are akin to human marriages arranged in youth by a third party without consulting the partners—they can be consummated but have small chance of success.

The importance of a pedigree lies in the knowledge we have of the individual animals involved. A fifteen-generation pedigree means nothing if we know nothing about the dogs mentioned. It is more important to extend your knowledge of three or four generations than to extend the pedigree itself. Of real guidance in breeding is a card-index system, such as was used at Fortunate Fields by Humphrey and Warner. This system should indicate clearly the faults and virtues of every pedigree name for at least three generations, with available information as to dominant and recessive traits and the quality of each animal's progeny. At the moment, such a system is practically impossible to achieve. There is little enough known, genetically, about living animals, and the virtues of dogs that are gone are distorted by time and sentiment. Here is a real project and a challenge for the Parent Club (forgive us our trespass) which would be of vastly more worth than the R.O.M. since true pedigree recordings, correctly developed, can represent a really valuable progeny test of ancestors. To be truly efficacious, near ancestors, as well as litter mates, must also be examined for endowed traits, and percentages in regard to these traits correlated and recorded in the pedigree index. From these indexes, graphs could be plotted which would indicate trends within the breed as a whole. To accomplish this design completely, a geneticist would have to be employed and furnished with absolutely truthful information. Incidently, the Puppy Futurities, inaugurated by our progressive and hard-working Parent Club, give the fancy a fair, though necessarily incomplete, idea of what existing "bloodlines" are producing.

The breeding of fine dogs is not a toy to be played with by children. For some of us it forms a nucleus of living, in the esthetic sense. We who give much of our time, thought, and energy to the production of superior stock are often disgusted and disillusioned by the breeding results of others who merely play at breeding. So often individuals long in the game advise the novice never to inbreed, but only to line-breed, since in this way the least harm can be done. There has been too much harm done already by novice breeders who should not have been encouraged to breed at all, except under the direct supervision or advice of an experienced or knowledgeable dog man.

The people who compose what we term The German Shepherd dog "fancy," belong to one of three categories: the novice, the amateur, and the professional. The novice is one who has recently become enamored of the breed, a tyro, a beginner. Many of them remain in that category indefinitely, due to lack of sincerity or reluctance to learn. Others, eager to absorb all they can, soon rise above the original status.

The professional is one who makes his livelihood from the dog game. His living or employment depends in whole or part upon his kennel activities. A professional must know his business well in order to make it a success, and the earnest professional generally does, though he may occasionally be guilty of breeding for the market.

Numerically, the largest category is that of the amateur. To these individuals the breeding, showing, or training of Shepherds is a serious hobby. Here are the students of the breed, the people who, in most instances, are well informed, yet avid for new knowledge that will aid in breed betterment.

Our novice is many times a charming person who loves his dogs passionately, provides them with more fancy vitamins and supplements than honest food, and treats them with a sloppy sentimentality that even a human baby would resent. He simply can't wait to breed his lovely bitch and have those adorable puppies. Of course he hasn't the time to acquire a bit of knowledge about the breed, or about the animals in his bitch's pedigree or the stud to which he is going to breed. How then will he have

Ch. Churlswood Tosca of Brinton
A lovely, feminine English bitch who made her championship in top competition.

the time or knowledge to care for the pregnant bitch and the subsequent litter properly? Yet inevitably he does find time to listen to the pseudo-professional advice of several self-confessed authorities. In due time this novice is possessed of from seven to ten of the cutest puppies you ever saw, which will in turn be sold to other novices (Heaven help them) as show and breeding prospects.

By far the greatest menace to the future of the breed is a particular type of wealthy novice. Possessed of the wherewithal to keep and breed any amount of dogs, and kennelmen to take care of them, this novice blunders arrogantly forward by virtue of the authority vested in him by his bank-books and, unhampered by knowledge, breeds indiscriminately, producing

Ch. Amigo v. Hoheluft
(sire)
Ch. Pfeffer v. Bern
(dam)
Arla v. Verstamme

From a fine litter that passed their grand heritage on to their progeny.

litter upon litter of worthless stock. By the law of averages an occasional animal is produced that could qualify S.G. By cramming show classes with other of his mediocre stock and shipping, with professional handlers, to parts of the country where major wins can be made with fewer entries, he soon has champions which are extensively advertised at stud for other novices to breed to. In the end this novice generally surprisingly and suddenly blossoms out as a full blown "authority" and judge.

What has been written above is not to be construed as a sweeping condemnation of all novices. Without a constant influx of neophyte breeders, the breed would not be in the high place it is today. Many so-called novices bring to their new breed interest a vast store of canine knowledge collected by an inquiring mind and contact with other breeds.

To repeat, the novice is generally advised by the old-time breeder to begin his new hobby with a line-bred bitch, as this is the cautious approach which leaves the least margin for error. But what of that novice who is essentially what we call a born "dog man?" That individual who, for lack of better definition, we say has a "feel" for dogs, who seems to possess an added sense where dogs are concerned.

Gero v Haus Elkemann, SchH. III, FH.

(sire) Tell v. Colonia Agrippina   (dam) Regina v. Colonia Agrippina

A top show dog of beautiful type, he is also a successful sire.

Veit v. Busecker-Schloss, SchH. III
Litter-brother to Valet he also passes on the excellencies of his breeding.

If this person has an inquiring mind, normal intelligence, and has been associated with other breeds, then the picture of him as the true novice changes. The old-timer will find many times that this "novice" frequently possesses information that the old-timer did not even know existed. This is especially true if the tyro has been exposed to some scientific learning in fields relative to animal advancement. Even experience, which is the old-timer's last-ditch stand, is negligible, for this knowledgeable "novice" can disregard the vagaries of experience with foreknowledge of expectancy.

In most instances this type of novice doesn't begin to think of breeding, or even owning, a specimen of the breed until he has made a thorough study of background, faults, virtues, and genetic characters. To him, imitation is not a prelude to success. Therefore the line-bred bitch, modeled by another's ego, is not for him. The outcross bitch, whose genetic composition presents a challenge and which, by diligent study and application of acquired knowledge, can become the fountainhead of a strain of his own, is the answer to his need.

Some of what you have read here in reference to the novice may have seemed to be cruel caricature. Actually, it is not caricature, but it *is* cruel and is meant to stress a point. We realize that to some novices our deep

Perle v. Romerblut, SchH. II
A lovely, imported German bitch of real quality and fleet gait.

absorption in all the many aspects of breed betterment may seem silly or ridiculous. But wanton breeding once before almost destroyed our German Shepherds, and we who love the breed must diligently guard against a repetition of that disaster. The genetic repercussion of breeding stupidity can echo down through generations, making a mockery of our own intense, sometimes heartbreaking, and often humble, striving toward an ideal.

CHAPTER 6

THE GERMAN SIEGER SHOW

The Sieger show is the dreamed of Mecca of every serious Shepherd dog fancier. There, in Germany, the country of the breed's birth, this great annual specialty show draws the elite of the Shepherd world, and the decisions made by the judges influence generations of Shepherds to come, molding unborn dogs to specific conformation and temperament through the genetic pattern of progenitors selected at the Sieger show.

From America one can reach the land of the Lorelei by plane or boat and the preparation for the trip is always, in itself, exciting. We, the Harts, have used both means of transportation, having jetted to Frankfort for the 1963 show and, in 1964, embarked via the Dutch flag ship, S.S. *Rotterdam*, for Holland where we picked up a Peuguot station wagon (which we had bought in New York sight unseen), and drove leisurely down to Cologne (Koln) for the Sieger show. Our trips to Sieger shows, which begin as simple, albeit stimulating, two-day visits to these Shepherd shrines, inevitably get out of hand to become severely bloated with "geographic spread" and we find ourselves viewing wonders in far places greatly removed from Germany in time and place. As a matter of fact, we have just returned from Africa and a marvelous year on the Costa del Sol in southern Spain where our insatiable wanderlust inveigled us after our last Sieger show.

But, for the moment, we must turn a deaf ear to the siren songs of other lands and return to our objective, the Sieger show (Siegerhauptzuchtschau) in Germany. From all over the world people and dogs converge upon the city where the show is to be held. Approximately twenty-five nations have representative specimens of the breed entered in this great show; forty to fifty dogs, representing many different countries, cultures and peoples, from Pakistan to Uruguay, from Norway to India. Of course the greatest number of dogs are from all the sections of Germany itself and these animals comprise the bulk of the 600 to 1,000 German Shepherd dogs to be evaluated within the two day span of the Sieger show.

The number of dogs entered has increased steadily and in recent years the growth has been so marked that it is now necessary to select a city to house the show which has a race track within its borders or nearby, for only such an establishment can accommodate the tremendous influx of canines and lovers of the breed that converge upon the grounds of the Sieger show. The host city takes on an air of suppressed excitement (or perhaps this emotion exists only in the minds of the excited, visiting individual) and on the streets one sees many fine Shepherd dogs with their owners. While viewing the inevitable medieval Cathedral you will meet a judge or breeder from Canada, California or Connecticut who has heard through the grapevine, and imparts the invaluable information to you *sotto voce* and with a knowing wink, that a specific dog is "in" and will be selected as the next Sieger on Sunday. Never, but *never*, do these prophesies prove true.

Before we leave our hotel for the show grounds there are some pertinent facts of which we should be aware for a fuller understanding of the events we will witness during these two days. The dogs themselves, in the aggregate, are the finest of their breed in the world. To qualify for entrance to the two important Gebrauchshundklasses (Working Dog classes, a class for each sex) from which, on the second and last day of the show, will emerge the year's Sieger and Siegerin (Grand Champions), a Shepherd dog must have received an award of "Excellent" ("V"-Vorzüglich), or a minimum "Very Good" ("SG"-Sehr Gut) at one of the regional shows. Another requirement is that every animal entered in these classes must have earned at least one working degree, or (for dogs entered from other countries) the equivalent. These utility grades are known as Schutzhunde degrees (I, II, and III), and are comprised of a trio of tests that embrace tracking or trailing (Nase), general obedience (Unterordnung), and protection or man-work (Schutzdienst). Another qualification for entrance in this important class is that the dogs be mature; they cannot, therefore, be less than twenty-four months of age.

The Young Dog Class (Junghundklasse), divided for the sexes as are all classes, is open to animals of from eighteen to twenty-four months of age. This class will supply the Youth Sieger (and Siegerin from the comparable female class) for the current year. For dogs between the ages of twelve and eighteen months there is the Jugendklasse, or Youthful Class. One other class is also judged at the Sieger show, the interesting H G H, Sonderklasse, a special class for dogs and bitches actually and actively employed as herding dogs.

Competition other than in the principle classes named above is arranged in the Zuchtgruppen or Kennel Contest, in which groups of dogs of close uniformity typical of their particular strain, are entered by kennels; and the Breeding Groups (Nachkommengruppen) where the progeny of well known stud dogs are exhibited and assessed and the sire individually rated according to the quality and uniformity of his get.

Precedent decrees that the Working Dog Class, Males (Ruden), be judged each year by the first chairman (President) of the ruling body of the breed in Germany, the Verein für Deutsche Schäferhunde (SV), and the Working Class Bitches are to be appraised by the second chairman of the board. As a result of this old custom Dr. Werner Funk of Hamburg,

Painted from sketches made in the Bavarian Alps near Garmisch Partinkerchen, this watercolor by Ernest H. Hart depicts the German Shepherd doing the job it was bred to do. Here the bitch leads her son toward the flock to introduce him to his future charges.

FREI v. ENIGSFELD, SchH. II

(sire) Mutz a.d. Kuckstrasse   (dam) Ilse v. Dummerbach

Typical of his breeding, Frei is an impressive male who had not quite
reached maturity when this photo was taken.

BARRY v. RIEDGOLD, SchH. III

(sire Jonny v.d. Riedgold, SchH. III

(dam) Casta v. guten Ruf, SchH. III

A typical hard, driving, working dog type, Barry has achieved high awards constantly in Germany, but in the U. S. it is doubtful if he could win. VA6 at the '64 Sieger Show, Barry mirrors the genetic pattern of grandsire, Alf v. Nordfelsen.

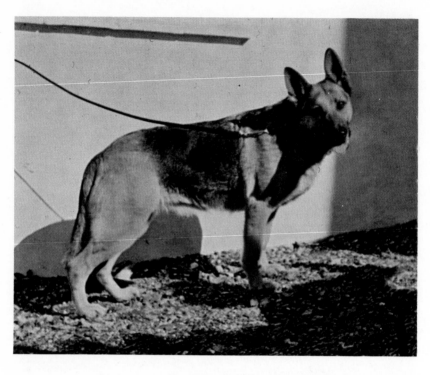

DELLA vom DEVRIENTHOF, SchH. I, HGH.

(sire) Volker v. Zollgrenzschutz-Haus, SchH. III, CACIB

(dam) Antje v. Ahnenschloss, SchH. III

Her dam was Berlin Siegerin and Della is the best daughter of her celebrated sire. A "VI" bitch in conformation and performance, she has twice been Leistungshuten Siegerin (Herding), and Diensthund-leistungssiegerin of Berlin. Imported and owned by Mr. and Mrs. Ernest H. Hart.

Shadows are beginning to elongate in the mature bitch class ring as the Siegerin and other VA bitches are about to be selected. Note the balanced beauty of the high ranked bitch in the foreground.

ALF v. SCHWALESTADT, SchH. III

(sire) Bur v. Stoerstrudel   (dam) Bionda v. Lomborn

This dog has been a top competitor in Sieger competition. He is a dry, excellent moving male with flashy coloration.

CONDOR vom SIXTBERG, SchH. II, AD.

(sire) Volker v. Zollgrenzschutz-Haus, SchH. III, CACIB

(dam) Caret v. Elfenhain, SchH. I

A "VI" German import, Condor's great nobility, mental and physical balance, and impressive masculinity, are the product of generations of top German breeding. Volker's greatest son, his wonderful character parallels his powerful working dog type. Owned by Mr. and Mrs. Ernest H. Hart.

A top VA bitch at the Sieger Show. Beautifully balanced and in excellent show ring bloom, she illustrates the type for which German breeders strive.

One of the rings at the Sieger Show. The size of the ring can be estimated by the distance to the spectators on the other side.

AXEL v. PFINZLAND, SchH. I

(sire) Casar v. Drosselhorst   (dam) Kascha v. Walzbachquelle

Axel received a high "V" at the 1963 Sieger Show. Bred by Fritz Muller, he is a medium sized dog with rich pigmentation and a marvelous temperament.

Ulk Wikingerblut, SchH. III, AD.

(sire) Troll v. Richterbach, SchH. III, FH.   (dam) Natja Wikingerblut, SchH. II

This import, an American and Canadian Champion and Canadian Grand Victor, is the son of a celebrated import and U. S. Grand Victor. Ulk's multitude of show ring wins are a tribute to his quality. Owned by Ralph S. and Mary C. Roberts.

Witz v. Haus Schutting, SchH. III

(sire) Karlo v. Hannastein, SchH. II   (dam) Trojana v. Colonia Agrippina, SchH. I

Bred by Dr. Werner Funk and owned by Karl Muller in Tokyo, Witz has been a powerful stud force in Germany.

one of the most famous judges and breeders of German Shepherds in the world (the von Haus Schutting Kennels), has for years, as president of the SV, judged the most important male class at the annual Grand Championship show and bestowed the most coveted award in Shepherdom upon his eventual choice, the title of Sieger.

In such huge classes judging must, in some respects, be rather arbitrary. For instance, one lacking tooth is considered a fault, regardless of the reason, accidental or congenital, that is the cause of its absence. A weak ear could be the result of damage sustained in that area during a kennel fight but, whatever the cause, it is faulted as not being the wanted, typical ear. If there is any small margin of doubt about a dog's character or temperament, the animal is set down. In Germany no concessions are made where temperament is concerned. Any slight deficiency in strength of nerves or character is severely penalized.

The other five secondary classes (including the Sonderklasse and excluding the two Gebrauchshundklasses already discussed) are evaluated by men of undeniable integrity whose full knowledge of the breed and long experience in judiciary assignments at important shows make them qualified to cope with the almost overwhelming quality and quantity in Sieger show classes. We will be able to purchase a catalogue at the show grounds (for ourselves and to fill the requests of friends in the fancy back home) which will impart full information on every dog entered. On Friday night don't forget to remove the film (comprised of a multitude of shots of "the Cathedral") from your camera and reload with a fresh roll so that you can return home with photos of the many fabulous dogs you will see and wish you owned.

Saturday dawns, sometimes cloudy and damp, but more often sunny and brightly beautiful and, filled with suppressed excitement and pleasant expectation, we are off to the Sieger show. Cars, people, and dogs crowd everywhere outside the main gates to the track. After purchasing a ticket and entering inside the grounds, the commercial booths will first draw our attention. Leashes, collars, including the torquatus training type, are on display, and large tables or hanging racks offer padded attack sleeves, jackets and full suits, monstrous in their bulk, like clothing tailored for alien creatures of some far planet. Dog food, only recently making its appearance in Europe, is displayed in booths much as it is at dog shows in our country. But most German breeders, I'm sure, still feed the diet that has nourished generations of Shepherds in the Fatherland, soaked oats, tripe, milk and oatmeal. Commemorative first cover envelopes bearing special stamps and a picture of last year's Sieger are on sale, and there are Shepherd dog pins and emblems of all kinds and for all purposes.

We enter under the "Eingang" sign into the infield of the stadium where

Gero v. Katharinentor. SchH. III, FH.
(sire) Casar v.d. Malmannsheide, SchH. III, FH. (dam) Barbel v. Escherdamm, SchH. II
He gave richness of pigmentation and uniformity in type to his get. Important in many
German pedigrees, Gero is an example of the "Axel" "R" litter, Osnabrucker Land
cross.

the huge rings are located on the springy grass. Above us clouds race across the blue sky, grouping, pausing for a moment then breaking into shards and segments and hurrying away, seemingly as excited as the people below in the racing arena. There are small stands back from the rings, where one may buy a hot rinderwurst (frankfurter) with sauerkraut on a thick slab of home-made bread, and wash it down with Cognac, Coca-Cola, or Kirshwasser.

And everywhere there are dogs, tied to fences, lolling in the shade of bushes, or walking with their owners. Dogs and people, moving toward specific goals in erratic patterns, and the people, unless they are the rare individual whom you may know, are a faceless, two-legged mass attached by an umbilical-like leash to the many magnificent dogs. Ah, the dogs, the handsome, powerful, panting dogs, each more beautiful, more graceful than the last. Your head swivels madly, your eyes dining voraciously on this feast of canine majesty as we follow the crowd, with many pauses to hurriedly check the number of a passing dog in our catalogue for identification and breeding. We select one of the gigantic class rings (usually the

Gebrauchshundklasse Ruden) to make our visual stand. Surrounding us, ten or more deep, and continuing in the same number all around the great circle, is a colorful moving mass of humanity from all parts of the globe; faces highcheeked, heavyjowled, smooth shaven, bewhiskered, brown, black, yellow, white, almond eyed, blue eyed; from lands of snow or sand, fjords and forests, mountains and plains, they have come from wherever planes will fly, to see, to compare, to be stirred by, and to pay homage to, the German Shepherd dog.

Meanwhile, the other rings also have their massed complement of eager observers as the judges emerge from under their huge sun umbrellas or small tents (the latter a recent innovation) and, armed with pens and pads and with their entourage of stewards, guest judges and runners, begin their important assignments. The dogs of these huge classes are broken up into smaller, more easily manipulated groups, and are trotted around the ring, brought forward separately for individual examination, and temperament tested by the firing of guns and the movement of the judge and his cohorts around them, then trotted around the ring again in the

Groll vom Sixtberg, SchH. II, AD.

(sire) Witz v. Haus Schutting, SchH. III   (dam) Caret v. Elfenhain, SchH. I

A top young, "V" male of the same breeding that produced the "H" litter, vom Sixtberg.

constant and seemingly interminable movement of dogs that will endure for these two days. The judge watches keenly, compiles his notes, compares views with various individuals of his retinue and, in general, goes about the very intense and exacting business of dog judging.

At the luncheon break we join others at the nearest restaurant, probably one at the track, and are enveloped in a mass of genially shouting and laughing people and quiet, well-mannered dogs. Eventually we'll find room to squeeze into a well-filled table and attempt to make conversation with smiling strangers in a language we don't speak, while the dogs sleep under the table crowding our feet oblivious to the cheerful cacophony. And though the moving, mouthing, hearty people crushing around us are not of our country, our culture or way of life, and though their tongue is alien to our ears, yet they are not complete strangers, for we share and find a close brotherhood in our intense interest in, and love for, the German Shepherd dog.

The day finally ends and we hurry back to our hotel to shower and change so that we can arrive at the welcoming banquet early enough to

Bob vom Riedkanal, SchH. III
(sire) Dick v.d. Malmannsheide, Sch. III   (dam) Werra vom Riedkanal, SchH. II
A top "V" show dog and excellent sire who gives to his progeny his rich pigmentation, excellent front assembly and iron back. Bob is well liked as a sire in Germany.

Andra Daheim, SchH. I

(sire) Condor v. Hohenstamm, SchH. III   (dam) Spree Daheim, SchH. I

Daughter of a former German Sieger, this lovely, imported bitch and American Champion, mirrors the best of her line. Owned by Charles H. Kaman.

insure our finding a good seat. This banquet is one of welcome and good-fellowship and consists of much noise, drinking beer, many speeches, drinking beer, singing, drinking beer, meeting people whose interests at the moment parallels ours, and good talk in many tongues and artful charades, about German Shepherd dogs and, of course, drinking beer.

Very late, gurgling with good Deutschland brew, and Shepherd-saturated, we stagger back to the hotel leaving an early call at the desk so that we can hurry through our continental breakfast and arrive at the show grounds early enough on Sunday morning to watch the special sire and get (Nachkommengruppen) judging.

Gradually, through the ordered confusion, this last day of the show reaches toward its dramatic climax. The best animals have been selected and given their highly prized awards in the Jugend and Junghund classes. Since the animals that are entered in these classes are still immature, the highest award is an "SG" (Sehr Gut—Very Good). But there is a de-signation of select "SG" dogs of the highest quality to segregate them from animals of lesser quality who yet deserve an "SG" award. Dogs lower in the scale of perfection who have received "G" (Gut—Good), "A" (Ausreishend—Sufficient), "M" (Mangelhaft—Faulty) and "O" (Failed—Zero) had been excused the day before. The Youth Sieger and Siegerin have been selected from the Junghundklasses, and the coveted "V's" (Vorzuglich—Excellent) if any, awarded in the HGH Sonderklasse, accompanied by lesser awards.

Shadows paint indigo shapes across the track as the final decisions are

Halla vom Sixtberg, SchH. I

(sire) Witz v. Haus Schutting, SchH. III   (dam) Caret v. Elfenhain, SchH. I

A fine young "V" bitch, a successful repeat of the "G" litter vom Sixtberg. Out of the great producing bitch, Caret v. Elfenhain.

made in hushed silence. The dogs are still moving, moving, trotting steadily around the ring accompanied by their bone-weary handlers. Then an excited clamor and mass movement agitates the tightly packed crowd, greeting the final selection of the Sieger and Siegerin in their respective rings. The new Sieger, and his feminine counterpart, followed by the Excellent Select ("V-A"—Vorzuglich Auslese) animals, placed according to the judge's selection ("V-A1," "V-A2," etc.) and usually numbered up to eight, trot around the rings in order as announced and identified over the loudspeaker system. Photographers and people with cameras (there *is* a distinction) rush up and maneuver for place to take photos of these great dogs.

After the "VA" class there are listed the top "V" (Excellent) dogs, followed by "V" animals slightly less exalted, then the "SG" (Very Good) that are in the upper bracket of this classification, and so on, down the line to oblivion.

Then, as the sun sinks reluctantly over the grandstand, the major awards are made in front of a gaily colored backdrop of wind-whipped flags, where the new king and queen of Shepherdom, with their tired but happy handlers, standing on a graduated, Olympic-award-type platform and bedecked with victor's wreaths, are awarded the cups and crowns of sovereignty.

"The King is dead! Long live the King!"

Another Sieger show has added its international and glamorous influence to canine history. As we leave the grounds in the gathering dusk,

Hanko v.d. Hetschmuhle, SchH. II
(sire) Witz v. Haus Schutting, SchH. II   (dam) Eva v.d. Hetschmuhle, SchH. III
German Sieger, 1965. A good moving, harmonious animal, Hanko is owned by an
American. His breeding shows a double cross to Hein v. Richterbach. Owner: Bart B.
Chamberlain, Jr.

exhausted but exhilarated and, at last, completely Shepherd-satiated, we
pick up a quickly mimeographed list of all the animals shown and the
rating they have received here at the Sieger show, a last gesture to evoke
a paean of praise to the consummate Teutonic efficiency of the Verein
für Deutsche Schäferhunde, SV.

CHAPTER 7

IMPORT vs. AMERICAN-BRED

No other breed of dog is as extensively bred and used over the earth's surface as is our German Shepherd dog. The breed is international in scope, and the pleasure it brings surely passes the limited confines of nationalism, language, or alien habit. Yet we still have in this country a strong and influential group which says, "American-breds are the finest! Imports will only bring us grief! They will undo all we've accomplished in type and soundness!"

This is a wail that is both true and false. A voice crying in the wilderness of intolerance. A voice that constantly cries, "American-bred," yet conversely boasts of famous imports found in the pedigrees of their stock. It is an illogical premise certainly, bringing to mind another voice which with equal inconsistency, vehemently exclaims, "Thank God I am an atheist."

Certainly we have had, and still have, many great American-breds. Of course some imports can bring us undesirable lines of inheritance, but then we, too, have some undesirable patterns of inheritance here at home. No, we don't know what is behind the import—that is, unless we take the trouble to find out. Foreign judges' reports can be found in European Shepherd-dog magazines and translated (*Zeitung des Verein für Deutsche Schäferhunde, S.V.*). Pedigrees can be studied and warnings and advice by survey wardens in the breeding partners to be used can be found. What the forebears have done and what they've produced can be discovered and assimilated. The history of the import can be quite comprehensive to the diligent seeker.

As a matter of definite fact more can be learned about any import than about most American-bred dogs, and the information gleaned will be the unbiased and objective report of authorities.

The first informative document to consider is the imported animal's official pedigree. This is composed of a double length sheet of paper which, when folded in the middle, becomes a front cover, an inside double-page spread, and a back cover. The color of the paper alone gives us information. If it is pink then the breeding that produced the animal was sanctioned by the parent club, the Verein für Deutsche Schäferhunde (SV), as being a good and advantageous breeding. If the pedigree is white it means the dog's parents were not passed by the Breed Survey.

In the upper right-hand corner of the pedigree is typed the Körklasse (Breeding Survey class) in which a knowledgeable examiner representing the SV has designated this dog to belong. Anything lower than a Körklasse

ONE SECTION OF A GERMAN PEDIGREE

I designation in this category should be looked at with a jaundiced eye for any animal worth breeding to should have a Körklasse I rating. In this same space is typed the years during which he (or she) will be considered Angekört, or suitable as a breeding partner, usually a matter of two years which can be extended when it has lapsed by another Angekört examination (unless the animal's breeding record indicates that it is detrimental to the breed). Also listed are the dog's training degrees.

Besides the usual information, such as: the dog's name, registration number, whelping date, sex, and the breeder's name and address, this first page also describes the color and quality of the animal's coat, relates the inbreeding, if any, in the four generations of its pedigree, and lists the names and colors of the subject's litter mates, advising whether there were any with long coats or any males that exhibited orchidism.

By opening the pedigree to the double inside page we find a comprehensive four generation pedigree. Each ancestor's registry number and training degrees are listed and the presence (or absence) of a star next to the name indicates whether or not the dog was Angekört (recommended for breeding).

For the first two generations (both parents and the four grandparents) the pedigree supplies the years each animal was certified Angekört, the animal's color, a short but thorough description of the dog including virtues and faults, its conformation rating, and the names, colors, training degrees and conformation ratings of all its litter brothers and sisters. On the far right of this double-page spread is a key dictionary to all abbreviations found in the pedigree, and underneath this is a space for remarks in which are generally recorded the scores the animal made in its training degrees and the rating it received from the judges. The back sheet of the folder is for transferal of ownership and lists SV rules and regulations concerning the pedigree, registration and new ownership of the animal.

So far you have received valuable knowledge about this imported dog and his ancestry from the animal's pedigree. But this is only one of the informative documents that comes with the import. There are also his exhibition cards which list date and judge of the show, catalogue number, breeder, owner, sire and dam, the class shown in, his rating in that class, and the signature of the officiating judge. Other cards list the dog's scores in his training degrees and are in the nature of diplomas indicating his rating as a working dog. Report cards of the animal's placement in working competitions are also often included if the dog had taken part in any of the many contests of this kind held in Germany.

Now comes the *pièce de résistance*, the dog's Kör (Breed Survey) report. This is a sheet of heavy paper filled completely on both sides with pertinent data about this animal. First the dog is named, with his breeding, breeder,

Ch. Nyx of Longworth

A fine show dog and top producing bitch.

Ch. Oakledge's Donna
A show bitch of quality

Ch. Willette of Grafmar, U.D.T.
A champion in show and obedience

A GROUP

of

CHAMPION

AMERICANBRED

BITCHES

OF THE PAST

Ch. Ada v. Berg
Double Pacific Coast Victrix.

Ch. Minx of San Miguel
1950 Canadian Grand Victrix

owner, Körclass rating and training degrees. Following this section the examiner has written a short, succinct but complete description of the animal. The balance of this page, approximately one third of the total space, and all of the other side of the document is an extremely detailed analysis of the animal covering every inch of its physical aspect, standing and in motion, measurements, weight, comparative size of bone, eyes, teeth, etc. Not a single inch of the dog's physical properties are left without close and careful scrutiny. Also microscopically examined and reported upon is his temperament and character, his willingness, nerves, reaction to agitation and, when under pressure, aggressiveness, sharpness, and response to his handler's commands.

The Kör report ends with a recommendation or warning as to what must be looked for in the breeding partners of this dog. As the foregoing indicates, there is a wealth of information to be garnered about the imported dog, information of the most valuable kind, priceless knowledge that makes him known to us with far more accuracy than the American-bred dog.

Incidently, in order to be considered fit for breeding at all, and to be allowed to be used for breeding by the SV, a dog must have been shown and awarded a minimum classification of "G" ("Gut" or "Good"), and passed the test and obtained a working qualification.

The truth regarding this controversial subject can perhaps be best arrived at, clarified, and understood by an analysis of our American-breds to ascertain where the excellencies of their inherited qualities were derived.

We can all agree that Nox of Ruthland was one of our great modern American-breds, an outstanding show specimen and a dominant and valuable sire. He, his litter brother Noble, and the many fine animals that came from the same breeding or repeats of that breeding, were, of course, sired by the great Pfeffer von Bern, a German import. The dam of Nox and his illustrious sisters and brothers was Carol of Ruthland, and she was sired by Ferdl von der Secretainerie and out of Devise von Haus Schütting, both imports. The gorgeous bitch Lady of Ruthland, whom many fanciers considered the living embodiment of the ideal American-bred Shepherd, was also sired by Pfeffer von Bern and out of a fine imported bitch, Frigga von Kannenbackerland. The fine Pfeffer sons and daughters, grandsons and granddaughters, and those inbred or line-bred upon him, could stretch toward infinity. Consider also how valuable those Pfeffer bitches were in breeding to newly arrived imports, producing as they did an array of fine animals, many of whom became champions.

On the Pacific Coast, in the Midwest, and in many other areas of the country, Pfeffer's half brother, the imported Odin von Busecker Schloss, was used extensively, siring many great dogs and producers. Another import, the gray Chlodulf von Pelztierhof, was also used frequently on the coast in combination with Odin and other foreign-bred animals; Rocky Reach, San Miguel, and many other kennels in that area are rich in the genetic lines of those imports.

The following typical pedigree of a coast-bred champion, in this particular case Kirk of San Miguel, owned by Cosalta Kennels, can give us an idea of how the imports mentioned were used in that area.

San Miguel's Baron of Afbor	San Miguel's Ilo of Rocky Reach	Arno of San Miguel
		Franza of Rocky Reach
	Afra of Panamor	Colonel v. Haus Hodes
		Christel v. Scholarskamp
Judy of San Miguel	Quest v. Winnfeld	Chlodulf v. Pelztierhof
		Eda v. Winnfeld
	Anne of San Miguel	Chlodulf v. Pelztierhof
		Ramona of Cosalta

Arno of San Miguel was sired by the imported Chlodulf von Pelztierhof. Franza was the daughter of Odin von Busecker Schloss and granddaughter of another import on her dam's side. Christel von Scholerskamp and Quast von Winnfeld are both foreign-bred.

In the East, a typical American-bred, Hussar of Maur-Ray, shows the following use of imported stock in his breeding, particularly in strong line-breeding to Pfeffer von Bern. Brando von Heidelbeerberg is also an import.

Viking v. Hoheluft	Nox of Ruthland	Pfeffer v. Bern
		Carol of Ruthland
	Lady of Ruthland	Pfeffer v. Bern
		Frigga v. Kannenbackerland
Leda of Ireton	Noble of Ruthland	Pfeffer v. Bern
		Carol of Ruthland
	Donna of Ireton	Brando v. Heidelbeerberg
		Rita of Ireton

The quality of the "D" von Bern litter, through Pfeffer, Odin, and Lucie von der Drei-Kronen, combined with Sieger Arras aus der Stadt Velbert

Cato v.d. Wiekau, Sch.H. II
(sire)
Rolf v. Osnabrueckerland
(dam)
Hanna v. Rittrum

A "V" German dog and Rolf son, exhibiting the type dominance of this line.

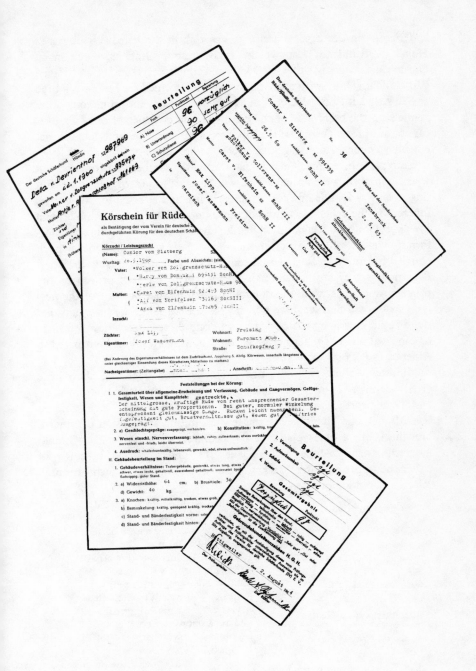

GERMAN KÖR REPORT AND RATING CARDS

and Ferdl von der Secretainerie, groups rich in the heredity patterns of Hoheluft, Ruthland, Longworth, Liebestraum, Grafmar, Grettamarc, Dornwald and many other well-known kennels of yesterday and today. Chlodulf and Odin, with other imported lines, formed the basic stock bred at San Miguel, Rocky Reach, Mi-Noah's, Seamair, and numerous other kennels on the other side of the country. The evidence of our own eyes cannot but prove, then, that the top American-bred sires and dams of that era all stemmed from imported stock, either directly or through line-breeding or inbreeding. It is true that during the somber years of two great wars no imports were available and yet America produced fine stock. But this stock was founded on foreign inheritance and selected for the virtues inherent in the genetic structure of those imports which we had. Through Pfeffer, Odin, and Chlodulf, by judicious selection, a beauty and uniformity were established in our American-breds such as had never been equaled before. Why then should some of us be fearful of using imported dogs now if they are fine animals whose worth has been proven by the progeny test? It is wholly reasonable to assume that in some of the new imports we will find what we need to correct the faults we have and that there could be among the newcomers to our shores dogs whose worth to us can rival that of the former great imports which fashioned our breed in America as it exists today.

Admittedly there are some fine American-bred dogs that show little or no German breeding for many generations, animals bred from good basic, Longworth, Edgetown, Dornwald, Grafmar, Rocky Reach, Cosalta, San Miguel, etc. bloodlines (some few exhibiting an infusion of English breeding), but a quick check of the pedigrees of most of the winning, modern, American-bred animals shows strong imported breeding in either the upper or lower bracket or both. A sampling of such breeding, selected at random, follows.

"F" litter Arbywood	Troll v. Richterbach (imported)
	Frigga of Silver Lane
Lahngold's Ike	Bernd v. Kallengarten (imported)
	Lahngold's Rhemba
Lavaland's Ingo	Wotan v. Richterbach (imported)
	Copper Canyon's Intrigue
Wilva Don's Nordic	Bill v. Kleistweg (imported)
	Afra v. Wormser Weg (imported)
Llano Estacado's Gengis	Axel v. Poldihaus (imported)
	Llano Estacado's Cece
Winaki's Nicolette	Manno v. Stuveschacht (imported)
	Winaki's Gina
Von Nassau's Mark of the Fang	Frack v.d. Burg Arkenstede (imported)
	Von Nassau's Delight
Rittmeister's Alaric	Immo v. Niederschwarzbach (imported)
	Hedgemeer's Freya

Ch. Vetter of Dornwald
(sire)
Ch. Pfeffer v. Bern
(dom)
Ch. Fritzie of Gwynllan
A great Americanbred sire
and showdog, to his get he
gave lavishly of his own
superb quality.

Gr. Vic. & Ch. Tawnee v.
Liebestraum
(sire)
Judo v. Liebestraum
(dam)
Vonda v. Liebestraum
Grand Victrix 1951. A
lovely, Americanbred bitch.

Ch. Naida of Browvale
(sire)
Ch. Nox of Ruthland
(dam)
Ch. Vicki of Hoheluft
Double Nox breeding,
strongly Pfeffer. Beauty of
type which we must not
forget.

There are a host of other dogs, too numerous to list here, and many new animals about to step into the limelight that are the products, in whole or part, of the fine German breeding now available in this country.

Let us now survey the background of the imports which are arriving today in greater numbers than ever before. To do this we must first go back a bit and evaluate the environment which molded them. At the end of the last world war, Germany's economy was as thoroughly smashed as some of her cities. The *Verein für Deutsche Schäferhunde*, during Hitler's regime, had become the playtoy of the ex-paperhanger's satellites. When the war had drawn to its logical conclusion, this situation was quickly remedied by the earnest German breeders. But the breed in the mother country was in very poor shape. Many dogs had been killed in service or during the bombings and the subsequent Allied invasion. Many more had been destroyed because of the lack of food. Some representatives of the best of the German stock survived, but these were in pitiable condition. Even though the war was over, conditions were such that it was almost impossible to find food for dogs when there was not enough food for humans. And what food there was, was not rich enough in essentials to produce proper growth without deficiencies in the young, or give strength and proper nourishment to the lactating mother. Nevertheless, the German breeders earnestly set about the almost insurmountable task of bringing the breed back to its former excellence through that stock which was left to them. The best was bred and the progeny selected from to be fed as well as it was humanly possible under the existing conditions. Outcross breeding was resorted to frequently, since there could be no great selection of line-bred stock from that which was available. Then, too, cross-bred animals had greater vigor, which enabled them to attain a maximum of growth and fertility from the poor food available.

Worth-while animals began to appear, heterozygous certainly, but prepotent in the transmission of their own genetic qualities. Food became a bit more plentiful and varied as time passed. Soon it became patent that certain individuals were dominant in the virtues which the breeders wanted. They then began to line-breed or inbreed upon those individuals whose prepotency and valuable genetic qualities were established. Pedigree lines began to draw together, showing a semblance of the perpetuation of wanted characters by genetic concentration.

As you can well imagine, during the war years and immediately thereafter the weak and the worthless had been weeded out by both man and environment. So the animals which the Germans had left to form the nucleus from which to breed were the most vigorous and temperamentally sane of their basic stock. Physically they were not what they would have been had proper diet and medical means been available. They showed the effects of generations of malnutrition in their lack of size, poor bone, their lack of resistance to disease and parasitic infestation. The amazing thing was that they survived at all. This nucleus with which the German breeders were left to begin again must have been tough and basically sound, both mentally and physically, for surely they had gone through the acid test of the survival of the fittest.

Beginning in about 1949, dogs whose fundamental worth was without question began to make their appearance at German shows. They exhibited the results of the German breeders' determined efforts to bring the breed back to the full glory of its former excellence in the mother country. The survival factor, vigor, the ability to withstand severe punishment, both mental and physical, is the birthright of these dogs. The very fact that they exist at all is evidence of this fact. Couple these truths with their breeding heritage and the structural excellence and temperament of the best specimens and you have an animal which can certainly bring great value to the breed in any country in the world.

Many of these dogs are now making their way to our shores, Shepherds which have been bred by earnest breeders under a strict breeding regime. Some are of no value to us, since to err is human and the German breeders, even with experienced counsel, can still make mistakes. Others are fine specimens in themselves, but will not produce their own virtues when bred to our bitches. But there are, and there will be, specimens which are great dogs, genetically able to produce their own worth, and possibly more, in our country. These are the dogs we must use to correct deficiencies physical or mental in our own stock, and strengthen the general value of our breed.

Let us now attempt to evaluate the qualities of the American-bred and the import with an eye to breed betterment in America.*

We, in America, possess some truly fine bitches, based on the "bloodlines" mentioned before in this chapter. We do not have as many producing males of equal caliber. Since our breeding is genetically limited by general relationship, we who have bitches to breed are hard put to find a stud which does not carry, in either a dominant or recessive state, the same faults which our bitches possess. Generally speaking, we can stand improvement in shoulder, wither, back, teeth, movement, and temperament. We can also see the beginning of a trend toward overrefinement. We do have good angulation, bone, ears, expression, feet, front, middle-piece, and general over-all quality and uniformity. We could overcome all our failings by staying within our own genetic scope and breeding an immense number of dogs, watching for those whose genes have changed or mutated toward the

* What you are about to read was truer a dozen years ago than it is today. The proportion of fully American bred bitches was greater then than now. But the use of imports with American breds as written here is still pertinent.

115

Ch. Rosant v. Holzheimer Eichwald,
Sch.H. III
(sire)
Claudius v. Hain
(dam)
Uda v. Holzheimer Eichwald

Excellent in conformation, this import has had successful show careers in both Germany and America.

Astor v. Hexenstanz, Sch.H. III
(sire)
Alf v. Kronselhoehe
(dam)
Britta v. Haus Fauser

A fine imported stud with a very successful American show career.

Ch. Brando v. Aichtal, Imp.
(sire)
Claus v. Haus Werle
(dam)
Wika v. Aichtal

Grand Victor 1954. A prominent imported winner in American show rings.

improvement we want. Then, by intense selection over a period of years we might, in time, arrive at some of the improvement so needed. This method would entail untold expense and possibly interminable years.

The single easy way to effect a change is to breed to an animal possessing the virtues we seek, hoping to find some of these new qualities in the get, and by selection and continued breeding for these qualities, eventually fix them in our strains. Obviously, then, we must turn to the import.

The better imports have firmness of back, good mouths, fine shoulder placement, high withers, good movement, and strong, though sometimes plain, heads. They also bring us typical temperament and strong, sane mentality. The breeding basis of these dogs, you will find, is sometimes broader than that of our own stock, but they are not the result of completely indiscriminate or outcross breeding. A study of their pedigrees, with a knowledge of the animals involved, will unfold a pattern of type-breeding based on individual worth, compensation breeding as a corrective measure, and breeding, as far as possible, from prototypes of top and tested dogs, which will generally appear several times within the first four or five generations. These better imports will also come from a line of Shepherds the majority of which have been rigidly tested as to mental and physical fitness and have been qualified for breeding by the *Korung*, or survey.

You will also find that, almost universally, the pedigrees of the imports will show much of the same basic stock our own animals possess. Although he was bred in Germany, the breeders there did not have access to Pfeffer von Bern. But the animals behind Pfeffer, the animals which gave him his greatness, will be found far back in many German pedigrees.

Yes, the best of the imports can give us much in the way of improvement. On the other side of the ledger though, there is the danger that unless they are used properly, they can bring us much misery. We have had, and still have, animals that approach greatness. Through them we have arrived at almost universal uniformity. A close inspection of the imported dogs as a whole presents no such picture. Type varies as consistently in these imports as it remains constant in our own stock. By breeding to the import, we run the risk of losing this uniformity, we have striven to attain. Yet it seems that this is the price we must gamble on paying if we are to achieve the virtues which we lack. By breeding these dogs back into our own lines and selecting vigorously for the desired improvement in conjunction with our own good type, we can achieve gain without loss. So many of our American-breds are so strongly line-bred or inbred that prepotency will result regardless of the breeding partner used. It becomes, then, a process of selection for small steps in the direction we seek.

We definitely need many of the virtues which the better imports can provide. But simply because they are imports from across the waters is not

reason, in itself, to use them as breeding animals. The only safe approach is to use a dog which has been used on other bitches, like in type and breeding to the one we contemplate breeding him to. In this manner we can evaluate his usefulness to us and determine whether he is producing the given improvements we want, or is passing on some hidden genetic factor which, linked with unwanted recessives in the bitch, will destroy the type we seek.

Many have been disappointed when they have bred to imports, finding a great variation in type in the progeny which, upon development, are recognized as being inferior to both sire and dam. This must be expected in many cases, since betterment cannot be achieved with one breeding or in one generation. To succeed in our objective of borrowing needed virtues possessed by the import to graft upon our American-bred stock, we must breed judiciously, using our finest representative bitches, select wisely, and realize that it will take more than one generation, perhaps two or three, to establish the new improvements in stock so strongly stamped by a type which we have established over such a long period of time and so many generations. The one immediate improvement we can generally depend upon is character.

The value of the import, therefore, lies in what he can give us that will benefit our breeding as a whole, and not in some nebulous glamor that seems to be attached to the animal which has come from abroad. Much harm can come from imports which have nothing to give, but an immense amount of good can be derived from considered breedings to fine imports whose hereditary characteristics are known and who are genetically constituted to inject needed improvements into our own breeding program.

Germany produces a steady stream of vigorous, handsome, intelligent Shepherd dogs and fine show specimens are always available, at a price. But only a very few of the numerous top show animals that come to the fore each year are great, or even good, producers. Those that are, you can be assured, are very difficult indeed to purchase.

The breeders in the fatherland know that it is much easier to breed a

top show dog than a top producer, and those animals that can give consistently to their progeny the best of their own genetic heritage are greatly valued and are generally not sold out of the country. Great producers *can* be bought, but only through chance, through friendship, or when the powers-that-be in the SV feel that they have enough stock carrying the hereditary design of a specific producer.

A great stud may possibly be purchased when he is too young to have as yet proven his potential as a sire (or, in the case of a bitch, proven her value as a producing brood matron), or when the animal is rather old and leaves enough of his proven get behind him. All dogs carry unwanted faults in their gene-complex, and even the greatest of breeding animals will, in certain matings, produce these faults so that, if the dog lives long enough (and this is particularly true of stud dogs), he eventually becomes a figure of controversy in reference to his producing value. Such dogs can be bought, though generally when past their prime in years. Physically, and of course mentally, though carrying a bit of age, they will be strong, vigorous animals, due to the German regime of husbandry.

Dogs can be bought that have not produced well in Germany or come from families that are not noted for good production, but these dogs could perhaps become good breeding partners when used with American-bred stock. Remember, when the Germans declare that, "*Shepherd dog breeding is working dog breeding*" they mean it. No matter how beautiful a dog may be, if he does not possess working qualities and come from a good "*family*," the German breeders don't want him. In the Sieger shows the genetic quality of the animal and its working attributes are considered against its physical appearance. They are fully aware of the fact that the top, selected animals will be widely used as producers, and no matter how beautiful in conformation a dog may be, outward appearance is no indication of breeding worth. Therefore, and inevitably, the Shepherds selected for top honors in the important German shows are animals that have beauty, working ability, and come from good "*families*."

Many fanciers would like to own an imported dog. If you are one of those who does, consider first the reason for your desire and the end to be achieved. Don't import a Shepherd simply to own a dog possessing that nebulous aura of false worth which we in this country often give to the product stamped "European." Evaluate your desire realistically. Is it a show dog you want? a guard dog? or a dog of different immediate bloodlines to use in your breeding? When you have answered yourself to your own satisfaction, then ask yourself another question. Might it not be possible for me to find an animal here in America which will suit my needs as well as an import would? If it is an imported show dog you desire, remember that a top-winning German show dog in his prime cannot be purchased for "peanuts," and anything less than a top dog in Germany cannot win here in competition with our better American-breds. The same can be said of the imported producer. If your choice is a guard dog, you must be reasonably sure that you will be able to handle such an animal after you have received him. Fully trained German dogs are not of the same caliber as the products of our obedience rings. They are highly efficient protectors whose proficiency is absolute when properly handled, but can be dangerous in foolish or untutored hands.

We can be coldly objective about the imported dog until we own one and then emotionalism has its way. A fine mature animal of good breeding, temperament, character, and with Schutzhund training becomes almost priceless to the owner. The newly imported dog will take a bit of time to become completely acclimated to its new environment but will almost immediately and quietly fit into your family life. Their training makes them beautifully behaved and absolutely dependable under all circumstances and your voice will function like a marionette's wire, exacting immediate obedience. You will feel completely secure in the animal's instant reaction to your every command, and you will be so terribly proud to have this wonderful dog as your own. You will give your heart to this Shepherd and receive, in turn, all of the dog's sweet love and proud obeisance. To possess a fine, fully trained import is a unique experience in dog ownership. Ask the man who owns one.

If, after honestly evaluating your needs, you find that an import is the only answer, and you can afford that answer, then you must reach a person who has the right contacts in Germany and the knowledge and honesty to evaluate truthfully the dogs available (many fine dogs are available if the price offered is enough). It is not advisable to import a puppy as a potential show dog regardless of how good he is reported to be or how well bred. Only adult animals, whose quality can be evaluated from German judges' show reports, should be considered if your desire is an imported show dog. The cost of a German show dog which consistently qualifies "V," or

Harper of Oldway

An English champion who has done some fine winning on his native soil.

Atlas v. Piastendamm, SchH. II

(sire) Ulbert v. Piastendamm SchH. III   (dam) Clarice v.d. Teufelslache SchH. I

This big, powerful, gray dog was imported and made his championship in this country. He is the sire of another fine sire and import, Raps v. Piastendamm.

"Excellent," should not exceed 6,000 to 8,000 marks, or the equivalent of $1,500 to $2,000.

Of course many "V" dogs sell for much more if the buyer will bid higher. In fact today a "V" dog will usually sell for export in the neighborhood of from $2,500 to $5,000 (particularly at the Sieger show). Dogs which receive a "V" Auslese (VA) rating, which is the very select class rating for the top animals at the Sieger show (generally only given to from five to eight animals), are usually priced at from $3,500 to $10,000 (this is only assuming that any of these dogs can be bought at all). The Sieger, if he can be bought, will bring all that the traffic will allow. Mutz a.d. Kuckstrasse, Sieger 1963, and the last Sieger to be bought after winning this exalted honor, sold to a Shepherd enthusiast and breeder in Karachi, Pakistan, for an estimated $15,000. Herr Josef Wassermann, breeder and owner of the fabulous Youth Sieger, double German Sieger and World Sieger, Volker v. Zollgrenzschutz-Haus, has been offered and refused a small fortune for this dog.

A Shepherd that has been consistently awarded high S.G. (Sehr Gut, meaning, Very Good) can be bought for from 1,000 to 4,000 DM (German marks). A mark is the equivalent of 25¢, U.S. money, so the high S.G. dog can be purchased for from $250 to $1,000. An ordinary S.G. dog, holding an SchH.I degree, is worth about $200 with each extra training degree worth from $50 to $100 more. All grown dogs must have earned at least one training degree or they cannot be shown in the regular classes in Germany.

You must not, however, expect the S.G. dog to do much, if any, winning in American show rings. A German dog without real show quality, yet typical and possessing all the basic protection training degrees, Sch. I, II, III, can be purchased for $150 to $200.

In addition to the purchase price of your import, you must add transportation costs, insurance, health certificate, rabies inoculation, and crate costs. If you ship by air, the bill will come to approximately $125 to $150 to New York. If your import comes by boat, the cost will be about $50. The other charges listed above will add approximately $25 to your total outlay.

Not too many of us can afford the cost of a top import, as you can see. But if your bankbook feels no strain and you import a really top Shepherd possessing valuable inheritable material, then you will find great pleasure and profit in your purchase, and quite possibly, by importing this dog, you may have contributed greatly toward the improvement of the breed in America.

CHAPTER 8

FEEDING

Your Shepherd is a carnivore, a flesh eater. His teeth are not made for grinding as are human teeth, but are chiefly fashioned for tearing and severing. Over a period of years this fact has led to the erroneous conclusion that the dog must be fed mostly on muscle meat in order to prosper. Wolves, jackals, wild dogs, and foxes comprise the family Canidae to which your dog belongs. These wild relatives of the dog stalk and run down their living food in the same manner the dog would employ if he had not become attached to man. The main prey of these predators are the various hoofed herbivorous animals, small mammals and birds of their native habitat. The carnivores consume the entire body of their prey, not just the muscle meat alone. This manner of feeding has led some zoologists to consider the dog family as omnivorous (eater of both plant and animal matter), despite their obvious physical relationship to the carnivores.

You would assume, and rightly so, that the diet which keeps these wild cousins of the dog strong, healthy, and fertile could be depended upon to do the same for your Shepherd. Of course, in this day and age your dog cannot live off the land. He depends upon you for sustenance, and to feed him properly, you must understand what essential food values the wild carnivore derives from his kill, for this is nature's supreme lesson in nutrition.

The canine hunter first laps the blood of his victim, then tears open the stomach and eats its contents, composed of predigested vegetable matter. He feasts on liver, heart, kidneys, lungs, and the fat-encrusted intestines. He crushes and consumes the bones and the marrow they contain, feeds on fatty meat and connective tissue, and finally eats the lean muscle meat. From the blood, bones, marrow, internal organs, and muscle meat he has absorbed minerals and proteins. The stomach and its contents have supplied vitamins and carbohydrates. From the intestines and fatty meat he gets fats, fatty acids, vitamins, and carbohydrates. Other proteins come from the ligaments and connective tissue. Hair and some indigestible parts of the intestinal contents provide enough roughage for proper laxation. From the sun he basks in and the water he drinks, he absorbs supplementary vitamins and minerals. From his kill, therefore, the carnivore acquires a well-rounded diet. To supply these same essentials to your Shepherd in a form which you can easily purchase is the answer to his dietary needs.

BASIC FOODS AND SUPPLEMENTS

From the standpoint of nutrition, any substance may be considered food which can be used by an animal as a body-building material, a source of energy, or a regulator of body activity. From the preceding paragraphs we have learned that muscle meat alone will not fill these needs and that your Shepherd's diet must be composed of many other food materials to provide elements necessary to his growth and health. These necessary ingredients can be found in any grocery store. There you can buy all the important natural sources of the dietary essentials listed below.

1. PROTEIN: meat, dairy products, eggs, soybeans.
2. FAT: butter, cream, oils, fatty meat, milk, cream cheese, suet.
3. CARBOHYDRATES: cereals, vegetables, confectionery syrups, honey.
4. VITAMIN A: greens, peas, beans, asparagus, broccoli, eggs, milk.
5. THIAMINE: vegetables, legumes, whole grains, eggs, muscle meats, organ meats, milk, yeast.
6. RIBOFLAVIN: green leaves, milk, *liver*, cottonseed flour or meal, egg yolk, wheat germ, yeast, beef, chicken.
7. NIACIN: milk, lean meats, liver, yeast.
8. VITAMIN D: fish that contains oil (salmon, sardine, herring, cod), fish liver oils, eggs, fortified milk.
9. ASCORBIC ACID: tomatoes, citrus fruits, raw cabbage (it has not been established that ascorbic acid is necessary for dogs).
10. IRON, CALCIUM, AND PHOSPHORUS: milk and milk products, vegetables, eggs, soybeans, bone marrow, blood, liver, oatmeal.

The first three listed essentials complement each other and compose the basic nutritional needs. Proteins build new body tissue and are composed of amino acids, which differ in combination with the different proteins. Carbohydrates furnish the fuel for growth and energy, and fat produces heat which becomes energy and enables the dog to store energy against emergency. Vitamins and minerals, in general, act as regulators of cell activity.

Proteins are essentially the basis of life, for living cells are composed of protein molecules. In this connection, an interesting scientific experiment was conducted some time ago which led to an important discovery. A young scientist attempted to duplicate the conditions which, it is assumed, prevailed upon the earth before life began. Cosmological theory indicates that the atmosphere at that time (approximately two thousand million years ago, give or take a year) would have been poisonous to all the living organisms that exist today, with the exception of certain bacteria. When the experiment had been completed, it was found that amino acids had formed. These chemicals are the building blocks of proteins, and proteins are the basis of life. No, science has not yet produced actual life by building proteins. It is still rather difficult to even define life, let alone manufacture

Ch. Derry of Longworth
(sire)
Ch. Marlo v. Hoheluft
(dam)
Ch. Nyx of Longworth

Prominent show and stud dog from a famous litter of champions.

it. But we can sustain and give growth to living forms by proper feeding procedures.

The main objective in combining food factors is to mix them in the various amounts necessary to procure a balanced diet. This can be done in a number of ways. The essential difference in the many good methods of feeding lies in the time it takes to prepare the food and in the end cost of the materials used. Dogs can be fed expensively and they can be fed cheaply, and in each instance they can be fed equally well.

There are various food products on the market packaged specifically for canine consumption. The quality of these foods as complete diets in themselves ranges from poor to excellent. The better *canned*, or *pudding*, foods are good but expensive for large breeds such as ours, since the moisture content is high and your Shepherd must consume a large amount for adequate nourishment. Compact and requiring no preparation, the canned foods are fine for use at shows or when traveling—though for traveling an even better diet is biscuits, lean meat, and very little water. The result is

Kurt v. Fraubeck
(sire)
Judo v. Fraubeck
(dam)
Fraubeck's Gale v.d. Burg

"Temperament plus . . ."

less urination and defecation, since the residue from this diet is very small. The diet is, of course, not to be fed over any extended period of time because it lacks food value.

Biscuits can be considered as tidbits rather than food, since much of the vitamin and mineral content has been destroyed by baking. The same holds true for *kibbled* foods. They are fillers to which must be added, fat, milk, broths, meat, vegetables, and vitamin and mineral supplement.

By far the most complete of the manufactured foods are the *grain foods*. In such a highly competitive business as the manufacturing and merchandising of these foods, it is essential for the manufacturer to market a highly palatable and balanced ration. The better grain foods have constantly changing formulas to conform to the most recent result of scientific dietary research. They are, in many cases, the direct result of controlled generation tests in scientific kennels where their efficacy can be ascertained. A good grain food should not be considered merely a filler. Rather, it should be employed as the basic diet to which fillers can be added. Since the grain food is bag or box packaged and not hermetically sealed, the fat content is necessarily low. A high degree of fat would produce quick rancidity. Therefore fat must be added to the dry food. Milk, which is one of the finest of foods in itself, can be added along with broths or plain warm water to arrive at the proper consistency for palatability. With such a diet we have a true balance of essentials, wastage is kept to a minimum, stools are small and firm and easily removed, and cost and labor have been reduced to the smallest equation possible to arrive at and yet feed well. The *pellet type* food is simply grain food to which a binding agent has been added to hold the grains together in the desired compact form.

There is one observation that must be made in reference to the evaluation of any commercial food and that is the difference to be found between the experimental animal and the German Shepherd (and many other breeds of medium and large dogs). These foods are, as mentioned before, the result of controlled tests, but the living controls used are generally individuals of a breed smaller than the Shepherd, easier keepers and generally much more voracious eaters pound for body pound. Beagles are one of the breeds most usually used in this capacity for the good and valid reasons named above. Larger breeds need a bit more nutritional value in their daily meals than do Beagles. They must build bigger bone, their rate of growth is slightly more explosive, and they grow over a longer period of time than does the Beagle. Most Shepherds have hearty appetites (if they haven't been babied), but they do not eat with the abandoned gusto of most any hound dog, and are definitely more fastidious than are Beagles. A Shepherd bitch, feeding a litter of puppies, may need up to 300% more nutrition than she does normally.

Fat should be introduced into the dog's diet in its pure form. Proteins and carbohydrates are converted into fat by the body. Fat also causes the dog to retain his food longer in the stomach. It stores vitamins E, K, A, and D, and lessens the bulk necessary to be fed at each meal. Fat can be melted and poured over the meal, or put through the meat grinder and then mixed with the basic ration.

Just as selection is important in breeding, so ratio is important in feeding. The proper diet must not only provide all the essentials, it must also supply those essentials in the proper proportions. This is what we mean by a balanced diet. It can be dangerous to your Shepherd's well being if the ratios of any of his dietary essentials are badly unbalanced over a period of time. The effects can be disastrous in the case of puppies. This is the basic reason for putting your faith in a good, scientifically balanced grain dog food.

There is an abundance of concentrated *vitamin supplements* on the market specifically manufactured for dogs.* They are undoubtedly of real worth—if your dog needs a supplement. Dogs fed a balanced diet do not need additional concentrated supplements, with the exception, perhaps, of the rare individual. If you feel that your dog is in need of a supplement, it is wiser to consult your veterinarian for advice and specific dosage. Check the label of the dog food you buy to make sure that it has all the necessary ingredients. If it has, you will generally not find it necessary to pour in concentrated vitamin supplements. Another of the supplements widely in use today, packaged under various trade names, embodies the elements of what was initially called A.P.F., or animal protein factor. This is a powder combining various antibiotic residues with the composite vitamin B_{12}. The role of this supplement in dog feeding has not, as yet, been adequately established. Theoretically, it is supposed that this supplement produces better food utilization and the production of extra body fat, which accounts for better growth and weight. On the other hand, it is also thought that it can affect the normal balance of intestinal flora, and overdoses can produce undesirable effects. Nature is generally generous in her gift of vitamins, minerals, and other nutritional essentials, and all can be found, in adequate abundance, in the balanced diet. We do not want to rule out supplements, but we do want to stress that they should be used with care.

In many instances kennel owners feel that their animals, for various reasons, need a supplementary boost in their diet. Some are in critical stages of growth, bitches are about to be bred or are in whelp, mature dogs are being frequently used for stud, and others are recuperating from illness.

---

* PALTONE, is a very good nutritional tonic and dietary supplement in malt-like powder form. Pervival, Vionate, etc., are also good supplements.

In such cases supplements can be added to the food, but in reasonable amounts. Some breeders like to supply the supplements through the medium of natural nutritional material rather than chemical, concentrated, commercial supplements. Brewers' yeast, alfalfa meal, and similar natural agents, can be mixed separately in a container and judicious quantities added to the basic diet.

Calcium and *phosphorus* in pure chemical form must be handled with care when used in the dog's diet. Toxic conditions can be caused by an overabundance of this material in the bloodstream. Green, ground, edible bone meal is a much better product to use where it is thought necessary. Most good grain foods have an abundance of this inexpensive element in correct balance. Milk is a highly desirable vehicle for balanced calcium and phosphorus as well as many other nutritional needs.

The feeding of excessive phosphorus is a common cause of metabolic bone disease and the accompanying susceptibility to symptomatic lameness, fractures and bone brittleness due to hyperphosphatemia, which results in the reduction of blood calcium to a percentage far below normal. Felines and canines of the larger species, kept in Zoos, exhibited dramatic changes and excessive bone resorption when consistently fed meat diets, which contain up to twenty times more phosphorus than calcium. *

Cod liver oil is another product that, if given to excess over a period of time, can cause toxicity and bone malformation. It is better and cheaper to employ a fish liver oil concentrate such as percomorph oil. In this oil the base vehicle has been discarded and the pure oil concentrated, so that a very small dosage is required. Many owners and breeders pour cod liver oil and throw handsful of calcium and supplementary concentrates into the food pans in such lavish amounts that there is a greater bulk of these than of the basic food, on the theory that, if a little does some good, a greater amount will be of immense benefit. This concept is both ridiculous and dangerous.

An occasional pinch of *bicarbonate of soda* in the food helps to neutralize stomach acidity and can prevent, or alleviate, fatigue caused by a highly acid diet. Bones need never be fed to dogs for food value if the diet is complete. Poultry bones should never be fed. They splinter into sharp shards which can injure gums or rip the throat lining or intestines. Once in the stomach they are dissolved by strong gastric juices. It is on their way to their ultimate goal that they do damage. The same is also true of fishbones. Soft rib bones are excellent to feed your dog periodically, not necessarily as nourishment, but to clean his teeth. The animal's teeth

---

* CALPHO-D tablets, from the Haver-Lockhart Laboratories, can be used to supply extra calcium and phosphorus in balanced form during pregnancy. This preparation also contains Vitamin D_2.

Rickets in a Shepherd
pup, the result of a
dietary deficiency.

pierce through them completely, and in so doing tartar will be removed and the teeth kept clean of residue. These soft rib bones can be considered the canine's toothbrush.

Table scraps are always good, and if your dog is a good eater and easy keeper, give him any leftovers in his food pan, including potatoes. The diets of good feeders can be varied to a greater extent without unfavorable repercussions than can the diets of finicky eaters. *Fish* is a good food, containing all the food elements which are found in meat, with a bonus of extra nutritional values. *Muscle meat* lacks many essentials and is so low in calcium that, even when supplemented with vitamin D, there is grave danger of rickets developing. In its raw state, meat is frequently the intermediate host of several forms of internal parasites. *Meat by-products* and *canned meat*, which generally contains by-products, are much better as food for dogs than pure muscle meat. Incidentally, *whale meat*, which is over 80 per cent protein, could well replace horse meat, which is less than 50 per cent protein, in the dog's diet.

Water is one of the elementary nutritional essentials. Considering the fact that the dog's body is approximately 70 per cent water, which is distributed in varying percentages throughout the body tissues and organs, including the teeth and bones, it isn't difficult to realize the importance of this staple to the dog's well being. Water flushes the system, stimulates

129

gastric juice activity, brings about better appetite, and acts as a solvent within the body. It is one of the major sources of necessary minerals and helps during hot weather, and to a lesser degree during winter, to regulate the dog's temperature. When a dog is kept from water for any appreciable length of time, dehydration occurs. This is a serious condition, a fact which is known to any dog owner whose animal has been affected by diarrhea, continuous nausea, or any of the diseases in which this form of body shrinkage occurs.

Water is the cheapest part of your dog's diet, so supply it freely, particularly in warm weather. In winter if snow and ice are present and available to your Shepherd, water is not so essential. At any rate, if left in a bucket in his run, it quickly turns to ice. Yet even under these conditions it is an easy matter to bring your dog in and supply him with at least one good drink of fresh water during the day. Being so easily provided, so inexpensive, and so highly essential to your Shepherd's health, sober thought dictates that we should allow our dogs to "take to drink."

Breeders with only a few dogs can sometimes afford the extra time, expense, and care necessary to feed a varied and complicated diet. But it is easy to see that to feed a large kennel in such fashion would take an immense amount of time, labor, and expense. Actually, the feeding of a scientifically balanced grain food as the basic diet eliminates the element of chance which exists in diets prepared by the kennel owner from natural sources, since overabundance of some specific elements, as well as a lack of others, can bring about dietary ills and deficiencies.

Caloric requirements vary with age, temperament, changes in temperature, and activity. If your dog is nervous, very active, young, and kept out of doors in winter, his caloric intake must be greater than the phlegmatic, underactive, fully grown dog who has his bed in the house. Keep your Shepherd in good flesh, neither too fat nor too thin. You are best judge of the amount to feed him to keep him in his best condition. A well-fed Shepherd should always be in show "bloom"—clear-eyed, glossy-coated, filled with vim and vigor, and with enough of an all-over layer of fat to give him sleekness without plumpness.

FEEDING TECHNIQUES

The consistency of the food mix can vary according to your Shepherd's taste. It is best not to serve the food in too sloppy a mixture, except in the case of very young puppies. It is also good practice to feed the same basic ration at every meal so that the taste of the food does not vary greatly at each feeding. Constant changing of the diet, with supplementary meals of raw or cooked meat, tends to produce finicky eaters, the bane of the kennel and private owners' existence. Never leave the food pan before your Shepherd for more than thirty minutes. If he hasn't eaten by then, or has merely

Ch. Traute v. Bern
(sire)
Bodo v.d. Brahmenau
(dam)
Vicki v. Bern
German Siegerin 1937.
Balance beauty and fleetness.

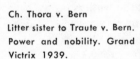

Ch. Thora v. Bern
Litter sister to Traute v. Bern.
Power and nobility. Grand
Victrix 1939.

Ch. Attilas Argos C.D.X.
(sire)
Waldo v. Baumchen
(dam)
Freude v. Richrath
Deep pigmentation, iron
temperament. Full advantage was not taken of his
genetic worth.

131

nibbled, the pan should be removed and not presented to him again until his next feeding time. This same policy should be followed when breaking a dog to a new diet. If he has become a canine gourmet, spoiled by a delicate diet, he may sometimes refuse to eat for two or three days. But eventually, when his hunger becomes acute enough and he realizes his hunger strike will not result in coddling and the bringing forth of his former delicacies, he will eat with gusto whatever is put before him. Remember, your Shepherd is not a lap dog—he is a big and powerful working dog and should not be babied. Where there are several dogs to create mealtime competition, there is little danger of finicky eaters regardless of what is fed.

Keep your feeding utensils clean to eliminate the danger of bacterial formation and sourness, especially in warm weather. Your food pans can be of any solid metal material. Agate, porcelain, and the various types of enamelware have a tendency to chip, and are therefore not desirable.

Every kennel owner and breeder has his own pet diet which has proven successful in the rearing and maintenance of his stock. In each instance he will insist that his is the only worth-while diet, and he cannot be blamed for so asserting, since his particular diet has nourished and kept his own stock in top condition over a period of years. Yet the truth is, as we have mentioned before in this chapter, that there are many ways to feed dogs and feed them well, and no one diet can be said to be the best.

Perhaps it would be enlightening to the reader to explain how the dogs are fed in the kennels of both authors, as well as the feeding procedure used in a much larger kennel than either of ours. The results of these three different diets have all been excellent. There have been no runts, the growth factor in each instance has been entirely adequate, and none of the animals bred or raised have shown any signs of nutritional lack. All the dogs raised on these diets have developed normally into the full flower of their genetic inheritance, with lustrous coats, fine teeth and bones, and all possessing great vigor and stamina. Incidentally, what has been written in this chapter is applicable mostly to grown dogs, though the three feeding formulas to follow include puppy feeding as well. A more comprehensive study of puppy feeding will be found in the chapter dealing specifically with puppies.

Diet Number 1

This diet is employed by Captain Goldbecker at his Beckgold Kennels. Dietol, an oil product, is given the pups in the nest on the second day after whelping; two drops to each puppy. The amount is gradually increased, until the second week each pup is receiving ten drops of the oil. The third week, twenty drops are given, and this is continued until a full pint has been consumed.

At twelve to fourteen days, for a litter of six puppies, a cereal is cooked with one-eighth of a pound of butter or margarine, or a good special puppy meal is substituted for the cereal. To this is added one-half a can of evaporated milk, two poached eggs, cow's milk, and two tablespoonsful of Karo syrup. This is fed twice daily to supplement dam's feedings.

At three weeks, the same diet is given three times a day.

At four weeks, the same diet, given four times a day. At this time, chopped beef, rich in fat, is added, and two eggs are cooked in with the cereal.

Between the fifth and sixth weeks the puppies are weaned. During this period, two feedings are the same as the diet fed during the fourth week, and two other feedings are composed of a good grain dog meal, moistened with broth or soup, to which has been added a heaping handful of chopped beef which is at least 25 per cent fat. This food mixture is supplemented by three tablespoons of refined cod liver oil and a heaping tablespoon of a mixture of bone meal, soybean meal, brewer's yeast, and a small amount of salt.

Three meals are fed as described above at three months and continued until the pups have reached the age of five months, the only variation being the use of small kibbles occasionally replacing the basic cereal or meal at two of the meals.

From five months until twelve to fourteen months, two large meals are given, one in the morning and one at night, using the same diet as above, augmented by any and all table scraps, from potatoes and sauerkraut to cake.

From fourteen months on the dog is fed once daily in the summer. In fall and winter the diet consists of a light breakfast of warm cereal, milk, and Karo syrup. The main evening meal is composed of grain meal or, occasionally, kibbles or pellets, moistened in soup or warm water, a pound of ground fatty meat, one tablespoonful of cod liver oil or Dietol, and a heaping tablespoon of the mixed supplement mentioned previously (bone meal, soybean meal, and yeast). To this is added table scraps of every description, except fowl bones and fishbones.

During the winter months occasional stews of beef or lamb and fresh vegetables are cooked and relished by the Beckgold Shepherds.

Diet Number 2

At the Katherneschloss Kennels of Ernest H. Hart, the following diet is followed.

Dietol is given each puppy in increasing amounts as it grows, beginning with two drops for Shepherd puppies. This oil is rich in vitamin K, which is an essential vitamin for puppy survival.

At sixteen days the pups are given their first supplementary feeding.

From then on the Dietol is incorporated in their meals. A puppy grain meal, Pampa, is used as a base, to which is added a tablespoonful of Pelargon, a Nestle's dried milk product which has been enriched and acidified so that it more closely approaches the taste of the bitch's milk than does plain cow's milk. (Incidentally, if you've brought a puppy home who refuses to eat, try this product mixed with warm milk or sprinkled over the food mixture. In almost every instance it will do the trick.) Warmed cow's milk and about 10 per cent melted fat is added to the Pampa and Pelargon. Stir to the consistency of cream and allow them to eat all they can hold.

At three weeks the same mixture is fed three times a day.

At four weeks, the same mixture is fed four times a day. The fat content is raised to about 15 per cent. The consistency of the food is slightly thickened, and a natural supplement, composed of alfalfa leaf meal, irradiated yeast, and ground bone meal, is added sparingly. The ratios of these ingredients, mixed together in a large jar for continued use are: two tablespoonsful of alfalfa leaf meal to one tablespoonful of yeast and three-quarters of a tablespoonful of bone meal.

At six weeks the pups are completely weaned and fed five times daily. Four of the meals are the same mixture as used at four weeks, with a small amount of canned meat added for taste and a scent appeal. The meals are increased in size with the growth of the pups. The last meal, the fifth at night, consists of warmed milk, half natural cow and half evaporated. After eight weeks the Pelargon is discontinued and powdered milk is used instead.

Five feedings are given until three months. Four feedings from then up to five months.

From five months until eight months, three feedings are given, eliminating the late evening milk meal. The dog is switched then from Pampa to a regular grain meal (in this instance either Lifespan or Kasco, since both

Werra z.d. Sieben-Faulen, SchH. II
(sire)
Etu v. Zierenberg
(dam)
Blanka v. Obervieh!and
An outstanding German show and producing bitch.

are easily available and are good grain foods). Milk is added to all other meals in powder or liquid form.

Two meals, from eight to eighteen months, are fed and thereafter one meal, unless, as is generally the case, the individual thrives better on two meals. From a pint to a quart of whole milk in the morning is always good.

Table scraps of all kinds are used whenever available, exclusive of fowl bones and fishbones. The schedule as outlined above is not necessarily a rigid one. Fish, stews, eggs (yolks only if raw, whole egg if cooked), liver, and a host of other foods are occasionally incorporated into the diet. But this is the one main day in, day out diet.

Diet Number 3

This diet is used by a breeder of Coon Hounds, which are approximately the same size as Shepherds. During the hunting season they are hunted extensively, running miles and miles of woodland nightly, trailing their quarry. Bitches are bred regularly, whelping large litters of healthy pups.

At sixteen to eighteen days supplementary feeding is begun, consisting of Pampa (or a like product) and warmed evaporated milk. This mixture (of creamy consistency) is fed three times a day.

At seven weeks the puppies are completely weaned and receive four feedings daily as described above. Fat is now added to the diet to the amount of 20 per cent of the dry weight of the complete ration.

This amount of fat is incorporated into the diet until the puppies are three to four months of age. At this time the pups are changed to a tested adult grain meal and the fat incorporated raised to 25 per cent of the dry total. The pups are then fed twice daily, with hot water replacing the milk, until fully grown.

With full growth only one daily feeding is given, consisting of the same diet as above.

Relative to these diets, it must be remembered that the authors (Beckgold and Katherneschloss Kennels) are essentially what are termed "back-yard"

Ch. Chlodulf v. Pelztierhof, Imp.
(sire)
Edi a.d. Leineweberhoffe
(dam)
Bella v.d. Lohbrugger-Hohe
A basic stud force on the Pacific Coast.

breeders. Neither kennel is a puppy factory, only from one to perhaps three litters being bred a year. At Beckgold you will seldom find more than one or two dogs and occasionally some puppies. Katherneschloss Kennels houses three or four imported Shepherds,* exclusive of puppies and occasional young stock. In comparison the larger kennel houses sixty or more Redbones, as well as a large number of Beagles used in dietary and other experimentation. Breeders with only a few dogs can generally afford the extra time, expense, and care necessary to feed varied and complicated diets, but to feed a kennel of sixty dogs on complicated diets would take an immense amount of time and labor, not to mention expense, and is therefore not feasible.

To the authors, working with a limited amount of stock, every breeding made is the result of intense study and much discussion, since every breeding made is eminently important and must not be wasted. Then, to complement the results of breeding, a complete and balanced diet is necessary to follow through and bring the resulting get to a correct and healthy maturity.

Remember always that feeding ranks next to breeding in the influence it exerts on the growing dog. Knowledgeable breeding can produce genetically fine specimens, selection can improve the strain and the breed, but, without full and proper nourishment, particularly over the period of growth, the dog cannot attain to the promise of his heritage. The brusque slogan of a famous cattle breeder might well be adopted by breeders of Shepherds. The motto is, "Breed, feed, weed."

* The grown dogs are kept in the house and live as part of the family.

CHAPTER 9

GENERAL CARE

When you own a dog, you own a dependent. Though the Internal Revenue Department does not recognize this fact, it is nevertheless true. Whatever pleasure one gets out of life must be paid for in some kind of coin, and this is as applicable to the pleasure we derive from our dogs as it is in all things. With our dogs we pay the toll of constant care. This Shepherd which you have taken into your home and made a part of your family life depends completely upon you for his every need. In return for the care you give him, he repays you with a special brand of love and devotion that can't be duplicated. That is the bargain you make with your dog: your care on one side of the scale, his complete idolatry on the other. Not quite a fair bargain, but we humans, unlike our dogs, are seldom completely fair and unselfish.

Good husbandry pays off in dollars and cents too, particularly if you have more than one or two dogs, or run a semicommercial kennel. Clean, well-cared for dogs are most often healthy dogs, free from parasitic invaders and the small ills that bring other and greater woes in their wake. Good feeding and proper exercise help build strength and resistance to disease, and a sizable run keeps your canine friend from wandering into the path of some speeding car. Veterinarian bills and nursing time are substantially reduced, saving you money and time, when your dog is properly cared for.

Cleanliness, that partner to labor which is owned by some to be next to godliness, is the first essential of good dog care. This applies to the dog's surrounding environment as well as to the dog himself. If your Shepherd sleeps in the house, provide him with a draft-free spot for his bed, away from general household traffic. This bed can be a piece of rug or a well-padded dog mattress. It doesn't particularly matter what material is used as long as it is kept clean and put in the proper place.

Feeding has been comprehensively discussed in the previous chapter, but the utensils used and the methods of feeding come more specifically under the heading of general care, so we will repeat these few facts mentioned in the previous chapter. Heavy aluminium feeding pans are best, since they are easily cleaned and do not chip as does agate or porcelain. Feed your dog regularly in the same place and at the same time. Establish a friendly and quiet atmosphere during feeding periods and do not coax him to eat. If he refuses the food or nibbles at it sparingly, remove his food and do not feed again until the next feeding period. Never allow a pan of food to stand before a healthy dog for more than thirty minutes

Judge Ernest H. Hart putting up the lovely young bitch, Hexe's Bella of Highland Hills. This fine female went on to some nice wins in strong Eastern competition.

under any circumstances. Should your Shepherd's appetite continue to be off, consult your veterinarian for the cause.

If you are feeding several dogs in an outside kennel, it is good practice to remain until all are finished, observing their appetites and eating habits while you wait. Often two dogs, kenneled together and given the same amount and kind of food, show different results. One will appear thin and the other in good condition. Sometimes the reason is a physiological one, but more often observation will show that the thinner dog is a slower eater than his kennel mate; that the latter dog gulps down his own food and then drives the thin dog away from his food pan before his ration is fully consumed and finishes this extra portion, too.

Never, never, force feed a healthy dog simply because he refuses an occasional meal. Force feeding and coaxing make finicky eaters and a finicky feeder is never in good coat or condition and turns feeding time into the most exasperating experience of the day. Rather than forcing or coaxing, it is better to starve your dog, showing no sympathy at all when he refuses food. If he is healthy, he will soon realize that he will experience hunger unless he eats when the food pan is put before him and will soon develop a normal and healthy appetite. Immediately upon removing the food pans, they should be thoroughly washed and stacked, ready for the next mealtime.

During hot weather, be certain that your Shepherd has a constant supply of fresh, clean water. In winter, water left outside in runs will freeze solid and be of no use to the dogs, so it is best to provide fresh water two or three times a day and remove the pail after the dogs have had their fill. Always provide water within an hour after feeding.

It has been the experience of most dog people that animals kept or kenneled outdoors, both winter and summer, are healthier and in better condition generally than their softer living housedog brethren. Light and the seasons have a great deal to do with shedding and coat condition. The outdoor dog, living in an environment approaching the natural, has regular shedding periods, after which his new coat comes in hard, strong, and glossy. Housedogs, living in conditions of artificial light and heat seem to shed constantly, and seldom possess the good coat exhibited by the Shepherd who lives outdoors. The housedog is much more susceptible to quick changes in temperature, particularly in the winter when he is brought from a warm, furnace-heated house, into the frigid out-of-doors. Never forget that your Shepherd is a strong and powerful working dog, not a lap dog, and treat him accordingly. Babying an individual of a breed of such high intelligence can produce a nuisance or a canine hypochondriac.

PLANNING YOUR RUN

Even the housedog should be provided with an outside run and house, a domain of his own to keep him in the sun and air and protect him from disturbance by children or other dogs. There, in his run, he is safe from accident, and you know he can't run away to become lost, strayed, or stolen. There, also, you can be sure he is not soiling or digging in your neighbor's newly planted lawn, a situation which can strain, to put it mildly, any "good-neighbor policy." Provide shade in some section of the run against the hot summer sun. Natural shade from trees is the ideal, of course, but artificial shade can be provided by a canvas overthrow placed strategically.

The run should be as large as your property will permit. Twenty by forty feet is a good size for one or two dogs, but if space permits it, a longer run is preferable. If you are building a kennel of several runs, remember that the length is more important than the width, and connecting runs in a row can be cut down to ten feet or less in width if the length provided is ample.

The best surface for your run is a question open for argument. Breeders in Germany prefer packed-down fine cinders for their run surface, claiming that this material provides good drainage and is the best surface for a dog's feet, keeping them compact and strong. Actually, heredity and, to a lesser degree, diet are the prime factors that produce good feet in dogs, but a dog's feet will spread and lose compactness if he is kept constantly on a soft or muddy surface. Cinders do make an excellent run, but this surface also makes an admirable place in which parasitic eggs and larvae can exist and thrive, and they are almost impossible to clean out from such a surface, short of resorting to a blowtorch. Here in America we favor cement runs. They are easy to clean and present a good appearance. But again, we have a porous surface into which the minute eggs of parasites can take refuge. Only by daily scrubbing with a strong disinfectant, or periodic surface burning, can concrete runs be kept free of parasitic eggs and larvae.

Gravel and plain dirt runs present the same disadvantage, plus the difficulty of efficiently gathering stools from such surfaces. Dirt runs also become muddy in rainy weather and dusty in dry weather, making it necessary to change bedding often, and producing, as formerly mentioned, a deleterious effect upon the animal's feet. It would seem, then, that none of these run surfaces is the perfect answer to our problem. But there is yet another run surface which can give us better control over parasitic re-infestation. On this run we employ washed builders' sand for the surface. The dog generally defecates in a limited area, almost always at the end of his run farthest from the run door and his own house. Stools can easily be removed from the sand surface, and by digging down and removing one or two inches of sand below the stool, parasitic invaders are also removed. Fresh sand is filled into the spaces left by cleaning. The sand soon packs down and becomes a solid surface. The grains drop easily from the dog's feet and are not carried into his house to soil his bedding. This sand is not expensive, and periodically the whole surface can be removed and fresh sand brought in and leveled. An ideal run would be one with a cement base which can be washed down with disinfectants or a strong borax solution (which will destroy hookworm larvae) whenever the surface sand is completely removed and before a fresh sand surface is provided.

BUILDING YOUR RUN

If you plan to build the run yourself, you might consider the "soil-cement" surface as a base rather than true cement. Soil-cement is a subsurface employed on light-traffic airfields and many suburban roads; it is inexpensive, durable, and easily built without special knowledge or equipment. First remove the sod on the area to be converted into a run, then loosen the soil to a depth of about four inches with a spade and pulverize the soil, breaking up any lumps with a rake. Scatter dry cement at the rate of two-thirds of a sack of cement to a square yard of surface and mix in thoroughly with the soil until the mixture has a floury texture.

140

Adjust your hose to a mist spray and water the surface until the soil-cement mixture will mold under pressure, and not crumble. Follow by raking the entire mixture to full depth to assure uniform moisture, and level at the same time. Now you must work quickly, compacting the run with a tamper and then rolling with a garden roller. All this must be done within a half hour or the surface will harden while still uneven. After rolling, the surface should be smooth and even. Mist-spray again, then cover with a coating of damp sawdust or soil for a week, after which the run can be used. Remember to keep a slight slope on all run surfaces so that water can drain off without puddling. Soil-cement is also excellent for paths around, or to and from, the kennels.

CLEANING YOUR RUN

In removing stools from a run, never rake them together first. This practice tends to spread worm eggs over a greater area. Shovel each stool up separately, and deposit it in a container. When the run is clean, carry the container to a previously prepared pit, dump the contents, and cover with a

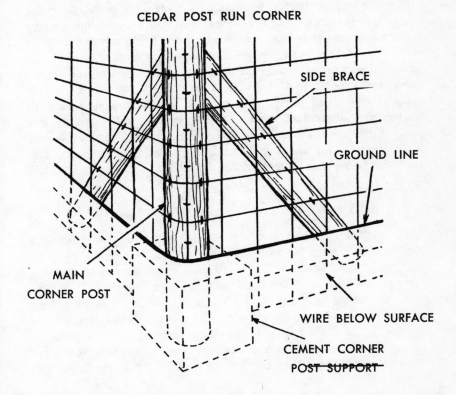

CEDAR POST RUN CORNER

SIDE BRACE

GROUND LINE

MAIN CORNER POST

WIRE BELOW SURFACE

CEMENT CORNER POST SUPPORT

layer of dirt. Hose out the container and apply disinfectant, and the job is done with a minimum of bother. In winter, due to snow and ice, very little can be done about run sanitation. But those who live in climates which have definite and varied seasons have the consolation of knowing that worm eggs do not incubate nor fleas develop during cold weather. Therefore they must only do whatever is possible in run cleanliness for the sake of appearance and to keep down odors.

FENCING YOUR RUN

Fencing the run is our next problem. The ideal fencing is heavy chain link with metal supporting posts set in cement, and erected by experts. But if your pocketbook cries at such an expenditure (and the cost is not small), you can do your own fencing, cutting the cost drastically by purchasing cheaper wire, using cedar posts for supports, and girding your loins for a bit of labor. Hog wire, six-inch stay wire fencing, fox wire, or fourteen gauge, or two-inch-mesh poultry wire all can be used. Whatever fencing you employ, be sure it is high enough to rise six feet above ground level and is of a heavy enough gauge to be substantial. A mature Shepherd can easily scale fencing which is less than six feet high. Dig post holes, using horizontally stretched string as a guide to keep them evenly in line, and dig them deeply enough to hold the posts securely. Leave approximately six feet of space between each post hole. Paint the section of the post which is to be buried in the hole with creosote, or some other good wood preservative and set the posts in the holes. Concrete and rock, poured into the hole around the post, will provide a firm base. A horizontal top rail strengthens the run materially and will make for a better job. Brace all corner and gate posts as shown in the illustration. When your posts are in and set, borrow a wire stretcher for use in applying the wire fencing to the posts. This handy instrument can make the difference between a poor and a good job.

YOUR DOG HOUSE

The dog house can be simple or elaborate, reaching the extremes from a barrel set on cement blocks, to a miniature human dwelling, complete with shingles and windows. The best kind of house comes somewhere in between these two extremes. Build the house large enough, with sleeping quarters approximately three by five feet, and three feet high at the highest point. Incorporate a front porch one-and-a-half to two feet deep and the five-foot width of the house. If the house is correctly situated, the porch roof offers shade from the sun and the porch itself a place to lie in rainy or snowy weather. Make the skeleton framework of two by threes, first building the two side sections, allowing six inches of extra height on the uprights for floor elevation. Incorporate the porch size in the over-all length of the side pieces and remember the back slope over the sleeping portion, which will accommodate the hinged roof.

Next build the floor frame and cover it with five-eights-inch outdoor plywood, or tongue and groove siding. Cover the sides with the same material you use for the floor. If you allow your two-by-three-inch framing to show on the outside of the house, you will have a smooth inner surface to attach your floor platform to. Keep the floor the six inches above ground level provided by your side uprights and brace the floor by nailing six-inch pieces of two by threes under the floor and to the inside bottom of the side uprights. Frame in the door section between the porch and the sleeping quarters, framing for a door four to six inches from the floor (to hold in the bedding), eighteen inches wide and two feet high. Nail your plywood, or tongue and groove siding, over this framework, of course leaving the opening for the door, and nail the same wood across the back and the porch roof, thus closing the house in all around except for the roof section over the sleeping quarters. Build this section separately, with an overlay of four inches on the two sides and the back. Attach an underneath flange of wood on both sides and the rear, in from the edges, so that the flanges will

Ch. Tackleway Rock of Novem

A winning English stud. The low station this male exhibits is typical of most of the winning English stock of this era.

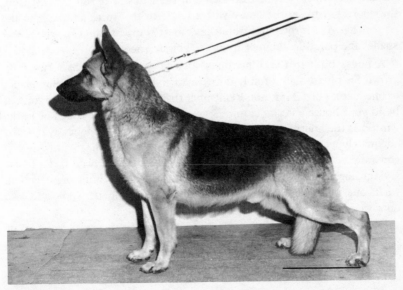

143

fit snugly along the three outside edges of the house proper to keep out drafts and cold. Hinge this roof section to the back edge of the porch roof and cover the entire roof part with shingles or heavy tar paper, with a separate ten-inch flap stripped along and covering the hinged edge. Paint the house (blue or blue-gray paint is said to discourage flies), and it is finished.

If you wish, you may insulate with board insulation on the inside, or double flooring can be provided with insulating paper between the layers. In cold weather a gunny sack or a piece of canvas, rug or blanket, should be tacked at the top edge of the doorway to fall across the opening, thus blocking out cold air. If the house is big enough, an inside partial wall can be provided at one side of the door, essentially dividing the inner portion into a front hall with a weather-blocking partition between this hall and the sleeping quarters. If you build the house without the porch, you will find it necessary to build a separate platform on which the dog can lie outside in the sun after snow or rain. Should your ambitions embrace a full-sized kennel building with office, etc., it might be wise to investigate the prefabricated kennel buildings which are now on the market.

This house that you build, because of its size, is not an easy thing to handle or carry, so we suggest that you build it as close to the site you have picked for it as possible. The site should be at the narrow end of the run, with just a few inches of the porch jutting into the run and the greater bulk of the house outside of the run proper. Situate the house at the door end of the run, so that when you approach the run, the dog will not track through his excreta, which will be distributed at the end of the run farthest from the door. Try to set the house with its side to the north and back to the west. This gives protection from the coldest compass point in winter and shades the porch in summer from the hot afternoon sun.

A house built to the dimensions advised will accommodate two fully grown Shepherds comfortably if the weather-block partition is eliminated, or one mature dog if it is not. Remember that the smaller and lower you can build your house without cramping your dog, the warmer it will be in the winter. If the house is not too large, is well built, and the doorway blocked adequately, you will be surprised by the amount of heat the dog's body will generate in cold weather to keep his sleeping quarters warm. To house several dogs, the necessary number of houses can be built or, if you so wish, one house doubled in length, with a dividing partition and two doorways, to service two separate runs.

Bedding for the sleeping box can consist of marsh grass, oat, rye, or wheat straw, or wood, pine, or cedar shavings. The latter is said to discourage fleas and lice and possesses an aromatic odor. If any of the other materials are used, shake a liberal supply of flea powder in the bedding

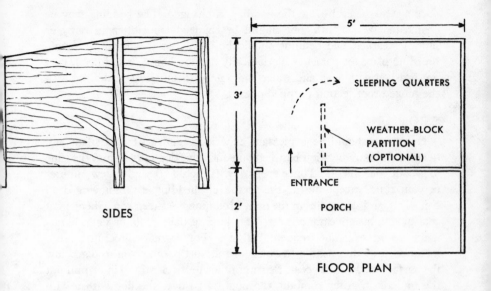

SIDES

5'

3'

SLEEPING QUARTERS

WEATHER-BLOCK
PARTITION
(OPTIONAL)

ENTRANCE

2'

PORCH

FLOOR PLAN

FINISHED HOUSE

E.H.H.

once a week or each time the bedding is changed. The bedding may be changed once a month, but should be changed more often in rainy or muddy weather. Old bedding should be burned so it will not become a breeding place for parasites. Periodically the dog house should be cleaned out, washed with soap and water and a good disinfectant, and aired with the hinged roof section propped open.

GROOMING

Grooming should be a pleasant experience and a time of silent and delightful communication between you and your dog. Try to find the time to groom your Shepherd once every day. It should take only a few minutes of your time, except during the season of shedding. By removing dead hair, dust, and skin scales in the daily grooming, you keep your Shepherd's coat glossy, his appearance neat. This kind of daily grooming also eliminates the necessity of frequent bathings. For ordinary grooming use a metal comb with a handle. A comb of this sort permits you to dig below the surface of the outer coat. Be careful not to irritate the skin or pull out the undercoat. After combing thoroughly, go over the dog with a wire grooming glove and finish with a stiff-bristled brush. During the shedding season, a coarse-toothed hacksaw blade pulled through the coat is handy for removing loose hair below the coat surface, while an ordinary rubber heel, applied with the curved inside edge against the coat, will help remove loose hair on the surface. During the grooming procedure, beginning skin disease can be seen and nipped in the bud.

To get a shining, beautiful quality coat on your dog amazingly fast use one of the sources of unsaturated fatty acids. Nutriderm, from the Norden Laboratories, Inc. is one source. It contains a highly assimilable source of unsaturated fatty acids and supportive vitamins. The result, as seen in your dog's coat, is almost miraculous.*

BATHING

You may bathe your dog or puppy any time you think it necessary, as long as you do not think it is necessary too frequently. Be careful in chilly weather to bathe him in a warm room and make sure he is completely dry before you allow him to venture out into the cold outdoors. When you bathe your dog, you soak him down to the skin and remove the protective oils from his coat. When a dog is exposed to rain and snow, the dampness is shed by the outer coat and kept from your Shepherd's skin by his undercoat. Therefore he is not likely to be affected by natural seasonal conditions. Be careful, however, that he is not exposed to these same conditions directly

* There are now several other similar products being merchandised under various brand names.

after a bath, as there is danger of his contracting a cold. During the time of shedding, a bath once a week is not too often if the weather is warm. It helps to remove loose hair and skin scales, as does the grooming that should follow the bath when the dog is completely dry. As mentioned above, your Shepherd's coat is water-resistant, so the easiest way to insure the removal of deep dirt and odors caused by accumulated sebum is by employing a chemicalized liquid soap with a coconut-oil base. Some commercial dog soaps contain vermin poisons, but an occasional prepared vermicidal dip, after bathing and rinsing, is more effective and very much worth while. When bathing, rub the lather in strongly down to the skin, being careful not to get soap in the dog's eyes. Cover every inch of him with heavy lather, rub it in, scrape the excess off with your hands, rinse and dry thoroughly, then walk him in the sun until he is ready for grooming. There are paste soaps available that require no rinsing, making the bathing of your Shepherd that much easier, or you may wish to use liquid detergents manufactured specifically for canine bathing. Prepared canned lathers, as well as dry shampoos, are all available at pet shops and are all useful in keeping your Shepherd clean and odorless.

There are many dog people who do not believe in frequent bathing because it tends to remove the oil from the dog's coat and can result in dry skin, dandruff, and skin itch. If you are in this category and wish to keep your Shepherd clean and fresh-looking without fully bathing him, you can do so by employing the following procedure. First, fill a pail with luke-warm water and swish a bar of a bland cosmetic soap through the water until it is very slightly cloudy. Dip a large towel in the water and throw it over your Shepherd's back in much the same manner as a drying blanket is draped over a horse. Begin rubbing the moisture through your Shepherd's coat from behind his ears down his neck, back, croup, etc., until you have rubbed him all over and completely. Then rinse the towel in fresh water, wring it out, and repeat the procedure until the first liquid application has been completely removed. Following this, rub the dog down briskly with a dry towel, comb him, combing in the direction of the lay of his coat, and allow him to dry in the sun if possible. Do not permit him to roll in dirt or earth, a habit which seems to be the particular delight of most dogs after bathing or grooming.

If your dog has walked in tar which you find you cannot remove by bathing, you can remove it with kerosene. The kerosene should be quickly removed with strong soap and water if it is not to burn and irritate the skin. Paint can be washed off with turpentine, which must also be quickly removed for the same reasons. Some synthetic paints, varnishes, enamels, and other like preparations, which are thinned with alcohol, can be removed by the same vehicle. If the paint (oil base) is close to the skin, linseed oil

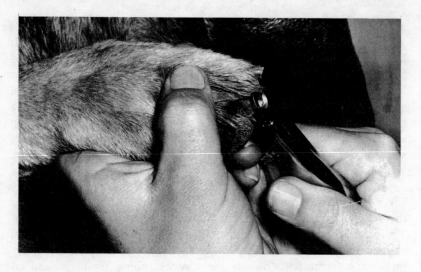

Be careful not to nick the vein when you trim the nails.

will dissolve it without irritation. Should your Shepherd engage in a tête-à-tête with a skunk, wash him immediately (if you can get near him) with soap and hot water, or soak him with tomato juice if you can find enough available, then walk him in the hot sun. The odor evaporates most quickly under heat.

A box of small sticks with cotton-tipped ends, which are manufactured under various brand names, are excellent for cleaning your Shepherd's ears. Drop into the ear a mixture of ether and alcohol, or of propylene glycol, to dissolve dirt and wax, then swab the ear clean with the cotton-tipped stick. Surplus liquid will quickly evaporate.

CARE OF TOENAILS AND TEETH

Keep your Shepherd's nails trimmed short. Overgrown nails cause lameness, foot ailments, spread toes, and hare feet. If your dog does a great deal of walking on cement, nail growth is often kept under control naturally by wearing off on the cement surface. Some Shepherds seem to possess a genetic factor for short nails which never need trimming, but the majority of our dogs need nail care. To accomplish this task with the least possible trouble, use a nail cutter specifically designed to trim canine nails and cut away only the horny dead section of the nail. If you cut too deeply, you will cause bleeding. A flashlight held under the nail will enable you to see the dark area of the blood line so you can avoid cutting into it. If you should tap the blood supply in the nail, don't be overly alarmed, simply keep the dog quiet until the severed capillaries close and the bleeding stops.

Munsel's solution or a styptic pencil applied to the bleeding nail helps to hurry coagulation. After you have cut the nails, file them smooth with the use of an ordinary carpenter's file. File from above with a downward, rounding stroke. If a nail has bled from trimming, do not file it for at least twenty-four hours.

Soft rib bones fed twice a week will help prevent tartar from forming on your dog's teeth. His teeth pierce the bones, scraping off tooth residue in the process, keeping his teeth clean and white. If tartar should form, it can be chipped off with the same kind of instrument your dentist uses on your teeth for that purpose, or your veterinarian can clean them efficiently and without bother to you. Check your dog's mouth every other week for broken, loose, or abscessed teeth, particularly when he has passed his prime. Bad teeth must be tended by your veterinarian before they affect your Shepherd's general health.

FLIES

During the summer months certain flies, commonly called "deer" flies, bite at the tips of a Shepherd's ears, causing great discomfort, the formation of scabs, subsequent baldness, and sometimes infection in that area. A good liquid insecticide, one of the many recently developed for fly control, should be rubbed or sprayed on the dog's ears as often as necessary to keep these pests away. Skin-disease salve which contains sulphur and oil of turpentine as a vehicle is also efficacious against flies, particularly if D.D.T. flea powder is shaken on top of the salve, where it adheres, giving extra protection. Oil of Benzoin and oil of Cade, painted on the ears, are also effective.

RATS

If rats invade the kennel area, they should be eradicated as quickly as possible. Not only are they disease carriers, but they are an affront to our more delicate senses. To get rid of them, set out small pans of dog meal near their holes every night for several nights until you have them coming to these pans to feed. Then mix Red Squill with the dog food they are being fed, eight measures of dog meal to one of Red Squill. After a single night's feeding of this poisonous mixture, you will generally rid your premises of these gray marauders. Red Squill is a drug that is non-poisonous to all animals except rodents, so it can be used around the kennel with safety.

TRAVEL

When traveling in hot weather with your dog, never leave him in a closed car in the sun alone. Death takes its grisly toll each summer of dogs so treated. Carry his water pail and food dish with you and take care of his needs as you do your own when on the road. If you intend changing his diet to one more easily fed when traveling, begin the change a few days before your trip so he can become accustomed to it. Gaines Research Division publishes a list of approximately 3,500 hostelries across the country that will accept dogs—a handy booklet for the dog-loving traveler to have.

If you find it necessary to ship a Shepherd to another section of the country, make sure the crate you use is large enough in all dimensions to keep the dog from being cramped during his journey. Check to see that there are no large openings or weak sections which might break in transit and allow the dog's limbs to project out of the crate. Consult your veterinarian or your local express agency for data on state health certificates. Supply the dog with a pan, rigidly attached to the crate, for water, and throw a few dog biscuits on the floor of the crate for the dog to gnaw during his journey to alleviate boredom. Be sure there are air holes in strategic

Take your Shepherd with you when you travel. But make sure that you have everything necessary for his comfort and well-being.

locations to provide air and ventilation. If possible, the top surface of the crate should be rounded, rather than flat, to discourage the parking of other crates on top of the dog crate. Strips of wood, nailed horizontally along the outside of the crate and projecting out from the surface, will prevent adjacent crates, or boxes, from being jammed tightly against the dog crate and thus blocking and defeating the purpose of the ventilation holes.

A periodic health check of your Shepherd by your veterinarian can pay big mental and monetary dividends. When you take him for his examination, remember to bring with you samples of his stool and urine for analysis.

EXERCISE

Exercise is one of the facets of canine care that is many times neglected by the owner. The Shepherd, in particular, needs his share of muscular activity if he is to develop properly that floating, easy trot which is a part of his breed being. Dogs need a great deal more exercise than humans, so taking your dog for a walk on leash cannot be considered exercise from the canine standpoint. If you can allow him to run free when you take him out, he will get more exercise, but still just a bare modicum of what is necessary. If you teach him to chase a ball and retrieve it, he will get still more exercise, while you can take your ease. But the best way to provide a Shepherd with correct and substantial exercise is to train him to trot beside a bicycle. In this manner he will receive the steady movement which will give him co-ordination, muscular fluidity, and tightness. Begin this type of exercise at about seven months. At this age, a mile a day is sufficient. Train him to run at the right side of the bicycle, to protect him from traffic. As he grows older, the amount of ground covered should increase, so that at maturity he is covering five to six miles a day with comparative ease. Pedal slowly, keeping the dog in an easy, relaxed, and even trot, and when he shows signs of weariness, stop and lie on roadside grass to rest until it is time to resume again. If the weather is exceptionally hot, it is best to skip the exercise for that day, or wait until the cool of evening. Many owners who live in rural areas and allow their dogs the freedom of several acres assume that the animal is getting enough exercise by himself. This is seldom true, and even if the dog did virtually exhaust himself chasing rabbits or other wild creatures native to the area, the bounding, running explosion of energy employed in the chase cannot take the place of the steady trotting exercise which your Shepherd most needs.

Jumping over an obstacle a number of times in succession, and retrieving a length of rubber or plastic hose (not a stick or piece of tree limb which can cause injuries), if indulged in with great vigor and over long enough a

Condor v. Stoerstrudel, SchH. I, AD.
A German import, Condor became U. S. Grand Victor in 1963. Animated and of fine
temperament he is owned by Thomas L. Bennett and Fred W. Becker, Jr.

period during each exercising session, can be very beneficial in keeping your Shepherd in shape. German owners frequently use these methods to keep their animals in athletic condition.

We have considered in this chapter the elements of physical care, but we must not forget that your Shepherd needs mental care as well. His character and mental health need nourishment, grooming, and exercise, just as much as his physical being. Give him your companionship and understanding, teach him right from wrong, and treat him as you would a friend whom you enjoy associating with. This, too, is a part of his general care, and perhaps the most important part for both you and your Shepherd.

Remember that good general care is the first and most important part of canine ownership and disease prevention. The health and happiness of your Shepherd is in your hands. A small amount of labor each day by those hands is your dog's health and life insurance, and the premium is paid by your Shepherd in love and devotion.

CHAPTER 10

THE BROOD BITCH AND THE STUD

If we want to succeed in improvement within our breed, we must have an even greater trueness to breed type in our bitches than we have in their breeding partners. The productive value of the bitch is comparatively limited in scope by seasonal vagary and this, in turn, increases the importance of every litter she produces.

In America, over a span of fruitful years, we were fortunate in possessing many bitches of true and uniform type, and through them perpetuated the breed type we desired. In the last few years we have not seen this bitch quality as frequently, which leads to some anxiety as to the future of the breed on our shores. Undoubtedly this recent lack of substantial uniformity in true type is due to the crossing of American-bred strains and of breeding American-breds to imported animals, which always produces heterozygosity. Those of us who have lived with the breed through those years of splendid bitches will remember that wonderful type and retain it by selection as the various strains, now incorporated in our Shepherds' germ plasm, blend. It is the novice breeder who has not seen those many fine bitches of the past, and so cannot visualize them, who must be shown the path to that true type again.

To begin breeding we must, of necessity, begin with a bitch as the foundation. The foundation of all things must be strong and free from faults, or the structure we build upon it will crumble. The bitch we choose for our foundation bitch must, then, be a good bitch, as fine as we can possibly acquire, not in structure alone, but in mentality and character as well. She is a product of her germ plasm, and this most important facet of her being must be closely analyzed so that we can compensate, in breeding, for her hidden faults. Structurally, the good brood bitch should be strongly made and up to standard size. She should be deep and not too long in body, for overlong bitches are generally too long in loin and weak in back, and after a litter tend to sag in back line. She must possess good bone strength throughout, yet she should not be so coarse as to lack femininity. Weakness and delicacy are not the essence of femininity in our breed and should be particularly avoided in the brood bitch.

Your bitch will first come in season when she is between eight and twelve months of age. Though this is an indication that nature considers her old enough and developed enough to breed, it is best to allow her to pass this first heat and plan to breed her when she next comes in season. This should come within six months if her environment remains the same. Daylight, which is thought to affect certain glands, seems to occasionally influence the ratio of time between heats, as will complete change in environment. Scientific studies of the incidence of seasonal variation in the mating cycles of bitches indicate that more bitches come in heat and are bred during the months of February through May than at any other time of year. The figures might not be completely reliable, since they were assembled through birth registrations in the A.K.C., and many breeders refrain from fall and winter breedings so they will not have winter or early spring litters. Small breeds reach maturity much earlier than do our Shepherds, and bitches of these breeds can be bred at first heat, which generally comes at a younger age.

In Germany, a bitch is not bred until she has passed two seasons, but it is not necessary to wait this long. In fact, should you breed your bitch at her second season, it will probably be better for her, settling her in temperament and giving her body greater maturity and grace.

When your bitch is approaching her period of heat and you intend to breed her, have her stool checked for intestinal parasites, and if any are present, worm her. Feed her a well-balanced diet, such as she should have been getting all along. Her appetite will increase in the preparatory stage of the mating cycle as her vulva begins to swell. She will become restless, will urinate more frequently, and will allow dogs to approach her, but will not allow copulation. Within the bitch other changes are taking place at this stage. Congestion begins in the reproductive tract, the horns of the uterus and the vagina thicken, and the luteal bodies leave the ovaries.

The first sign of blood from the vulva ushers in the second stage of the

NORMAL BITCH MATING CYCLE

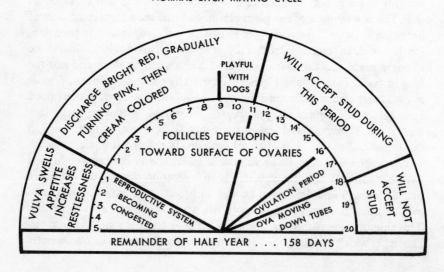

154

Ch. Vondaun Juno
Flashy, feminine, good moving English champion bitch.

mating cycle. In some bitches no blood appears at all, or so little that it goes unnoticed by the owner, and sometimes we find a bitch who will bleed throughout the cycle. In either circumstance we must depend upon other signs. The bitch becomes very playful with animals of her own and the opposite sex, but will still not permit copulation. This is, of course, a condition which is very trying to male dogs with which she comes in contact. Congestion within the bitch reaches a high point during this period. Ova develop within the follicles of the ovaries, and, normally, the red discharge gradually turns to pink, becoming lighter in color until it becomes straw color and is no longer obvious. Her vulva is more swollen, and she becomes increasingly more playful with males. This period is generally of about ten days' duration, but the time varies greatly with the individual. Rather than rely upon any set time period, it is best to conclude that this period reaches its conclusion when the bitch will stand for the stud and permit copulation. This generally occurs at about the tenth day, but can take place as early as the fourth or fifth day of this period or as late as the seventeenth day.

The third period in the cycle is the acceptance period. The bitch will swing her hind end toward the dog, her tail will arch and fall to the side, and she will permit copulation. Sometimes the stud may have to tease her for a time, but she will eventually give in. The bitch may be sensitive and yelp and pull away when the stud's penis touches the lining of the vagina. If this occurs several times, it is best to wait another day, until the sensitivity has left this region. A very definite indication that the bitch is in the acceptance period is the softness and flaccidity of the vulva, from which the firmness and congestion has gone. Within the bitch the ovarian follicles have been growing ever bigger, and approximately midway in the acceptance period, some of them burst and the eggs are ready for fertilization. If the bitch has a normal mating cycle, as shown on the diagram, the best time to breed her is about the thirteenth or fourteenth day of the mating cycle, when ovulation has occurred. This time also varies with the individual bitch, so that until you have bred your bitch once or twice and feel that you know the best time for her, it is better to breed her on the eleventh day and every other day thereafter until her period of acceptance is over. This last, of course, is generally only possible when the stud is owned by you. One good breeding is actually all that is necessary to make your bitch pregnant, providing that breeding is made at the right time. If copulation is forced before the bitch is ready, the result is no conception or a small litter, since the sperm must wait for ovulation and the life of the sperm is limited. The acceptance period ceases rather abruptly, and is signaled by the bitch's definite resistance to male advances.

If your bitch is a maiden, it is best to breed her this first time to an older stud who knows his business. When you bring her to the stud and if there are adjoining wire-enclosed runs, put the stud in one run and the bitch in the adjacent one. They will make overtures through the wire and later, when the stud is loosed in the run with the bitch, copulation generally occurs quickly. You may have to hold the bitch if she is flighty or reluctant, sometimes a problem with maiden bitches. If your bitch fails to conceive from a good and proper breeding, do not immediately put the blame on the stud. In most instances it is the fault of either the bitch or the owner of the bitch, who has not adequately timed the mating. Many bitch owners fail to recognize the first signs of the mating cycle and so bring their bitch to the stud either too early or too late. Normal physiology of the reproductive system can be interrupted or delayed by disturbance, disease, or illness in any part of the dog's body. A sick bitch will therefore generally not come in season, though it is time to do so, until after she has completely recovered and returned to normal. Bitches past their prime and older tend to have a shorter mating cycle and so must be bred sooner than usual to assure pregnancy.

During copulation and the resulting tie, you should assist the stud dog owner as much as possible. If the stud evidences pain when he attempts to force his penis in the vulva, check the bitch. In virgin bitches you may find a web of flesh which runs vertically across the vaginal opening and causes pain to the dog when his penis is forced against it. This web must be

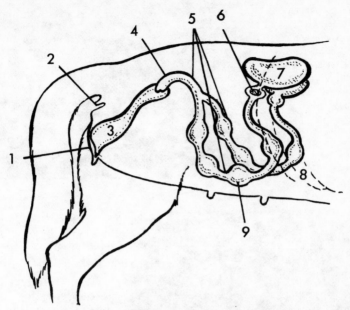

REPRODUCTIVE SYSTEM OF THE BITCH

1. Vulva. 2. Anus. 3. Vagina. 4. Cervix. 5. Uterus. 6. Ovary. 7. Kidneys.
8. Ribs. 9. Feotal lump.

broken by hooking your finger around it and pulling if a breeding is to be consummated. After the tense excitement of the breeding and while the tie is in effect, speak to the bitch quietly and keep her from moving until the tie is broken, then snap a leash on to her collar and take her for a fast walk around the block without pausing. After that she can be taken home in the car. If it is necessary to travel any great distance before she arrives again in familiar surroundings, it is best to allow her a period of quiet rest before attempting the journey.

Occasionally fertile bitches, whether bred or not, will have phantom pregnancies and show every physical manifestation of true gestation up to the last moment. In some cases a bitch may be truely bred and then, after a month, resorb her fetuses. The only way of differentiating between pseudo-pregnancy and fetal resorption is by palpation, or feeling with the hands, to locate the fetal lump in the uterus. This is a difficult task for one who has not had vast experience.

After you have returned home with your bitch, do not allow any males near her. She can become impregnated by a second dog and whelp a litter of mixed paternity, some of the puppies sired by the first dog and others sired by the second animal. Often a bitch is bred to a selected stud just be-

Ch. Ulla of San Miguel
(sire)
Judo v. Liebestraum
(dam)
Ch. Christel of San Miguel
Grand Victrix 1953. A
lovely bitch of true type
and quality.

Sandra v. Beckgold
(sire)
Ch. Questor Maximian v.
    Grossland
(dam)
Pert v. Hoheluft
A lovely bitch type, mirror-
ing the strong Pfeffer breeding of her dam.

Ch. Frigga v. Hoheluft
(sire)
Ch. Nox of Ruthland
(dam)
Ch. Lady of Ruthland
A grand bitch. Product of
familiar Pfeffer inbreeding
through two of his greatest
children.

fore ovulation. The sperm will live long enough to fertilize the eggs when they flush down. The next day, another male breeds to the bitch, the sperm of the two dogs mix within her and both become sires of the resulting litter.

Let us assume that your bitch is in good health and you have had a good breeding to the stud of your choice at the proper time in the bitch's mating cycle to insure pregnancy. The male sperm fertilizes the eggs and life begins. From this moment on you will begin to feed the puppies which will be born in about sixty to sixty-three days from ovulation. Every bit of food you give the bitch is nutritionally aiding in the fetal development within her. Be sure that she is being provided with enough milk to supply calcium, meat for phosphorus and iron, and all the other essential vitamins and minerals. A vitamin and mineral supplement should be incorporated into the food, used moderately. Her diet should be rich in protein and contain from 20 to 30% fat. She must be fed well for her own maintenance and for the development of the young *in utero*, particularly during the last thirty days of the gestation period. She should not, however, be given food to such excess that she becomes fat.

Your bitch, her run, and house or bed should be free of worm and flea eggs. She should be allowed a moderate amount of free exercise in the prenatal period to keep her from becoming fat and soft and from losing muscular tone and elasticity. If your bitch has not had enough exercise prior to breeding and you wish to harden and reduce her, accustom her to the exercise gradually and it will do her a great deal of good. But do not allow her to indulge in unaccustomed, abrupt, or violent exercise, or she might abort.

The puppies develop in the horns of the uterus, not in the "tubes" (Fallopian tubes), as is commonly thought. As the puppies develop, the horns of the uterus lengthen and the walls expand until the uterus may become as long as three and a half feet in a Shepherd bitch carrying a large litter. A month before the bitch is due to whelp, incorporate fresh liver in her diet two or three times a week. This helps to keep her free from constipation and aids in the coming, necessary production of milk for the litter. If the litter is going to be small, she will not show much sign until late in the gestation period. But if the litter is going to be a normal or large one, she will begin to show distention of the abdomen at about thirty-five days after the breeding. Her appetite will have been increasing during this time, and gradually the fact of her pregnancy will become more and more evident.

Several days before she is due to whelp, the whelping box should be prepared. It should be located in a dimly lit area removed from disturbance by other dogs, or humans. The box should be four feet square, enclosed on all sides by eight- to ten-inch high boards, either plank or plywood.

Boards of the same height must be added above these in about three weeks to keep the pups from climbing out. Four inches up from the flooring (when it is packed down), a one- by three-inch smooth wooden slat should be attached to the sides with small angle irons, all around as a rail, or a pipe rail can be used. This will prevent the bitch from accidentally squeezing to death any puppy which crawls behind her. On the floor of the box lay a smooth piece of rubber matting which is easily removed and cleaned when the bedding is cleaned or changed. The bedding itself should be of rye or oat straw, and enough of it supplied so that the bitch can hollow out a nest and still leave some of the nesting material under the pups.

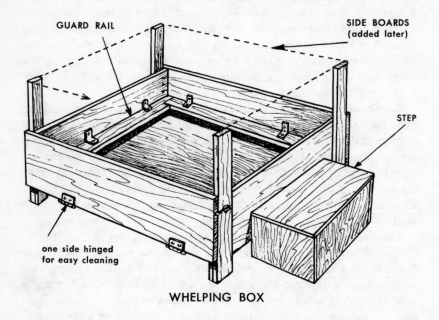

WHELPING BOX

Another method much used is to have several layers of newspapers in the bottom of the box so that they can be removed one or two at a time as they become soiled during whelping. After the litter is completely whelped, the straw bedding is provided and hollowed into a saucer shape so the whelps will be kept together in a limited area. The whelping box should be raised from the ground and a smaller box, or step, provided to make it easier for the bitch to enter or leave.

As the time approaches for the whelping, the bitch will become restless; she may refuse food and begin to make her nest. Her temperature will drop approximately one degree the day before she is ready to whelp, and she will show a definite dropping down through the abdomen. Labor begins with

160

pressure from within that forces the puppies toward the pelvis. The bitch generally twists around as the puppy is being expelled to lick the fluid which accompanies the birth. Sometimes the sac surrounding the puppy will burst from pressure. If it doesn't, the puppy will be born in the sac, a thin, membranous material called the fetal envelope. The navel cord runs from the puppy's navel to the afterbirth, or placenta. If the bitch is left alone at whelping time, she will rip the fetal caul, bite off the navel cord and eat the sac, cord, and placenta. Should the cord be broken off in birth so that the placenta remains in the bitch, it will generally be expelled with the birth of the next whelp. After disposing of these items, the bitch will lick and clean the new puppy until the next one is about to be born, and the process will then repeat itself. Under completely normal circumstances, your Shepherd bitch is quite able to whelp her litter and look after them without any help from you, but since the whelping might not be normal, it is best for the breeder to be present, particularly so in the case of bitches who are having their first litter.

If the breeder is present, he or she can remove the sac, cut the umbilical cord, and gently pull on the rest of the cord, assuming that the placenta has not yet been ejected, until it is detached and drawn out. Some breeders keep a small box handy in which they place each placenta, so they can, when the whelping is completed, check them against the number of puppies to make sure that no placenta has been retained. The navel cord should be cut about three inches from the pup's belly. The surplus will dry up and drop off in a few days. There is no need to tie it after cutting. You need not attempt to sterilize your hands or the implements you might use in helping the bitch to whelp, since the pups will be practically surrounded with bacteria of all kinds, some benign and others which they are born equipped to combat.

If a bitch seems to be having difficulty in expelling a particularly large puppy, you can help by wrapping a towel around your hands to give you purchase, grasping the partly expelled whelp, and gently pulling. Do not pull too hard, or you might injure the pup. The puppies can be born either head first or tail first. Either way is normal. As the pups are born, the sac broken, and the cord snipped, dry them gently but vigorously with a towel and put them at the mother's breast, first squeezing some milk to the surface and then opening their mouths for the entrance of the teat. You may have to hold them there by the head until they begin sucking.

Often several puppies are born in rapid succession, then an interval of time may elapse before another one is born. If the bitch is a slow whelper and seems to be laboring hard after one or more pups have been born, regular injections of Pitocin, at three-hour intervals, using a little less than one-half c.c., can help her in delivery. Pituitrin, one-half to one c.c., is a similar drug and the one most often used, though Pitocin brings less nausea and directly affects the uterus. Both these drugs should be administered hypodermically into the hind leg of the bitch at the rear of the thigh.* After the bitch has seemingly completed her whelping, it is good practice to administer another shot of the drug to make sure no last pup, alive or dead, is still unborn and to cause her to clean out any residue left from the whelping. Never use either of these drugs until she has whelped at least one pup.

Allow her to rest quietly and enjoy the new sensation of motherhood for several hours, then insist that she leave her litter, though she won't want to, and take her out to relieve herself. Offer her some warm milk. From then on, feed her as recommended during the gestation period, with the addition of three milk feedings per day. Sometimes milk appears in the udders before birth, but generally it comes in when the pups begin to nurse, since it is manufactured by glands, from blood, while the pups are at the breast.

Now is the time to cull the litter. Of course, all young which are not normal should be culled immediately at birth. If the bitch whelps six or less pups and all seem strong and healthy, no culling is required. If she has a particularly large litter, it does not pay, in the long run, to raise all the whelps. Allow her to keep six or seven of the best and sturdiest and cull the rest. Those which you have retained will grow better and be larger and stronger than if you allowed the entire large litter to live. Quiet puppies are healthy ones. Constant crying and squirming of the pups is a danger signal, and a check should be made to see what ails them. It may be that the bitch is not providing enough milk and they are hungry, or perhaps they are cold. Sometimes the trouble is parasitic infection, or possibly coccidiosis, or navel infection. Dr. Walter Koch, in 1950, at the University of Munich, Animal Institute, reported a bacillus, Aerogenes, which he claimed caused many deaths of young puppies. This bacillus infects from contact with the dam's rectum. It multiplies rapidly in the whelp's intestines, and the normal bacillus in the stomach and intestines seems to have no effect on the lethal bacillus. It begins with the first digestion of the pups and attacks the basic internal organs, exhibiting symptoms on the second or third day following birth. The pups develop cramps, fail to suck, whimper, and die within two or three days. The disease does not seem to be contagious to other well puppies. If there is something wrong with the pups, whatever it may be, you need professional advice and should call your veterinarian immediately.

Except for the removal of dew claws on the hind legs, the pups, if

* There are new drugs, for this purpose and others, constantly being discovered. Consult your veterinarian for the latest and best.

	1	2	3	4	5	6	7	8	9	10	11	12	13	14	15	16	17	18	19	20	21	22	23	24	25	26	27	28	29	30	31
Bred—Jan.	1	2	3	4	5	6	7	8	9	10	11	12	13	14	15	16	17	18	19	20	21	22	23	24	25	26	27	28	29	30	31
Due—March	5	6	7	8	9	10	11	12	13	14	15	16	17	18	19	20	21	22	23	24	25	26	27	28	29	30	31	1	2	3	4 *(April)*
Bred—Feb.	1	2	3	4	5	6	7	8	9	10	11	12	13	14	15	16	17	18	19	20	21	22	23	24	25	26	27	28			
Due—April	5	6	7	8	9	10	11	12	13	14	15	16	17	18	19	20	21	22	23	24	25	26	27	28	29	30	1	2 *(May)*			
Bred—Mar.	1	2	3	4	5	6	7	8	9	10	11	12	13	14	15	16	17	18	19	20	21	22	23	24	25	26	27	28	29	30	31
Due—May	3	4	5	6	7	8	9	10	11	12	13	14	15	16	17	18	19	20	21	22	23	24	25	26	27	28	29	30	31	1	2 *(June)*
Bred—Apr.	1	2	3	4	5	6	7	8	9	10	11	12	13	14	15	16	17	18	19	20	21	22	23	24	25	26	27	28	29	30	
Due—June	3	4	5	6	7	8	9	10	11	12	13	14	15	16	17	18	19	20	21	22	23	24	25	26	27	28	29	30	1	2 *(July)*	
Bred—May	1	2	3	4	5	6	7	8	9	10	11	12	13	14	15	16	17	18	19	20	21	22	23	24	25	26	27	28	29	30	31
Due—July	3	4	5	6	7	8	9	10	11	12	13	14	15	16	17	18	19	20	21	22	23	24	25	26	27	28	29	30	31	1	2 *(August)*
Bred—June	1	2	3	4	5	6	7	8	9	10	11	12	13	14	15	16	17	18	19	20	21	22	23	24	25	26	27	28	29	30	
Due—August	3	4	5	6	7	8	9	10	11	12	13	14	15	16	17	18	19	20	21	22	23	24	25	26	27	28	29	30	31	1 *(Sept.)*	
Bred—July	1	2	3	4	5	6	7	8	9	10	11	12	13	14	15	16	17	18	19	20	21	22	23	24	25	26	27	28	29	30	31
Due—September	2	3	4	5	6	7	8	9	10	11	12	13	14	15	16	17	18	19	20	21	22	23	24	25	26	27	28	29	30	1	2 *(Oct.)*
Bred—Aug.	1	2	3	4	5	6	7	8	9	10	11	12	13	14	15	16	17	18	19	20	21	22	23	24	25	26	27	28	29	30	31
Due—October	3	4	5	6	7	8	9	10	11	12	13	14	15	16	17	18	19	20	21	22	23	24	25	26	27	28	29	30	31	1	2 *(Nov.)*
Bred—Sept.	1	2	3	4	5	6	7	8	9	10	11	12	13	14	15	16	17	18	19	20	21	22	23	24	25	26	27	28	29	30	
Due—November	3	4	5	6	7	8	9	10	11	12	13	14	15	16	17	18	19	20	21	22	23	24	25	26	27	28	29	30	1	2 *(Dec.)*	
Bred—Oct.	1	2	3	4	5	6	7	8	9	10	11	12	13	14	15	16	17	18	19	20	21	22	23	24	25	26	27	28	29	30	31
Due—December	3	4	5	6	7	8	9	10	11	12	13	14	15	16	17	18	19	20	21	22	23	24	25	26	27	28	29	30	31	1	2 *(Jan.)*
Bred—Nov.	1	2	3	4	5	6	7	8	9	10	11	12	13	14	15	16	17	18	19	20	21	22	23	24	25	26	27	28	29	30	
Due—January	3	4	5	6	7	8	9	10	11	12	13	14	15	16	17	18	19	20	21	22	23	24	25	26	27	28	29	30	31	1 *(Feb.)*	
Bred—Dec.	1	2	3	4	5	6	7	8	9	10	11	12	13	14	15	16	17	18	19	20	21	22	23	24	25	26	27	28	29	30	31
Due—February	2	3	4	5	6	7	8	9	10	11	12	13	14	15	16	17	18	19	20	21	22	23	24	25	26	27	28	1	2	3	4 *(March)*

163

healthy, need not be bothered until it is time to begin their supplementary feeding at about three weeks. Dew claws should be removed on about the second day after birth. Puppies and their needs, dietary and otherwise, are discussed more fully in the chapter which follows.

There are several ills which might befall the bitch during gestation and whelping which must be considered. Eclampsia, sometimes called milk fever, is perhaps most common. This is a metabolic disturbance brought on by a deficiency of calcium and phosphorus in the diet. If you give your bitch plenty of milk and a good diet such as we have recommended, she should not be troubled with this condition. Should your bitch develop eclampsia—evidenced by troubled shaking, wild expression, muscular rigidity, and a high temperature—it can be quickly relieved by an injection of calcium gluconate in the vein.

Should your bitch be bred by accident to an undesirable animal, your veterinarian can cause her to abort by the use of any one of several efficient canine abortifacients. He can also aid old bitches who have been resorbing their fetuses to carry them full term and whelp with the aid of stilbestrol.

Mastitis, an udder infection, is a chief cause of puppy deaths. It is generally mistaken by the uninformed for "acid milk," a condition which does not exist in dogs because the bitch's milk is naturally acid. Mastitis is an udder infection which cuts off part of the milk supply and the whelps either die of infection, contracted from the infected milk, or from starvation, due to the lack of sufficient milk. It is not necessary to massage the dam's breasts at weaning time with camphorated oil. They will cake naturally and quickly quit secreting milk if left completely alone.

Growths, infections, injuries, cysts, and other and various ailments can affect the female reproductive system and must be taken care of by your veterinarian. The great majority of bitches who have been well cared for and well fed are strong and healthy, and the bearing of litters is a natural procedure—the normal function of the female of the species to bear and rear the next generation, and in so doing fulfill her precious destiny.

Ch. Nores v. Beckgold
(sire)
Ch. Quell v. Fredeholz
(dam)
Helga v. Beckgold

A top American bred showdog.
Canadian Grand Victor.

THE STUD DOG

Rittmeister von Stephanitz wrote: "Modern breeding research has taught us that it is not so much the appearance of an animal that indicates its breeding values, but rather its hereditary picture, which means the sum total of the qualities and characteristics which it has inherited from its ancestors." This statement is as true today as when it was written in 1930, and is particularly applicable to the stud dog.

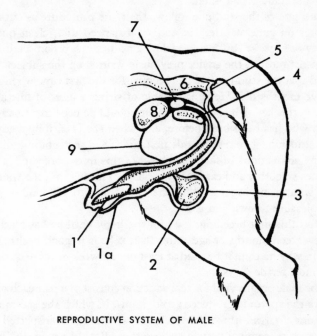

REPRODUCTIVE SYSTEM OF MALE

1a. Sheath. 1. Penis. 2. Testicle. 3. Scrotum. 4. Pelvic bone.
5. Anus. 6. Rectum. 7. Prostate. 8. Bladder. 9. Vas deferens.

If what we have said above about the unrivaled importance of the brood bitch is true, it may be difficult to understand why we pay so much attention to the male lines of descent. The reason is that stud dogs tend to mold the aspects of the breed on the whole and in any given country, or locality, to a much greater extent than do brood bitches. While the brood bitch may control type in a kennel, the stud dog can control type over a much larger area. The truth of this can be ascertained by the application of simple mathematics.

Let us assume that the average litter is comprised of five puppies. The brood bitch will produce, then, a maximum of ten puppies a year. In that same year a popular, good producing, well-publicized stud dog may be used on the average of three times weekly (many name studs, in various breeds, have been used even more frequently over a period of several years). This popular stud can sire fifteen puppies a week, employing the figures mentioned above, or 780 puppies a year. Compare this total to the bitch's yearly total of ten puppies, and you can readily see why any one stud dog wields a much greater influence over the breed in general than does a specific brood bitch.

The care of the stud dog follows the same procedure as outlined in the chapter on general care. He needs a balanced diet, clean quarters, and plenty of exercise, but no special care as does the brood bitch. Though it is against most of the advice previously written on the subject, we recommend that the stud be used in breeding for the first time when he is about twelve months old. He is as capable of siring a litter of fine and healthy pups at this age as he ever will be. He should be bred to a steady, knowing bitch who has been bred before, and when she is entirely ready to accept him. Aid him if necessary this first time. See that nothing disturbs him during copulation. In fact, the object of this initial breeding is to see that all goes smoothly and easily. If you succeed in this aim, the young dog will be a willing and eager stud for the rest of his life, the kind of stud that it is a pleasure to own and use.

After this first breeding, use him sparingly until he has reached sixteen or seventeen months of age. After that, if he is in good health, there is no reason why he cannot be used at least once a week or more during his best and most fertile years.

The male organs vital for reproduction consist of a pair each of: testicles, where the sperm is produced; epididymis, in which the sperm are stored; and *vas deferens*, through which the sperm are transported. The dog possesses no seminal vesicle as does man. But, like man, the male dog is always in an active stage of reproduction and can be used at any time.

When the stud has played with the bitch for a short period and the bitch is ready, he will cover her. There is a bone in his penis, and behind this bone is a group of very sensitive nerves which cause a violent thrust reflex when pressure is applied. His penis, unlike most other animals', has a bulbous enlargement at its base. When the penis is thrust into the bitch's vagina, it goes through a muscular ring at the opening of the vagina. As it passes into the vagina, pressure on the reflex nerves causes a violent thrust forward, and the penis, and particularly the bulb, swells enormously, preventing withdrawal through the constriction band of the vulva. The stud ejaculates semen swarming with sperm, which is forced through the cervix, uterus, Fallopian tubes, and into the capsule which surrounds the ovaries, and the breeding is consummated.

The dog and bitch are tied, or "hung," and the active part of the breeding is completed. The owner of the bitch should then stand at her head and hold her by the collar. The stud's owner should kneel next to the animals with his arm or knee under the bitch's stomach, directly in front of her hindquarters, to prevent her from suddenly sitting, while still tied. He should talk soothingly to the stud and gently prevent him from attempting to leave the bitch for a little while. Presently the stud owner should turn the dog around off the bitch's back by first lifting the front legs off and to the ground and then lifting one hind leg over the back of the bitch until dog and bitch are standing tail to tail.

Some studs choose merely to leave the mounted position and remain at the side of the bitch during the tie, either because they prefer it this way or because the lifting of the leg over the rump of the bitch as the body of the male is turned in the tail-to-tail position causes them pain, during the act or when the tie becomes terminated.

Dogs remain in this position for various lengths of time after copulation, but fifteen minutes to a half an hour is generally average. When the congestion of blood leaves the penis, the bulb shrinks and the animals part.

The stud dog owner should keep a muzzle handy to be used on snappy bitches. Many bitches, due to temperament, environment, or fright, may cause injury to the stud by biting. If she shows any indication of such conduct, she should be muzzled. Should she continue to attempt to bite for any length of time, it is generally because it is either too early or too late in the estrum cycle to consummate a breeding. If the bitch is small, sinks down when mounted, or won't stand, she must be held up. In some instances her owner or the stud's owner will have to kneel next to her and, with his hand under and between her hind legs, push the vulva up toward the dog's penis or guide the stud's penis into her vulva. Straw or earth, pushed under her hind legs to elevate her rear quarters, is effective in the case of a bitch who is very much too small for the stud.

As mentioned before, many novice bitch owners fail to recognize the initial signs of the oncoming heat period, or neglect to check, so that their knowledge of elapsed time since the first showing of red is only approximate. Many offer little aid in the attempt to complete the breeding, and talk incessantly and to no purpose, generally expressing wonder at their bitch's unorthodox conduct, but do little to quiet her. In many instances, particularly with a novice of the opposite sex, these actions are due to embarrassment. Regardless of the reason, remember to use the muzzle only on the bitch. We must always put the welfare of our dogs ahead of self.

There is not much more that can be written about the stud, except to caution the stud owner to be careful of using drugs or injections to make his dog eager to mate or more fertile. The number of puppies born in any litter is not dependent upon the healthy and fertile male's sperm, but upon the number of eggs the bitch gives off. Should your dog prove sterile, look for basic causes first. If there seems to be no physical reason for his sterility, then a series of injections by your veterinarian (perhaps of A-P-L, anterior-pituitary-like injections) might prove efficacious.

It is often a good idea to feed the dog a light meal before he is used, particularly if he is a reluctant stud. Young, or virgin, studs often regurgitate due to excitement, but it does them no harm. After the tie has broken, allow both dog and bitch to drink moderately.

Perhaps it would be well, in this chapter dealing with the brood bitch and the stud, to discuss two innovations which are closely related to the sexes and breeding: the *Register of Merit* (*R.O.M.*) and breed surveys.

The *R.O.M.* was born in a worthy effort to afford tyro, and experienced breeders as well, an easy access to a formulated rating of animals, living and dead, based upon their winning get. It is easily seen how such an idea could seem to the originators to be pregnant with wonderful opportunity for breed improvement, particularly since similar charting had proven eminently successful in other livestock fields. The work of compilation has undoubtedly been tedious and long, and it is a pity that such a worthwhile conception should whelp so dubious a litter. The primary purpose of the *R.O.M.* is based upon a false premise, therefore the complete value is lost. We do not mean to intimate that the listed *R.O.M.* animals are without worth. We are primarily interested in the values of the *R.O.M.* program itself, not in the animals which it has rated.

As it exists today, the *Register of Merit* merely tells us that certain dogs, through wide campaigning, wins, advertising, and possibly their own sterling worth, were bred extensively to many bitches, among which were a large number of fine quality, and the best of the resulting progeny were fortuitously sold to show-conscious buyers in areas where *R.O.M.*-designated shows could be reached. There is no indication of the percentage of mediocre or poor stock sired by these same studs, or the genetic faults which they possessed and transmitted. We do not know the number of bitches bred to each individual *R.O.M.*-rated stud, their genetic heritage, or type, the overall number of pups he produced over a given time and the percentage to reach *R.O.M.* show rings. The implications of the myriad blind spots in the *R.O.M.* throw a long shadow of meaning.

The great danger lies in the influence such a vague and untrustworthy compilation of pseudo-facts has on the novice, who views any dog labeled "champion" through a fog of blind, ecstatic worship which completely hides the animal's faults and heritage. How more dangerous it is then, to this same tyro, to hang a *R.O.M.* "tag" on a geographically available stud. Canny breeders know that *R.O.M.*-rated studs can give us, along with virtues, all the faults we have tried to eliminate through the years, from long coats, bad dentition, and structural faults, to poor character and temperament, unless bred to the right bitches. The knowledgeable breeder is also aware of the fact that there are dogs which have never basked in the limelight who can possibly produce better with particular breeding partners than well-known *R.O.M.* or champion studs. But the novice is led astray by glorified "tags" which blind him to true values and lead him to perpetuate faults which we have been striving to eliminate.

Identifying specific shows as *R.O.M.* shows is rather unfair to the owners of good dogs who are, by time or pocketbook, limited to exhibiting in certain small areas. Still, from the standpoint of the originators of the *R.O.M.*, it was eminently necessary to choose only shows, for this rating, where competition is strong and dependable specialty judges pass on the exhibited animals.

If all the studs in the country were given equal opportunity with bitches of equal quality which were compatible with the stud's breeding, and all the progeny of equal numbers of all the litters sired were given equal opportunitiy to be shown at *R.O.M.* shows, and the results tabulated and the studs rated by this tabulation, then the *R.O.M.* could prove of great value. This could, of course, never come to pass. As it stands today, the *R.O.M.* gives us some very slight evaluation of the worth of certain dogs, but since the percentages are based only upon the winning stock produced by any individual stud, and the valueless or mediocre stock produced by the same animal is not considered at all, we can only come to the conclusion that the *Register of Merit*, as a measure of true breeding worth, cannot be considered seriously. Much more can be, has been, and will be said on this subject. We have simply attempted to find the most pertinent facts in regard to the *R.O.M.* and evaluate them objectively. The *R.O.M.* ratings on bitches have much greater value because of the limited number of progeny to be considered.

Breed surveys have marked value if properly and objectively conducted. The basic idea of the breed survey (or *Angekoert*) is to evaluate your dog impartially so that you, the owner, can see him in true perspective, minus the blind spots which come to most breeders and owners and are the result of close familiarity. The first phase of the breed survey is a professional criticism of both physical and mental faults and virtues. The second phase is a recommendation concerning breeding partners, warning the breeder to guard against breeding to strains or individuals carrying certain genetic weaknesses which are also prevalent in the animal being surveyed. The eternal argument against breed surveys is that they represent only the opinions of a limited group of individuals who may or may not be completely qualified to give opinions. In Germany, breed surveys have immense value and the evaluations and recommendations are seldom criticized. But breed surveys have much less impact in America because of our way of living, thinking, and acting.

We have had breed surveys before in this country, but their value was made nil by a general disregard of recommendations, and the movement died of inertia. Should a group of truly knowledgeable Shepherdists of undeniable integrity and intelligence be gathered together for a breed survey, and the individuals making the survey be changed yearly, we would, in all probability, eventually have a worth-while picture of existing stock. It is quite possible that such a group could be formed and, over the years, make a necessary contribution to breed knowledge. But regardless of how accurately it might recommend and classify, it would be bucking American individuality, ego, and stubbornness against being pushed into a direction decided by others. We respect the findings and opinions of our peers, but insist upon our own decisions. Like the proverbial horse,

Ch. Archer of Brinton
Richly colored male champion from a top winning English kennel.

we can be led to water, but we cannot be forced to drink. Undeniably, this attitude must be exasperating to any group or groups who are, without profit or glory, attempting to set our steps on the right path. But it must also be remembered that many a horse has been founded by drinking too quickly and too much.

CHAPTER 11

YOUR SHEPHERD PUPPY

The birth of a litter has been covered in the previous chapter on the brood bitch. As we indicated in that discussion, barring accident or complications at birth, there is little you can do for your Shepherd puppies until they are approximately three weeks old. At that age supplementary feedings begin. But suppose that for one reason or another the mother must be taken from her brood: What care must be given to these small Shepherds if they are to survive? Puppies need warmth. This is provided partly by their instinctive habit of gathering together in the nest, but to a much greater extent by the warmth of the mother's body. If the mother must be taken from the nest, this extra warmth can be provided by an ordinary light bulb, or, better still, an infra-red bulb, hung directly over the brood in the enclosed nest box.

By far the most important requirement of these newborn pups is proper food. Puppies are belly and instinct, and nothing much more. They must be fed well and frequently. What shall we feed them, what formula can we arrive at that most closely approaches the natural milk of the mother, which we know is best? There are prepared modified milks for orphan puppies which are commercially available and very worth while, or you can mix your own formula of ingredients which will most closely simulate natural bitch's milk. To do this, you must first know the basic quality of the dam's milk. Bitches' milk is comparatively acid; it contains less sugar and water, more ash and protein, and far more fat than cow or human milk, so we must modify our formula to conform to these differences.

To begin, purchase a can of Nestlé's Pelargon, a spray-dried, acidified, and homogenized modified milk product. If you can't get Pelargon, try any of the spray-dried baby milks, but Pelargon is best since it is, like bitches' milk, slightly acid and rich in necessary nutritive substances. To one ounce of the modified milk product, add one ounce of fresh cream. Pour six ounces of water by volume into this mixture and blend with an electric mixer or egg beater until it is smooth. Larger amounts can be mixed employing the same basic proportions and kept refrigerated. This formula should be fed five or six times a day and, when fed, must be warmed to body heat. Many puppies refuse to drink a formula which has not been warmed to just the right temperature. Do not add lime water, glucose, or dextrose to the formula, for by so doing you are modifying in the wrong direction. An ordinary baby's bottle and nipple are adequate as the formula vehicle. Never drop liquids directly in the puppy's throat with an eye dropper or you invite pneumonia. A twelve-ounce puppy will absorb one

A good three month old male puppy.

ounce of formula; a one-pound puppy, approximately one and three-quarter ounces of formula; a two-pound puppy, two ounces; and a three-pound puppy, two and three-quarter ounces at each feeding. A valuable adjunct to the puppy's diet, whether formula or breast fed, is two drops of Dietol, dropped into the lip pocket from the first day of birth on, the amount to be increased with greater growth and age. A bottle trough, such as is pictured in the illustration, can be built for orphan pups. The trick here is to space the nipple holes so that the bodies of the pups touch when drinking.

Incidentally recent research seems to indicate that plain goat's milk heated to the proper temperature may equal any formula for the raising of orphan puppies.

If it is possible to find a foster mother for orphan pups, your troubles are over. Most lactating bitches will readily take to puppies other than their own if the new babies are first prepared by spreading some of the foster mother's milk over their tiny bodies. The foster mother will lick them clean and welcome them to the nest.

When the pups are two-and-a-half to three weeks old, the mother will often engage in an action which might prove slightly disgusting to the

173

neophyte, but which is an instinctive and natural performance to the bitch. She will regurgitate her own stomach contents of partially digested food for her puppies to eat, thus beginning, in her own way, the weaning process. If you have begun supplementary feeding in time, this action by the bitch will seldom occur. If you haven't, it is a definite indication that supplementary feeding should begin at once.

Puppies grow best on milk, meat, fat, and cereal diets. Growth is attained through proteins, but proteins differ, so that puppies fed on vegetable protein diets will not grow and thrive as well as those fed animal proteins. Vitamins E and K (found in alfalfa meal) are essential to the pups' well being and should be used in adequate amounts in the food ration. Remember that 70 per cent of the pup's energy is derived from fat intake, so supply this food element generously in the diet. Lime water should not be incorporated in the diet since it neutralizes stomach acidity, a condition which is necessary to the assimilation of fat. In experiments, puppies on fat-free diets developed deficiency symptoms characterized by anemia, weight loss, dull coats, and finally, death. Fat alone could not cure the advanced manifestation of the condition, indicating that some metabolic process was disturbed when complete fat removal in the diet was resorted to. But feeding butterfat plus folacin resulted in dramatic cures.

To begin the small puppy on supplementary feeding, place the pan of food before him, gently grasp his head behind the ears, and dip his lips and chin into the food. The puppy will lick his lips, taste the food, and in no time at all learn to feed by himself. Be careful not to push the head in so far that the pup's nose is covered and clogged by food.

Check the puppies' navels every day to see that infection has not set in. This infection comes from the scraping of their soft bellies on a rough surface and can generally be avoided if several thicknesses of cloth covers the floor of the nest box under the bedding.

Clip the sharp little nails to avoid damage to litter mates' eyes, which will open at about ten days. If the pups are born with hind dew claws, cut them off with manicure scissors about two days after birth. They need not be bandaged, as the bitch will keep the wound clean until it has healed. Have a fecal check made when the pups are about three-and-a-half weeks old. If they are infested with worms, worm them immediately. Do not attempt to build up the pups first if the parasitic infestation has made them unthrifty. It is best to rid them of the worms quickly, after which they will speedily return to normal health and plumpness.

The weeks fly by, and before you know it the puppies are at saleable age. The breeder, you can be sure, has not wasted these weeks. He has spent many hours in close observation of the litter and has centered his interest on one pup which he thinks shows the most promise. Either he will hold this pup for himself, sell him to a show-conscious buyer, or keep the puppy and sell it at a higher price when it has become more fully developed and its early promise becomes a fact. The strange part about this whole business of picking a young puppy from a litter is that the novice buyer many times stands a good chance of picking the best pup as the seasoned and experienced breeder. The reason for this seeming incongruity lies in the fact that in every litter there will be several pups which, if well bred and well cared for, appear to be potential winners at eight to ten weeks of age. Another reason concerns the ratio of sectional growth in young animals.

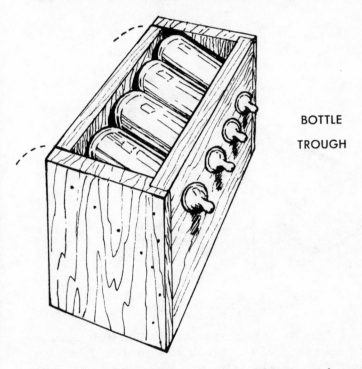

BOTTLE
TROUGH

Each pup, as an individual, will have a different growth rate and exhibit change in relative sections of the body, as well as in over-all growth, from day to day.

If you are the potential purchaser of a Shepherd puppy, or a grown dog for that matter, prepare yourself for the purchase first by attending as many shows as possible, especially outdoor shows where Shepherd specialty judges are officiating. Observe, absorb, and listen. Visit kennels which have well-bred, winning stock, and at shows and kennels make an unholy nuisance of yourself by asking innumerable questions of Shepherd people who have proved, by their record in the breed, that information gleaned from them can be respected. When you intend to purchase a new car, or an electrical appliance such as a refrigerator or washing machine, you go to sales rooms and examine the different makes, weighing their features and quality, one against the other. You inquire of friends who have different brands their opinion in regard to the utility value of the item, and, when you have made your up mind which brand is best, you make sure that you purchase the item from a reliable distributor. Do the same thing when you intend to purchase a dog. Before you make your journey to any breeder to buy a puppy, be sure to inquire first into the background of the breeder as well as the background of his dogs. What does this breeder actually know

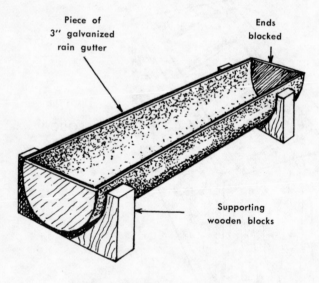

Piece of
3″ galvanized
rain gutter

Ends
blocked

Supporting
wooden blocks

PUPPY FOOD OR WATER TROUGH

about his breed? What has he formerly produced? What is his reputation amongst other reputable breeders? Does his stock have balanced minds as well as balanced bodies? Find the answers to these questions even before you delve into the ancestry of the puppies he has for sale. If the answers prove that this breeder is an honest, dependable person with more than a smattering knowledge of the breed, and that he has bred consistently typical stock, then your next step will be to study the breeding of his puppies to determine whether they have been bred from worth-while stock which comes from good producing strains. Examine stock he has sold from different breedings to other customers. Be careful of kennels which are puppy factories, breeding solely for commercial reasons, and don't be carried away by hysterical, overdone, adjective-happy advertisements.

When you have satisfied yourself that the breeder is a morally responsible person who has good stock, then you may sally forth to purchase your future champion. It is best, if possible, to invite an experienced breeder to accompany you on your mission. As mentioned before, even the most experienced Shepherdist cannot with assurance pick the pup in the litter which will mature into the best specimen. An experienced person can, however, keep you from selecting a very engaging youngster which exhibits obvious faults which quite possibly won't improve.

Assuming that the litter from which you are going to select your puppy is a fat and healthy one and it is a male puppy you have set your heart on having, ask the breeder to separate the sexes so you can examine the male pups only. Normal puppies are friendly, lovable creatures wanting immediate attention, so the little fellow who backs away from you and runs away and hides should be eliminated from consideration immediately. This also applies to the pup which sulks in a corner and wants no part of the proceedings. Watch the puppies from a distance of approximately twenty feet as they play and frolic, sometimes trotting and occasionally quitting their play for a fleeting moment to stand gazing at something of interest which has, for that second, engaged their attention. Don't be rushed. Take all the time necessary to pick the puppy you want. You are about to pay cold cash for a companion and a dependent who will be with you for many years.

If you have been lucky enough to have had the opportunity of examining both sire and dam, determine which puppies exhibit the faults of the parents or the strain. If any particular fault seems to be overdone in a specific pup, discard him from further consideration. Do not handle the pups during this preliminary examination. Look for over-all balance first and the absence of glaring structural faults, but remember that the good pup will show an exaggeration of all the excellencies you expect to be present in the mature animal. Shy or frightened puppies (and grown dogs) have a tendency to crouch a bit, giving the illusion of beautiful hindquarter angulation, where the bold dog who possesses equal angulation will appear straighter behind. Watch the pup's movement when at trot. A good one moves with a balanced, though ungainly, "bear cub" trot. Look particularly for a long reach in front, which indicates good shoulder angulation. Hindquarters often improve, except when the hock is straight and angulation is sorely lacking at this age, but front assemblies seldom change. A dog with good shoulders and reach can be depended upon to get the most from what he has when moving. Angulation, fore and aft, should be determined without handling, since a pup has a tendency to

Four-week old Shepherd pups.

crouch when set up for examination, exaggerating the angle of skeletal structure in these sections. The importance of the shoulder should be remembered by the novice, since the eye is usually first engaged by exaggerated rear angulation.

Make sure the back is short and straight, not roached or swayed. The ribs should be deep, well-sprung, and reaching far back, leaving a short, strong loin. The pup should be broad across the back and over the loin and croup, and the croup itself long and gently sloping to a tail that is not set high and hangs long and without curve to well below the hocks. High tail sets generally signify a future shortness in croup and can, in the mature animal, destroy the sweep of even an excellent croup. Sometimes the bulk of puppy fur obscures the true shape of the croup. In this case it can only be determined by handling and feeling. Many young puppies appear cow-hocked when standing if they possess very good or extreme rear-quarter angulation. This condition generally disappears with age, unless cowhocks is an inherited condition. Your Shepherd pup should exhibit a short hock, firm, well rounded and thickly padded feet, and heavy, strong bone. Avoid the pup who appears too tight and finished or mature at this age. Be careful too, of the novice's delight, the biggest, loosest, and clumsiest pup in the litter. The former will lack size, bone, and masculinity at maturity, and the latter will quite often never attain compactness or true fluidity in movement. The head should be wedge-shaped, fairly broad between the ears, with a strong muzzle, good-sized nose, and eyes dark and not too large or round. The toenails should be black. If they are light, it is sometimes an indication of a pigmentation lack which will manifest itself later when the pup is older and some of the black portions of the coat have receded.

By this time you have probably narrowed the field down to one or two pups. It is time now to hand examine the one or two youngsters who look the best to you. Stand each one upon a table individually in a show stance and examine the prosternum to determine whether it juts in front of the farthest forward point of the shoulder blade, as it should. Then examine

178

the mouth for tooth and jaw structure to determine the bite. In Shepherds, an overshot pup frequently levels off with growth if it is not a hereditary anomaly and is slight; but an undershot jaw seldom corrects itself to any great extent by maturity. Next, attempt to determine if the pup is sexually whole. At this age the testicles are descended into the scrotum but are often drawn up when the puppy is being handled, making it difficult to locate both testicles during examination. The buyer should have a written agreement with the seller to the effect that, should the pup prove to be subluxed, a monorchid, or cryptorchid, or should the ears refuse to stand fully and firmly within a reasonable length of time, the puppy can be returned and the purchase price refunded or the pup replaced by another of equal value.

If it is a female pup you want, look for the same values as outlined above in choosing a male. You would not, of course, go through the performance of determining sex as mentioned above. Female puppies are generally slightly smaller and show a degree of greater refinement than the males.

Remember that no one can pick a champion at eight weeks and no breeder can truthfully sell you a future winner at that age. All a breeder can guarantee is the health and breeding of the puppy, and the fact that he possesses the normal complement of eyes, ears and legs. The best you can do if you are observant, knowing, and lucky, is to pick the best pup in that particular litter, at that particular time.

If it is at all possible, it is best to purchase two pups at the same time. They furnish company for each other, eliminate lonesome serenades during the first few nights, and are competition at the food pan. If you bring home only one pup, provide him with a stuffed dog or doll in his sleeping box which you have taken to the breeder's with you and rubbed in the nest box. This will frequently give the puppy some sense of comfort and companionship and alleviate lonesomeness that brings on dismal howling during the

Correct scissors bite

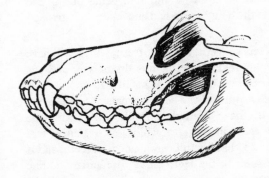

first night in his new home. A ticking alarm clock near the pup's bed will sometimes have the same effect.

In his new home, amidst strange surroundings, the pup will very often go off his feed for a time. This should not unduly alarm you unless his refusal to eat lasts so long that he becomes emaciated. If this occurs, ask your veterinarian for a good tonic, or change diets to tempt his palate. Never coax him or resort to forced feeding, or you will immediately spoil your pup and be a slave to him and his aggravating eating habits from that time forward. If he eats only one or two meals a day, instead of the several feedings he should have, he will survive until his appetite improves if he is otherwise healthy and vigorous. Should you find after a reasonable time and much scheming and effort that you have a naturally finicky eater, you must resign yourself to the fact that you have acquired a headache which can last for the duration of your dog's life and one which cannot be cured by aspirin. Only heroic measures can help you conquer this difficulty, and you must steel yourself and cast out pity if you are to succeed. He must be starved, but really starved, until he has reached a point where dry bread resembles the most succulent beef. Only by such drastic measures can a finicky eater be cured. Dogs who have the competition of other dogs, or even a cat, at the feed pan usually display a normal appetite. For this reason it is sometimes smart for the one-dog owner to borrow a friend's or neighbor's pet to feed with his own until such time as his own dog has acquired a healthful and adequate appetite.

Arrange for your pup to have lots of sleep, particularly after feeding, a difficult chore when there are youngsters in the home, but nevertheless very necessary to the well being of the pup. Make him feel at home so he will respond quickly to his new surroundings. It so often happens that a puppy retained by the breeder surpasses at maturity the purchased pup who was a better specimen in the beginning. This confounds the novice, yet has a reasonably simple explanation. The retained pup had no change in environment which would affect his appetite and well being during the critical period of growth, while the bought pup had and so was outstripped by his lesser litter brother.

Your puppy will have two sets of teeth, the milk teeth, which will have fallen out by the time he is approximately six months of age, and the permanent teeth, which he'll retain for the rest of his life. Loss of weight and fever may accompany the eruption of the new, permanent teeth, but is no cause for alarm. Anatomists have a simple formula to represent the number and arrangement of permanent teeth which, at a glance, will allow you to determine if your dog has his full complement of teeth, and if he hasn't, which ones are missing. In the teeth chart, the horizontal line represents the division between upper and lower jaw. We begin with the

incisors in the front of the dog's mouth and designate them with the letter
I. The canine teeth are labeled C, the premolars, P, and the molars, M.
The complete formula for a dog possessing all his teeth would be:

$$I \frac{3+3}{3+3} + C \frac{1+1}{1+1} + P \frac{4+4}{4+4} + M \frac{2+2}{3+3} = 42 \text{ teeth} \quad \begin{array}{l} \text{(20 in upper jaw)} \\ \text{(22 in lower jaw)} \end{array}$$

Often teething will cause your puppy's ears to droop after they have been
standing erect. If this happens, you can safely assume that once he has
finished this teething period, the ears will again erect themselves. If they
have never come erect up to this time and you can find no hereditary reason
for them not to, wait until the teething period is over; then, if they still
refuse to come erect, it is time to help them. On the inside of the ear, about
one-third up from the base, and at the outer edge, you will find a muscle
which seems to pull in and crimp the ear. Across this muscle, running
vertically along the outside edge of the inner ear, firmly tape a flat strip of
balsa wood, such as is used in toy aeroplane kits. Liquid adhesive can be
substituted for the tape if you have it available. Then anchor the ears in an
upright position with a strip of tape which runs across the top of the skull
between the ears and is attached at each end to the ears. Do not keep removing the tape and wood to see what effect it has had. Allow it to stay for
several days at a time without disturbance, during which period you may
resort to prayers in the hope that one or the other method will prevail and
the pup's ears come erect.

Occasionally, puppies develop lip warts which will disappear in a short
time, leaving no aftereffects. Remember to have your puppy immunized
against distemper and hepatitis and, as much as possible, keep him away
from other dogs until he is old enough to combat the diseases which take
their toll of the very young. Lastly, but of great importance, give your
pup the opportunity to develop that character and intelligence for which
the German Shepherd is justly famed. Give him human companionship
and understanding, take him with you in the car and amongst strangers.
Let him live the normal, happy, and useful life which is his heritage, and
that tiny bundle of fur which you brought home so short a time ago will
grow into a canine citizen of whom you will be proud to say, "He's mine."

THE SHEPHERD SERVES

Training to attack.

Hussan v. Haus Kilmark, U.D.T. and Margelen's Chiefton, U.D.T. These two fine shepherds held the U.S. Obedience Title for four straight years, 1950-51-52-53. Owner, trainer, Mrs. Winnifred G. Strickland.

Shepherd guarding U.S. Army installation. (U.S. Army Photo)

CHAPTER 12

FUNDAMENTAL TRAINING

Responsibility for the reputation of any breed is shared by everyone who owns a specimen of that breed. Reputation, good or bad, is achieved by conduct, and conduct is the result of the molding, through training, of inherent character into specific channels of behavior.

It is a distinct pleasure, to novice, old-timer, or the public at large, to watch dogs perform which have been trained to special tasks. Here is the ultimate, the end result of the relationship between man and dog. After watching an inspired demonstration, we sometimes wonder if, under a proper training regime, our own Shepherd could do as well. Perhaps he can if he is temperamentally fitted for the task we have in mind. No single individual of any breed, regardless of breed type, temperament, and inheritance, is fitted to cope with all the branches of specialized service. Nor does every owner possess the qualifications or experience necessary to train dogs successfully to arduous tasks. But every dog can be trained in the fundamentals of decent behavior, and every dog owner can give his dog this basic training. It is, indeed, the duty of every dog owner to teach his dog obedience to command as well as the necessary fundamentals of training which insure good conduct and gentlemanly deportment. A dog that is uncontrolled can become a nuisance and even a menace. This dog brings grief to his owner and bad reputation to himself and the breed he represents.

We cannot attempt, in this limited space, to write a complete and comprehensive treatise on all the aspects of dog training. There are several worth-while books, written by experienced trainers, that cover the entire varied field of initial and advanced training.* There are, furthermore, hundreds of training classes throughout the country where both the dog and its owner receive standard obedience training for a nominal fee, under the guidance of experienced trainers. Here in these pages you will find only specific suggestions on some points of simple basic training which we feel are neglected in most of the books on this subject. We will also attempt to give you basic reasons for training techniques and explain natural limitations to aid you in eliminating future, perhaps drastic, mistakes.

The key to all canine training, simple or advanced, is control. Once you have established control over your Shepherd, you can, if you so desire, progress to advanced or specialized training in any field. The dog's only

* See "How To Train Your Dog" by Ernest H. Hart, for full and comprehensive information on basic training.

boundaries to learning are his own basic limitations. This vital control must be established during the basic training in good manners.

Almost every Shepherd is responsive to training. He loves his master and finds delight in pleasing him. To approach the training problem with your Shepherd, to make it a pleasant and easy intimacy rather than an arduous and wearisome task, you must first learn a few fundamentals. In the preceding paragraph we spoke of control as the paramount essential in training. To gain control over your dog, you must first establish control over your own vagaries of temperament. During training, when you lose your temper you lose control. Shouting, nagging repetition, angry reprimand, and exasperation only confuse your canine pupil. If he does not obey, then the lesson has not been learned. He needs teaching, not punishment. The time of training should be approached with pleasure by both master and dog, so that both you and your pupil look forward to these periods of contact. If you establish this atmosphere, your dog will enjoy working, and a dog who enjoys his work, who is constantly trying to please, is a dog who is always under control.

Consistency is the brother of control in training. Perform each movement used in schooling in the same manner every time. Use the same words of command or communication without variance. Employ command words that are simple single syllables, chosen for their crispness and difference in sound. Don't call your dog to you one day with the command, "Come," and the next day, with the command, "Here," and expect the animal to understand and perform the act with alacrity. Inconsistency confuses your dog. If you are inconsistent, the dog will not perform correctly and your control is lost. By consistency you establish habit patterns which eventually become an inherent part of your Shepherd's behavior. Remember that a few simple commands, well learned, are much better than many and varied commands only partially absorbed. Therefore be certain that your dog completely understands a command and will perform the action it demands, quickly and without hesitation, before attempting to teach him a new command.

Before we begin training, we must first assess our prospective pupil's intelligence and character. We must understand that his eyesight is not as keen as ours, but that he is quick to notice movement. We must know that sound and scent are his chief means of communication with his world, and that in these departments he is far superior to us. We must reach him, then, through voice and gesture, and realize that he is very sensitive to quality change and intonation of the commanding voice. Therefore, any given command must have a definite tonal value in keeping with its purpose. The word "no" used in reprimand must be expressed sharply and with overtones of displeasure, while "good boy," employed as praise, should be

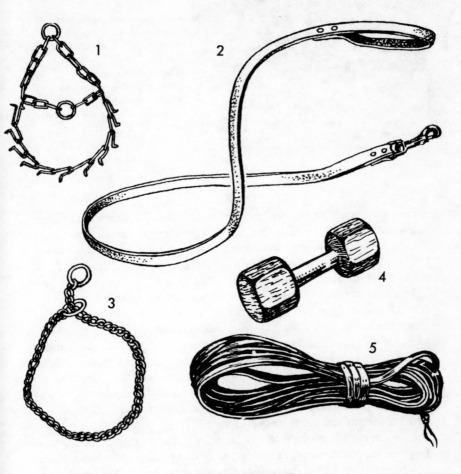

TRAINING EQUIPMENT

1. Torquatus, limited choke. 2. Six foot pliable leash. 3. Chain choke collar. 4. Dumb-bell (wooden). 5. Longe, or long leash. Items 2 and 3 are sufficient for simple basic training.

spoken lightly and pleasantly. In early training, the puppy recognizes distinctive sound coupled with the quality of tone used rather than individual words.

All words of positive command should be spoken sharply and distinctly during training. By this we do not mean that commands must be shouted, a practice which seems to be gaining favor in obedience work and which is very much to be deplored. A well-trained, mature Shepherd can be kept completely under control and will obey quickly and willingly when com-

Ch. Yasko vom Zenntal, SchH. III
(sire)
Xanto v. Osnabruckerland
(dam)
Mina v. Gerstenberg
1958 U.S. Champion and Grand
Victor, Yasko had wonderful temperament but was not a dominant sire.

mands are given in an ordinary conversational tone. The first word a puppy learns is the word-sound of his name; therefore, in training, his name should be spoken first to attract his attention to the command which follows. Thus, when we want our dog to come to us, and his name is Kurt, we command, "Kurt! Come!"

Intelligence varies in dogs as it does in all animals, human or otherwise. The ability to learn and to perform is limited by intelligence, facets of character, and structure, such as willingness, energy, sensitivity, aggressiveness, stability, and functional ability. The sensitive dog must be handled with greater care and quietness in training than the less sensitive animal. Aggressive dogs must be trained with firmness; and an animal which possesses a structural fault which makes certain of the physical aspects of training a painful experience cannot be expected to perform these acts with enjoyment and consistency.

In referring to intelligence, we mean, of course, canine intelligence. Dogs are supposedly unable to reason, since that portion of the brain which, in humans, is the seat of the reasoning power is not highly developed in the dog. Yet there have been so many reported incidents of canine behavior that seemingly could not have been actuated by instinct, training, stored knowledge, or the survival factor, that we are led to wonder if the dog may not possess some primitive capacity for reasoning which, in essence, is so different from the process of human reasoning that it has been overlooked, or is as yet beyond the scope of human comprehension.

Training begins the instant the puppies in the nest feel the touch of your hand and are able to hear the sound of your voice. Once the pup is old enough to run and play, handle him frequently, petting him, making a fuss over him, speaking in soothing and pleasant tones and repeating his name over and over again. When you bring him his meals, call him by name and coax him to "come." As time passes, he associates the command "come" with a pleasurable experience and will come immediately upon

Ch. Atstan Impressario
Another English champion and
fine stud dog.

command. Every time he obeys a command, he should be praised or rewarded. When calling your puppies to their food, it is good practice to use some kind of distinguishing sound accompanying the command—a clucking or "beep" sound. It is amazing how this distinctive sound will be retained by the dog's memory, so that years after it has ceased to be used, he will still remember and respond to the sound.

Some professional trainers and handlers put soft collars on tiny pups, with a few inches of thin rope attached to the collar clip. The puppies, in play, tug upon these dangling pieces of rope hanging from the collars of their litter mates, thus preparing the youngsters for easy leash breaking in the future. In training the pup to the leash, be sure to use a long leash, and coax, do not drag, the reluctant puppy, keeping him always on your left side. Never use the leash as an implement of punishment.

Housebreaking is usually the tragedy of the novice dog owner. We who have Shepherds are fortunate in this respect since, as a breed, they are basically cleanly in habit and quite easily housebroken. Many Shepherds which are raised outside in a run never need to be actually housebroken, preferring to use the ground for their act and seemingly sensing the fact that the house is not to be soiled. Dogs tend to defecate in areas which they, or other dogs, have previously soiled, and will go to these spots if given the chance. Directly after eating or waking a puppy almost inevitably has to relieve himself. If he is in the house and makes a mistake it is generally your fault, as you should have recognized these facts and removed him in time to avert disaster. If, after you have taken him out, he comes in and soils the floor or rug, he must be made to realize that he has done wrong. Scold him with, "Shame! Shame!" and rush him outside. Praise him extravagantly when he has taken advantage of the great outdoors. Sometimes if you catch him preparing to void in the house, a quick, sharp "No" will stop the proceedings and allow you time to usher him out. Never rub his nose in his excreta. Never indulge in the common practice of striking the puppy with a rolled up newspaper or with your hand. If you do, you may be training your dog either to be hand shy, to be shy of paper or to bite the newsboy. Your hand should be used only in such a way that your dog recognizes it as that part of you which implements your voice, to pet and give pleasure. In housebreaking, a "No" or "Shame" appropriately used and delivered in an admonishing tone is punishment enough.

A dog which will attain the size of a Shepherd is seldom broken to paper in the house. If your dog has been so trained and subsequently you wish to train him to use the outdoors, a simple way to teach him this is to move the paper he has used outside, anchoring it with stones. Lead the dog to the paper when you know he is ready to void. Each day make the paper smaller until it has completely disappeared, and the pup will have formed the habit of going on the spot previously occupied by the paper. Puppies tend to prefer to void on a surface similar in texture to that which they used in their first few weeks of life. Thus a pup who has had access to an outside run is easily housebroken, preferring the feel of ground under him. Smaller breeds are sometimes raised on wire-bottom pens to keep them free of intestinal parasites. Occasionally puppies so raised have been brought into homes with central heating employing an open grate-covered duct in the floor. To the pup the grate feels similar to his former wire-bottomed pen. The result, as you can well imagine, gives rise to much profanity and such diligence that the youngster is either rapidly house-broken or just as rapidly banished to live outdoors.

If your Shepherd is to be a housedog, a lot of grief can be avoided by remembering a few simple rules. Until he is thoroughly clean in the house confine him to one room at night, preferably a tile- or linoleum-floored room that can be cleaned easily. Tie him so that he cannot get beyond the radius of his bed, or confine him to a dog house within the room; few dogs will soil their beds or sleeping quarters. Feed at regular hours and you will soon learn the interval between the meal and its natural result and take the pup out in time. Give water only after meals until he is housebroken. Puppies, like inveterate drunks, will drink constantly if the means is available, and there is no other place for surplus water to go but out. The result is odd puddles at odd times.

"No," "Shame," "Come," and "Good boy" (or "girl"), spoken in appropriate tones, are the basic communications you will use in initial training.

If your pup is running free and he doesn't heed your command to come, do not chase him—he will only run away or dodge your attempts to catch him and your control over him will be completely lost. Attract his attention by calling his name and, when he looks in your direction, turn and run away from him, calling him as you do so. In most instances he will quickly run after you. Even if it takes a great deal of time and much exasperation to get him to come to you, never scold him once he has. Praise him instead. *A puppy should only be scolded when he is caught in the act of doing something he shouldn't do.* If he is scolded even a few minutes after he has committed his error, he will not associate the punishment with the crime and will be bewildered and unhappy about the whole thing, losing his trust in you.

Puppies are inveterate thieves. It is natural for them to steal food from the table. The "No!" and "Shame!" command, or reprimand, should be used to correct this breach of manners. The same commands are employed when the pup uses your living room couch as a sleeping place. Many times dogs are aware that they must not sleep on the furniture, but are clever enough to avoid punishment by using the sofa only when you are out. They will hastily leave the soft comfort of the couch when they hear you approaching and greet you in wide-eyed innocence, models of canine virtue. Only the tell-tale hairs, the dent in the cushion, and the body heat on the fabric are clues to the culprit's dishonesty. This recalls the tale of the dog who went just a step further. So clever was he that when his master approached, he would leap from the couch and, standing before it, blow upon the cushions to dislodge the loose hairs and cool the cushion's surface. The hero of this tale of canine duplicity was not identified as to breed, but we are sure that such intelligence could only have been displayed by a German Shepherd dog.

If, like the dog in the story, the pup persists in committing this misdemeanor, we must resort to another method to cure him. Where before we used a positive approach, we must now employ a negative, and rather sneaky, method. The idea is to trick the pup into thinking that when he commits these crimes he punishes himself and that we have been attempting to stop him from bringing this punishment down upon his head. To accomplish this end with the unregenerate food thief, tie a tempting morsel of food to a long piece of string. To the string attach several empty tin cans, or small bells, eight to ten inches apart. Set the whole contraption on the kitchen or dining-room table, with the food morsel perched temptingly on an accessible edge. Leave the room and allow the little thief to commit his act of dishonesty. When you hear the resultant racket, rush into the room, sternly mouthing the appropriate words of reproach. You will generally find a thoroughly chastened pup who, after one or two such lessons, will eye any tabled food askance and leave it strictly alone.

The use of mousetraps is a neat little trick to cure the persistent sofa-hopper. Place two or three set traps on the couch area the dog prefers and cover them with a sheet of newspaper. When he jumps up on the sofa, he

Ch. Alf vom Loherfeld, SchH. II

(sire) Alf v. Nordfelsen,   (dam) Nelke v.d. Starrenburg,

Sired by a famous German Sieger, Alf is typical of his breeding.

will spring the traps and leave that vicinity in a great and startled hurry.

These methods, or slight variations, can be used in teaching your pup to resist many youthful temptations such as dragging and biting rugs, furniture, tablecloths, draperies, curtains, etc.

The same approach, in essence, is useful in teaching the pup not to jump up on you or your friends and neighbors. You can lose innumerable friends if your mud-footed dog playfully jumps up on the visitor wearing a new suit or dress. If the "No" command alone does not break him of this habit, hold his front legs and feet tightly in your hands when he jumps up, and retain your hold. The pup finds himself in an uncomfortable and unnatural position standing on his hind legs alone. He will soon tug and pull to release his front legs from your hold. Retain your hold in the face of his struggles until he is heartily sick of the strained position he is in. A few such lessons and he will refrain from committing an act which brings such discomfort in its wake.

Remember that only by positive training methods can you gain control which is the basis of successful training, and these tricky methods do not give you that control. They are simply short-cut ways of quickly rectifying nuisance habits, but do nothing to establish the "rapport" which must exist between trainer and dog.

Teach your Shepherd always to be friendly with other people. The protective instinct is strongly inherited in our breed and specific training to develop it is not generally needed, unless the pupil is a mature animal undergoing special training for police, guard, or army duty.

During the entire puppy period the basis is being laid for other and more advanced training. The acts of discipline, of everyday handling, grooming, and feeding, are preparation for the time when he is old enough to be taught the meaning of the Sit, Down, Heel, Stand, and Stay, commands, which are the first steps in obedience training and commands which every dog should be taught to obey immediately. Once you have learned how to train your dog and have established complete control, further training is only limited by your own abilities and by the natural boundaries which exist within the animal himself.

Don't rush your training. Be patient with small progress. Training for both you and your dog will become easier as you progress. Make sure that whatever you teach him is well and thoroughly learned, and it will never be forgotten. Remember that your dog's inherited character and intelligence form certain limiting patterns. Some Shepherds can become competent Seeing Eye dogs, others cannot. Some can be trained as attack dogs, others are temperamentally unsuited to this task. Even though our Shepherds are descended from herding dogs, they have been bred away from that heritage, yet many can be expected to learn such pastoral tasks with a great degree of success. There does exist strains of the breed in Germany bred consistently and specifically for herding, and a puppy from such breeding could be expected to learn the art of herding easily, since his forebears had been selected for such work and it is his undeniable heritage.

We occasionally hear of the Shepherd being advocated for tracking or trailing. Here again we have a genetic limiting of ability in our breed. Though there may be individuals within the breed which show more marked ability in this respect, the faculty is limited and cannot compare to the inherent competence of breeds bred specifically for this ability. A Shepherd used for police work can follow an immediate and hot trail if he has been trained to do so, but a cold and complicated trail is beyond his olfactory powers. If we wish to hunt quail or pheasant, we use setters or pointers or whichever of the gun dog breeds we fancy, but we do not use a Shepherd, simply because gun dogs have been bred specifically for this work and to attempt to train a Shepherd to equal the gun dog's ability in the field would be ridiculous and without purpose. For true trailing ability, the Bloodhound is the breed supreme. Tracking, as a part of obedience work, is interesting and aids in developing our dog's mental powers, as do the various other obedience tests. Tracking, as an integral part of police work, is a necessary adjunct to the Shepherd's other abilities in this field. But only those who have had no other experience in true trailing would exaggerate our breed's ability in this field to the point of supremacy. Our breed is fit and capable of doing many things and doing them well. The Shepherd's service to mankind is so wide and varied that we have a multitude of outlets for his true abilities. Let us then stress the Shepherd's undeniable worth and inherited ability to perform in these various fields, rather than in some activity in which his capabilities are limited by breed pattern.

But to return to fundamental training, let us review the few and basic truths set forth in this chapter. Remember to use simple common sense when you approach the task of training. Approach it with ease and confidence. Control yourself if you wish to control your dog, for control is the vital element in all training. Realize the limitations as well as the abilities of your dog, and the final product of your training zeal will bring you pride in accomplishment, pride in yourself and your ability, and pride in your Shepherd.

Because of the many fine attributes that recommends the German Shepherd in the various areas of difficult and specialized canine work, your dog makes the ideal obedience breed. The combination of a good book on training, and working in a training class will bring you amazing and delightful returns in dog obedience work. If you are inclined toward this area of activity, write to The American Kennel Club, 51 Madison Avenue, New York, for their booklet, "Regulations & Standards for Obedience Trials."

Dr. Werner Funk (in black hat) officiating in the Gebrauchshundklasse Ruden ring from which the Sieger will eventually emerge. The gentleman in the gray suit is Dr. C. Rummel.

The Junghundklasse Ruden ring in 1964. The Junghund Sieger is Aro v. Worringer Reitweg, SchH. I, a son of Vello z.d. Sieben-Faulen. Reserve youth Sieger, behind Aro, is Black v. Lambertzeck, son of Jalk v. Fohlenbrunnen.

CAY EDLE v. HOLSTEN, SchH. III

(sire) Bur v. Stoerstrudel   (dam) Berna v. Lomborn

A richly pigmented male of excellent conformation, Cay's breeding
is similar to that of Alf a.d. Schwalestadt. This animal has been a
consistant "V" dog in Germany.

FLORA v. FURSTENHUGEL, SchH. II

(sire) Mutz a.d. Kuckstrasse   (dam) Elfi v. Furstenhugel

A very lovely German bitch. In the Gebrauchshundklasse Hundinner.
at the 1964 Sieger Show Flora received the high VA 4 rating.

HERA vom SIXTBERG

(sire) Witz v. Haus Schutting, SchH. II   (dam) Caret v. Elfenhain

As a very young bitch, the richness of her color and her balance gives promise of the beauty of her maturity. She was high S.G. in the Jugendklasse at the '64 Sieger Show. Her top producing, VI dam is also mother of the "C" (Condor, Carmen, etc.), "D," and "G" litters vom Sixtberg.

Big and masculine, this fine German stud has just left the Gebrauchshundklasse Ruden ring after being granted a "V" (Excellent).

BRIX v. GRAFENKRONE, SchH. III, AD.

(sire) Bar v.d. Weissen Pforte   (dam) Tatjana a.d. Weingegend

Brix is shown in Germany at the 1964 Sieger Show where he was V27.
Brought to this country the gray dog became Grand Victor in 1965.

The parade in the Gebrauchshundklasse Ruden (male) ring begins at the Sieger Show. In the foreground is Atlas v. Fasanenwinkel, followed by Siggo v. Buttlar.

DAGO v. SIXTBERG, SchH. III

(sire) Volker v. Zollgrenzschutz-Haus, SchH. III

(dam) Caret v. Elfenhain, SchH. I

At the 1963 Sieger Show, Dago was handled by his owner, Herr Wassermann. This dog is a younger brother (from an earlier litter) to Condor v. Sixtberg. Dago is now in this country.

Moving around the immense ring the handlers walk their dogs. Some are wearing track suits and sneakers. The orange judge's tent, which is halfway across the ring, can be seen at the right.

ZIBU v. HAUS SCHUTTING, SchH. III

(sire) Donar v. Firnskruppe   (dam) Niobe v. Haus Schutting

Awarded VA1, Zibu became German Sieger at the 1964 show. His get indicate his value as a sire. He closely reflects the type of his sire, but is firmer and shorter coupled.

CHAPTER 13

TRAINING FOR THE SHOW RING

So many things of beauty or near perfection are so often marred and flawed by an improper approach to their finish. A Renoir or an El Greco tacked frameless to a bathroom wall is no less a thing of art, yet loses importance by its limited environment and presentation. Living things, too, need this finish and preparation to exhibit their worth to full advantage. The beauty of a flower goes unrecognized if withered petals and leaves mar its perfection, and the living wonder of a fine dog is realized only in those moments when he stands or moves in quiet and balanced beauty. The show ring is a ready frame in which to display your dog. The manner in which he is presented within that frame is up to you.

If you contemplate showing your Shepherd, as so many of you who read this book do, it is of the utmost importance that your dog be as well and fully trained for exhibition as he is for general gentlemanly conduct in the home. Insufficient or improper training, or faulty handling, can result in lower show placings than your dog deserves and can quite conceivably ruin an otherwise promising show career. In the wider sense, and of even more importance to the breed as a whole, is the impression your Shepherd in the show ring projects to the gallery. Every Shepherd shown becomes a representative of the breed in the eyes of the onlookers, so that each dog becomes a symbol of all German Shepherd dogs when he is on exhibition. Inside the ring ropes, your dog will be evaluated by the judges as an individual; beyond the ropes, a breed will be judged by the behavior of your dog. So often the abominable behavior of an untrained animal irks even those whose interest lies with the breed. Think, then, what a warped impression of the breed must be conveyed, by this same animal, to the critically watching ringsider.

When you enter your Shepherd in a show, you do so because you believe that he or she is a good enough specimen of the breed to afford competition to, and perhaps win over, the other dogs entered. If your Shepherd is as good as you think he is, he certainly deserves to be shown to full advantage if you expect him to win or place in this highly competitive sport. A novice handler with a quality Shepherd which is untrained, unruly, or phlegmatic cannot give competition to a dog of equal, or even lesser, merit which is well trained and handled to full advantage.

Novice owners frequently bring untrained dogs to shows so that they can become accustomed to the strange proceedings and surroundings, hopefully thinking that, in time, the dog will learn to behave in the wanted manner by himself. Often the novice's training for the show ring begins in desperate and intense endeavor within the show ring itself. Confusion for both dog and handler can be the only result of such a program. Preparation for showing must begin long in advance of actual show competition for both dog and handler.

Let us assume that you have been fortunate enough to breed or purchase a puppy who appears to possess all the necessary qualifications for a suc-successful show career. Training for that career should begin from the moment you bring him home, or if you are the breeder, from the time he is weaned. This early training essentially follows the same pattern as does fundamental training in conduct. Again you begin by establishing between you and the puppy the happy relationship which, in time, becomes the control so necessary to all training. Handle the puppy frequently, brush him, examine his teeth, set him up in a show stance, and stroke his back slowly. Move him on a loose leash, talking to him constantly in a happy, friendly tone. Make all your movements in a deliberate and quiet manner. Praise and pat the puppy often, establishing an easy and happy rapport during this period. This is simple early preparation for the more exact training to come.

During this period the owner and prospective handler should take the opportunity to refresh or broaden his own knowledge. Reread the standard, and with this word picture in mind, build a mental reproduction of the perfect Shepherd: his structure, balance, gait, and movement. Critically observe the better Shepherd handlers at shows to see how they set and gait their dogs. Only by accumulating insight and knowledge such as this can you succeed in the training which will bring out the best features of your own future show dog.

Let us assume that your puppy is now old enough to show, or that you have acquired a young dog for whom you plan a show career. Beginning long before the show in which you are going to start him (several weeks at least), you introduce him to the "tidbit." This can be any bit of food which the dog relishes immensely and which is entirely different from the kind of food used in his regular diet. The tibdit, then, is a tasty piece of food which the dog likes and which is not given to him at any other time. Boiled liver, in chunks, is most generally used, but dogs can be shown with liverwurst, peanuts, turkey, or various other treats which the individual animal might particularly relish. If you choose liver as your tidbit, brown it in the oven for a few minutes after you have boiled it. This tends to remove the greasiness from the surface and keeps it from crumbling excessively, making it much easier to handle and carry in your pocket in the show ring.

Some dogs are alerted in the show ring by the use of a particular toy, such as a rubber mouse that squeaks when pressed. But the vast majority

Ch. Onyx of Edgetowne

Ch. Peter of Browvale

Ch. Klodo of Dornwald

A GALAXY

of

AMERICANBRED

MALE SHEPHERD

SHOW RING STARS

OF THE PAST

Ch. Jodo v. Liebestraum

Ch. Gernda's Ludwig

of handlers prefer to show a Shepherd through the medium of the tidbit. Several times a day when you and your dog are together, tempt him with the tidbit. Always make him stand, never sit, in front of you when you offer him this gourmet's delight. Hold the tidbit waist high and allow the dog to smell and taste it. When his complete attention is absorbed in attempting to nibble at this delicious morsel, move slowly backward, carefully watching the dog as he moves forward, until he has taken the proper balanced stance, with his front legs parallel to each other, his back level, and his left hind leg stretched back just enough to be comfortable. He is watching the tidbit and posing naturally, alertly, and in proper balance on a loose lead. At this point, you the handler, move forward to within approximately two feet of the dog and command him to "Stand, stay!" Keep his attention focused on the tidbit, speaking gently to him for a few seconds, then give him a small piece of the tidbit as reward and pet and praise him.

Continue this procedure, and, as you progress, make the dog stand motionless and alert for an ever-longer period of time before allowing him to taste the tidbit. When you give him the delicacy as a reward, move forward and present it to him; never allow him to break his pose and come forward to you. Always hold the leash in your left hand. Keep your left leg in front of your right and toward the dog to check him from advancing toward you. If he jumps up for the tidbit, raise your left leg so that your knee takes him in the chest, at the same time jerking strongly downward on the leash.

Another way of training for show, employing the same principles as outlined above, is to tie the end of the leash to a doorknob, then walk several feet away, turn and face the dog, and draw him to you with the tidbit as bait until he has moved forward into the proper show stance. Then command him to "Stand, stay!" as you walk toward him, coming to a halt when about two feet in front of him, and continue the training as described above. Always use a chain choke collar of sufficient length and a six-foot leash during training. Leashes made of woven khaki cloth straps, which are strong, pliable and easier on the hands and in handling than leather show leashes, can be purchased at this length.

It is time now to analyze what we have done and why we have done it. The reason for the tidbit is obvious. Holding it waist high and no higher, and standing no closer than two feet to the dog when using the tidbit, allows your Shepherd to stand naturally. It keeps him from straining his head and neck upward or reaching close above him, both of which postures make a break in the even flow of the neckline and connecting wither. Straining upward will also bring the dog's front feet forward, giving him a straight-shouldered appearance, and the strain of such a position will cause him to shift and break his stance.

With the Bavarian Alps in the background, this photo depicts three young, winning Shepherds from the Zollgrenzschutz-Haus Kennels. All three are from the same litter and sired by the World Sieger, Volker v. Zollgrenzschutz-Haus. From left to right; Caesar, Carmen, and Condor vom Sixtberg.

We will assume that you now have your dog trained to stand easily and naturally on a loose leash for a reasonable period of time, interested in the tidbit in your hand. The next step in show training is to teach your dog to move properly when on leash. Shepherds good enough to be shown generally possess the even, effortless trot which is a distinctive feature of the breed. It is your purpose now to control that beauty of movement so that it loses nothing when displayed in the show ring. Keeping the dog on your left side, move him forward at a slow trot, checking him sharply when he tends to pull out or break stride. Again, the leash should be kept loose. When you come to the end of the allotted run and turn to start back, do not jerk the dog around; instead give him more leash freedom and allow him to come around easily without a change of leads, meanwhile speaking to him quietly. When he has completed the turn, draw him to you with the leash and continue moving back to the starting point. At the finish, pat and praise him.

While you are teaching your dog the elements of ring deportment, take stock of the pupil himself. To do this correctly, you will need assistance. Have someone else put the dog through his paces, handling him as you have and as he will be handled in the show ring. Observe the dog carefully to determine when he looks his best. Should he be stretched out a bit when posing? Or does he have better balance and outline if his hind legs are not pulled too far back? At what rate of speed, when moving, does he perform his best?

Pretend that you are a judge. Envision the perfect Shepherd and, employing your knowledge of the standard as a yardstick, study your dog as though he were a strange animal. From this study you will see many things, tiny nuances, that will aid you in showing your Shepherd to the best possible advantage in open competition.

Once he has mastered the show training you have given him, you must take every opportunity to allow strangers and friends to go over your dog, much in the manner of a judge, while you pose and gait him, so he will become used to a judge's unaccustomed liberties. It would be well to enter your Shepherd in a few outdoor sanction matches now, to acquaint him with the actual conditions under which he will be shown. During all this time, of course, the character and temperament of your dog, as well as his physical assets, must be taken into consideration, as it must in all types of training, and the most made of the best he has.

Often a handler showing a dog which has not had sufficient training must use other methods to get the most from the animal. We must remember, too, that unless specifically trained to one particular method, a dog may be presented to better advantage when handled in an entirely different manner. It is necessary to attract the attention of some dogs by strange noises, either oral or mechanical. You will also often see handlers squat down on the right side of their animals and set the dog's legs and feet in the desired position. But dogs set up by hand in this manner generally lack the grace and flow of lines that the naturally posed dog shows to such good advantage.

There is, of course, that paragon of all show dogs, that canine jewel and handler's delight—the alert, curious animal who takes a keen interest in the world around him and stands in proud and easy naturalness at the end of his long leash, head and ears up, posing every minute he is in the ring. But remember, even this super-show dog has had some training in ring manners.

In some instances the dog's master stands outside of the ring in full view of his animal while someone else handles him in the ring. The dog will watch his master, keeping his head and ears up and wearing an alert expression. This is called "double-handling," and is sometimes frowned upon by other members of the showing fraternity.★

★ It has been the custom in Germany to permit any kind of handling (sometimes several individuals of a family running alongside dog and handler, shouting the animal's name), as long as the judge can truly assess the dog. This practice has been falling into disfavor in recent years.

THE IDEAL GERMAN SHEPHERD MALE

It is of the utmost importance that you never become blind to your dog's faults, but at the same time realize his good features and attempt to exploit these when in the ring. If your dog is a year old, or older, do not feed him the day before the show. This will make him more eager for the tidbit when in the ring. Make sure your dog is in good physical shape, in good coat, clean and well groomed. If a bath is necessary, give it to him several days before the show so the natural oils will have time to smooth the coat and give it a natural sheen. Be sure he is not thirsty when he enters the ring and that he has emptied himself before showing, or it will cramp his movement and make him uncomfortable.

School yourself to be at ease in the ring when handling your dog, for if you are tense and nervous, it will communicate itself to the dog, and he will display the same emotional stress. In the ring, keep one eye on your dog and the other on the judge. One never knows when a judge might turn from the animal he is examining, look at your dog, and perhaps catch him in an awkward moment.

Your Shepherd requires no trimming or primping to make him ready to show as do the representatives of so many other breeds. He is to be shown as nature made him, without any artificial means of beautification. If his nails need clipping, tend to it at least four days before show time so that if you should cut too deeply, the nail will have time to heal.

On the morning of the show, leave your home early enough so that you will have plenty of time to be benched and tend to any last minute details which may come up. When the class before yours is in the ring, give your dog a last quick brush, then run a towel over his coat to bring out the gloss. Should his coat be dull, a few drops of brilliantine, rubbed between the palms of your hands and then sparingly applied to the dog's coat, will aid in eliminating the dullness. Some handlers wipe a slightly dampened towel over the coat just before entering the ring to achieve the same effect.

Bring to the show with you: a water pail, towel, brush, comb, suppositories in a small jar, a bench chain, a chain choke collar, and a light six-foot leash for showing. If the dog has not emptied himself, insert a suppository in his rectum when you take him to the exercising ring. If you forget to bring the suppositories, use instead two paper matches, wet with saliva, from which you have removed the sulphur tips.

In the ring, the handler constantly endeavors to minimize his charge's faults while attempting to inveigle the judge into seeing his virtues. There are several little tricks which the knowing handler employs to accomplish his ends. If he is showing a dog with slightly soft ears, he holds the tidbit above and closer to the dog's head than recommended previously in this chapter. This causes the Shepherd to lift his head with his muzzle pointing upward, and the soft ears fall backward and appear fully erect and rigid. Should the dog stand east and west in front, the legs must be set correctly by hand. Grasp the dog by the elbow, not the forearm, and gently turn the elbow outward and away from the body until the feet rest parallel to each other. A dog showing lack of rear angulation is offered the tidbit with a pushing motion, while the handler crowds closer to the animal than usual. This causes the dog to sink slightly in the rear quarters, giving the illusion of greater angulation than is actually present. Many a top dog who possesses an excess of vigor and vitality will carry a high-held tail into the show ring, for which he will be unduly penalized due to the judge's inability to differentiate between a gay tail and a gay disposition. There is one corrective measure to overcome this seeming fault, which has been proven to be the best corrective by experience. Several days prior to the showing the handler should, upon every occasion that the tail is raised to the gay position, strike downward at the root of the tail with the edge of his hand with a strong, chopping motion. At the moment of contact the handler should command, in an admonishing tone, "Tail!" After a few such lessons, the

Ch. Vicki v. Hoheluft
(sire)
Ch. Nox of Ruthland
(dam)
Ch. Lady of Ruthland
Canadian Grand Victrix.
Size and quality typical of
her Pfeffer breeding.

Ingo Wunschelrute
(sire)
Arry v. Burghaldering
(dam)
Lona v. Aichtal
Grand Victor 1952. Import-
ed, he has had a great
American show career.

Ch. Afra v. Heilholtkamp
(sire)
Armin v. Trilke
(dam)
Fenja v.d. Eifferburg
Grand Victrix 1952. A big,
strong, imported bitch. Kennel mate of Ingo Wunchel-
rute.

dog will automatically lower his tail when only the command word is spoken. It is also good practice, with a dog of such vigor, to have someone who is not showing take him for a good long run before your class comes up. This will take the edge off his exuberance so he will handle with greater steadiness in the ring, and will not bring the handler into the ring in an exhausted condition.

Following is a chart listing the dog-show classes and indicating eligibility in each class, with appropriate remarks. This chart will tell you at a glance which is the best class for your dog.

DOG-SHOW CLASS CHART

CLASS	ELIGIBLE DOGS	REMARKS
PUPPY—6 months and under 9 months	All puppies from 6 months up to 9 months.	Puppy must be whelped only in U.S. or Canada.
PUPPY—9 months and under 12 months	All puppies from 9 months to 12 months.	Puppy must be whelped only in U.S. or Canada.
NOVICE	Any dog or puppy which has not won an adult class (over 12 months), or any higher award, at a point show.	After 3 first-place Novice wins, cannot be shown again in the class. Must be whelped in U.S. or Canada.
BRED BY EXHIBITOR	Any dog or puppy, other than a Champion, which is owned and bred by exhibitor.	Must be shown only by a member of immediate family of breeder-exhibitor, *i.e.*, husband, wife, father, mother, son, daughter, brother, sister.
AMERICAN-BRED	All dogs or puppies whelped in the U.S. or possessions, except Champions.	To be eligible for this class a dog must be whelped in the U.S. as a result of a mating which took place in the U.S.
OPEN DOGS	All dogs, 6 months of age or over, including Champions and foreign-breds.	Canadian and foreign champions are shown in open until acquisition of American title. By common courtesy, most American Champions are entered only in Specials.
SPECIALS CLASS	American Champions.	Compete for B.O.B., for which no points are given.

Each sex is judged separately. The winners of each class compete against each other for Winners and Reserve Winners. The animal designated as Winners is awarded the points. Reserve Winners receive no points. Reserve Winners can be the second dog in the class from which the Winners Dog was chosen. The Winners Male and Winners Female (Winners Dog and Winners Bitch) compete for Best of Winners. The one chosen Best of Winners competes against the Specials for Best of Breed, and the Best of Breed winner goes into the Working Dog Group. If fortunate enough to top this group, the final step is to compete against the other group winners for the Best in Show title.

When Best of Breed is awarded, Best of Opposite Sex is also chosen. A Shepherd which has taken the points in its own sex as Winners, yet has been defeated for Best of Winners, can still be awarded Best of Opposite Sex if there are no animals of its sex appearing in the ring for the Best of Breed award.

Ch. Kola v. Beckgold
(sire)
Erich v. Beckgold
(dam)
Dixie v. Bar-Orch

A fine American show bitch
of the past.

Champions are made by the point system. Only the Winners Dog and Winners Bitch receive points, and the amount of points won depends upon the number of Shepherds of its own sex the dog has defeated in the classes (not by the number entered). The United States is divided into five regional point groups by the A.K.C., and the point rating varies with the region in which the show is held. Consult a show catalogue for regional rating. A Shepherd going Best of Winners is allowed the same number of points as the animal of the opposite sex which it defeats if the points are of a greater amount than it won by defeating members of its own sex. No points are awarded for Best of Breed.

Ch. Nordraak of Matterhorn (sire)
Ch. Jory of Edgetowne (dam)
Charm of Dornwald II

Pacific Coast Grand Victor 1954. A magnificent American bred male now deceased.

To become a Champion, a dog must win fifteen points under a minimum of three different judges. In accumulating these points, the Shepherd must win points in at least two major (three points or more) shows, under different judges. Five points is the maximum amount that can be won at any given show. If your Shepherd wins a group, he is entitled to the highest number of points won in any of the working breeds by the dogs he defeats in the group if the points exceed the amount he has won in his own breed. If the show is a Shepherd Specialty, then the Best of Breed winner automatically becomes the Best in Show dog. The titles of Grand Victor and Grand Victrix are awarded annually to the Best of Breed and Best of Opposite Sex winners at the National Specialty Show sponsored by the German Shepherd Dog Club of America, Inc. (the Parent Club). No points are awarded at Match or Sanctioned shows.

Remember that showing dogs is a sport, not a matter of life and death, so take your lickings with the same smile that you take your winnings, even if it hurts (and it does). Tomorrow is another day, another show, another judge. The path of the show dog is never strewn with roses, though it may look that way to the novice handler who seems, inevitably, to step on thorns. Always be a good sport, don't run the other fellow's dog down because he has beaten yours, and when a Shepherd goes into the group, give him your hearty applause even if you don't like the dog, his handler, his owner, and his breeding. Remember only that he is a German Shepherd dog, a representative of your breed and therefore the best darn dog in the group.

We hope that this chapter will help the novice show handler to find greater ease and surety in training for show and handling in the ring and thus experience more pleasure from exhibiting. Competition is the spice of life, and a good Shepherd should be shown to his best advantage, for his own glory and for the greater benefit of our wonderful breed.

CHAPTER 14

SHOWS AND THE JUDGING SITUATION

The basic reason for the dog show, the object in the gathering together of representative animals of the breed in open competition, seems to have been mislaid in the headlong pursuit for ribbons, trophies, and points. These prizes undoubtedly lead to kennel-name popularity, which in turn produces greater and more profitable puppy sales and stud services, but they are not the end in themselves. They are given simply as tokens of achievement in a much larger pattern which has no direct relation to economy. The graded selection of various dogs according to individual quality by a competent, unbiased judge enables earnest breeders to weigh and evaluate the products of certain breedings and strains. It helps them to evaluate their own breeding procedures in relation to comparative quality, and to give them an idea as to which individuals, or breeding lines, can act as correctives to the faults inherent in their own breeding. Here the yard-stick of the official standard is used to measure the defects or virtues of individual animals and of the breed as a whole for the edification and tabulation of both the knowing breeder and the novice. This is what a dog show should mean to the exhibitor. But with the quality of judging so often displayed, it is no wonder that the showing of dogs has degenerated into a rat race for ribbons, points, and tarnished glory.

Essentially the judge should be an intermediary between the present and the future, because his decisions shape the trends for better or for worse. If these trends lead to undesirable results, there will be deterioration instead of an ever-closer approach to the breed ideal. The judge is a sounding board, a calculator of degrees of excellence, an instrument for computing worth. He can, with each assignment, give something of enduring value toward breed improvement. As such, he or she must not only be entirely familiar with the Shepherd standard, but must also understand every element of structure and balance. And almost more important, the judge must be able to see and evaluate each of those tiny nuances of quality which can establish the superiority of one animal over another of apparently equal excellence.

Judges should confine themselves to judging only those breeds with which they have had personal experience. A thorough reading of the standard and the appearance as an apprentice judge, three times, does not make anyone an authority on the breed. There should certainly be a more exacting test of ability before a person is granted a license to judge. We are all conscious of the fact that there are some people who could be in a breed all their lives, read every book published about the breed, and still not

Arno v. Fraubeck
(sire)
Ch. Dorian v. Beckgold
(dam)
Elle v. Fraubeck
Dorian's sensational winning son, now in South America. Formerly owned and shown by E. H. Hart.

Ch. Dorian v. Beckgold

(sire) Ch. Jeffrey of Browvale   (dam) Blondy v. Hoheluft

American and Canadian Grand Victor. "Nobility plus . . ." Handled by breeder and owner, Captain William Goldbecker. Morris and Essex, 1946.

qualify as competent judges, simply because they do not possess that special gift that brings clarity and sureness to decision. By the same token, there are perhaps others who do not judge who have that "feel" for a good dog, that gift to select surely which, when combined with knowledge and integrity, makes the completely competent judge.

In the interest of clarity and simplicity, as well as for the edification of the ringsider, a definite pattern of procedure should be adhered to by the Shepherd judge. All entries in any particular class should be lined up in catalogue order opposite the judge's table. The judge should step into the center of the ring and signal the handlers to circle the ring once or twice, with the dogs maintaining an easy trot. The class should then be halted and the dogs left at rest as the judge calls each dog separately to the center of the ring for individual examination. The judge should approach the dog from the front and, speaking kindly to him, begin his close examination. Unnecessary handling by the judge is poor practice. There is no reason, other than unsureness by the judge, for bouncing the animal's back like a mattress inspector, pulling the tail up or down, poking here and there as though frisking the dog for dangerous weapons, or any of the other ridiculous actions sometimes indulged in by judges. The Shepherd's coat is not so dense that the structure cannot be seen, and the dog is supposed to be viewed in a natural stance, not in the propped position of a terrier, hound, or sporting dog. Other than in the evaluation of teeth and testicles, the dog need not be touched. All other faults or virtues of a Shepherd can be readily seen by the trained eye when the dog is posed naturally at the end of a loose leash and when gaited.

After the individual animal has been examined in the center of the ring, the judge should ask to have him gaited at a slow trot, to and away from him, to evaluate movement coming and going. Following this, the dog should be gaited around the ring at a slow trot, to estabiish his quality in profile movement. When all the animals in the class have been individually examined as described, the entire class should be requested to walk around the ring several times and then to proceed at a slow trot until the judge has decided upon his placements.

The judge should not only pick his first four dogs, but place the others in the class in the order of their excellence as he sees them. He should know and, indeed, announce to the handlers of each of the first four dogs placed, the reasons for his selections. Should the judge be unable to explain his placings clearly and concisely, he should refrain from further Shepherd judging. If this procedure would become an A.K.C. rule, there would undoubtedly be several judges now officiating who would hesitate to accept future assignments. It should also be made mandatory, for the same reasons as mentioned above, for a judge to submit to the A.K.C. a written criticism of all dogs placed by him at any given show.

During the individual examination in the center of the ring, the judge can make notes covering each of the dogs brought before him for future reference. The procedure as outlined above can, of course, be varied to individual taste, but basically it is a standard and sound way of judging.

Though there are times when the judge is at fault, we must not forget that there are many times when the exhibitor's evaluation of the judge's placings is faulty. Too many exhibitors know too little about their own breed and are not competent to indulge in criticism. The very structure of dog-show procedure lends itself to dissatisfaction with the judge's decisions. The fact that there can be only three or fewer really satisfied winners in any breed judging, Winner's Male, Winner's Bitch, and Best of Breed, and that they are chosen by one individual who may or may not be competent, leaves a wide range of just or unjust recrimination for the exhibitor to air. Some of the post-mortem denunciation can be attributed directly to the psychological effect of the shows upon the exhibitors themselves.

Almost everyone, at some time or another, has had the urge to engage in some kind of competitive sport. Most exhibitors have arrived at that time of life when most competitive endeavor is too strenuous to be indulged in. Some have been frustrated nonathletes all their lives due to lack of muscular or physical prowess, or because sustained exertion did not fit their behavior patterns. Nevertheless, the fierce flame of competitiveness burns in them, and the dog-show ring provides a wonderful outlet to satisfy this need of expression. Some, without realizing it, find that the show ring provides an outlet for their normal desire to be important, if even for just a few fleeting moments, and it gives others an opportunity to be on the stage before an audience. The greater number of exhibitors are simply proud of their dogs and want to show them and have them evaluated in competition. Since there is no definite scoring for endeavor, merely a personal evaluation of their animals by an individual who can be right or wrong, tension is built and personalities clash.

The exhibitor has put into the show an enormous amount of time, thought, and heartaches in breeding, rearing, and preparation. With most exhibitors, the very fact that they are present signifies they consider their particular Shepherd fine enough to win. All this, coupled with the sad condition of the judging situation today, often tends to build up strong feelings which sometimes erupt into strong words.

Undoubtedly the whole procedure is of benefit to the exhibitor. He or she indulges in some measure of physical exercise, finds an outlet for the competitive spirit, and presently soothes built-up emotions by letting off vocal steam. But the end result is not good for the breed, since it results in confusion, especially to the novice who comes to the show to learn.

There will always be with us the chronic griper who must tear down another's dog with unfounded criticism after he has been defeated so that his own animal will appear better than it is. We must also deplore the custom of severe criticism and whispering campaigns against a consistent and deserving winner or stud. This insidious undermining of an animal of worth leads the novice to wonder how any judge had the temerity to put him up, which in turn casts reflections upon the judge's ability and further confounds the tyro who is seeking truth.

Many of the most prominent breeders who have been in the breed for years are judges as well. They are frequently criticized for their show-ring placements because they will put up animals of their own breeding or

Jola v. Burgunderhort, Imp.
(sire)
Arno v.d. Pfaffenau
(dam)
Asta v. Nibelungengold

Beautiful imported bitch of great quality and finish. A repeat of the "I" litter Burgunderhort breeding.

those of similar type to the strain they themselves produce. Undeniably, there are many instances in which a dog, handled or owned by an individual who is himself a judge, is given preference, since the breeder-judge officiating at the moment will, in the near future, show under the owner of the dog he has put up and expects the same consideration in return. This is but one of the many ways in which a judge may be influenced consciously or unconsciously. Regardless of the underlying cause, such practice must be condemned. But in most cases the breeder-judge who elevates animals of his own breeding or dogs of similar type cannot be summarily accused of lack of integrity. The type which he breeds must be the type of Shepherd he likes and his own interpretation of the standard. It

EXAMPLES OF STRUCTURAL FAULTS

The bitch at the top of the page displays the following faults: sway back, false front assembly (filled forechest disguises lack of proper shoulder angulation), too long in body, too long in loin, legs too short and bone spongy, weak pasterns, too short in neck, sickle hocks, tail curled and too high set.

The male at the bottom of the page has a poor head, snipey in muzzle and with apple skull, wet in neck, roach backed, shallow in body, and too high and square. He lacks bone, depth of body and his pasterns are too straight. He shows flat, mutton withers, too much tuck-up, too little angulation both in shoulder and hindquarter. He lacks forechest, his croup is too level, his tail too short, and he lacks pigmentation.

follows, therefore, that this is the type he will put up in all honesty. We may question his taste, knowledge, or interpretation of the standard, but not, in most instances, his ethics or honesty.

It is true that some judges seem to develop special prejudices on particular points of structure. For this reason it might have been wise to have included a numerical evaluation of points in the standard to check any tendency by a judge to overemphasize some minor fault which he particularly detests. Still, in some instances, this emphasis can be a boon, causing quick elimination of some fault which, if allowed to become concentrated, could become a definite menace to the perfection we strive for. Look at the photographs of former winners in the *Shepherd Dog Review* and notice particularly the absence of correct shoulder angulation.* If judges persist in elevating to the top animals possessing this or any other prevalent fault, the breeders unconsciously follow the trend and produce it, and it becomes incorporated as a dominant within the breed. When such a condition exists, the judges of the breed should be made aware of this tendency and, by penalizing it in the ring and vocally stressing this fact in evaluating the animal to its handler, do their share toward its elimination.

We are frequently told that the element of human variance in the interpretation of the standard is responsible for the wide difference of placings from one show to the next. Certainly this is true, but it should only be true to a limited extent. A judge's interpretation of the standard and his knowledge of what is a fault or a credit cannot vary so greatly from show to show if dictated alone by the human equation. Acknowledging the slight variance in placing which the individual judge's interpretation might cause, there is still no excuse for the wide discrepancy, and sometimes weird difference in placings, which we see occur too frequently. When we see this type of bad or biased judging, we can only assume that the arbitrator is either dishonest or ignorant and, in either case, is doing the breed great harm.

There are, thank goodness, quite a few qualified and earnest judges whose placings should be followed and analyzed, for it is through them that we can evaluate the breeding health of the Shepherd and know with confidence the individual worth of specific specimens. Judging is not an easy task. It does not generally lead to long and cozy friendships, for once an individual steps into the ring to begin his judiciary assignment, he is no longer an individual but becomes the impartial, wholly objective instrument of the standard. As such, friendship, personal likes or dislikes, cannot exist as facets of his make-up. He must judge the dogs before him as they

---

* The many fine imports (and the use of their genetic heritage) have given us vast improvement in shoulders.

211

are on that day without sentiment or favor. This is a task that demands complete subjection of self, high knowledge of the breed, and courage and integrity. It can be easily seen then, that not too many people could qualify in all these respects and so become completely proficient judges.

The *Shepherd Dog Review* fills a very real need for fanciers, both novice and veteran, by giving us a panoramic view of Shepherd activity throughout the country, complete with pictures of winners from the various sections. Some of the articles are of immense value to the earnest student of the breed, especially the occasional critiques by knowledgeable judges which give us their evaluation of certain animals. More of them should be published, since the retouched photographs and almost hysterical glorification of the descriptions in much of the advertising give us little in the way of a true conception of the dogs involved.

Incidentally, the show chairmen of show-giving clubs, particularly those who hold their shows during the winter months or during inclement weather when it is necessary to go indoors, should be reminded that the Shepherd is a large breed and that his gait is important to the judge's placings. Consequently a large ring is a necessity for easy judgment. Many judges do not care to judge indoor shows because of the small rings. Many fanciers will show only at outdoor shows, where rings are larger and their dogs have greater freedom of movement. It is definitely true that most Shepherds show to much better advantage out-of-doors than indoors.

The judging situation must be improved. A system should be set up whereby only those who have passed some rigid test would be qualified to judge the breed. As it exists today, instead of a process of selection tending toward breed improvement, we have nothing but unsureness leading to chaos. Were the ideal condition to exist, we, the breeders and owners, would submit our animals in open competition to the careful scrutiny of a truly competent authority whose integrity was beyond question. We would be able to compare our stock within the ring to see where we had erred. We would be able to measure the worth of breeding theory by the yardstick of a correct interpretation of the standard. We would know then what breeding lines were producing animals closest to the ideal and which individual dogs showed the highest degree of excellence; by thus creating, through the medium of the judge, an authority which we could depend upon, we could establish an easier path to the breed ideal.

CHAPTER 15

THAT QUESTION OF TEMPERAMENT

The first definition in Webster's of the word "temperament" reads: "Internal constitution in respect to balance or mixture of qualities or parts." This is, to say the least, a vague and general definition, and one which can stand considerable explanation and broadening when it is used with reference to the German Shepherd dog.

The word "temperament," in its general application, embraces character, sensitivity, discrimination, spirit, and intellect. It can denote either the absence or presence of one or more of these psychological traits. As a definitive, the word is therefore too wide in scope to have direct meaning. But we are not as concerned with the word as we are with its broad application. What is the true Shepherd temperament? How is temperament, good or bad, transmitted? Why does a Shepherd possess a temperament which can be specifically right or wrong for the breed? What are the essential faults of temperament? Where do these faults come from and can they be corrected? These are the questions which we must have answered if we would understand and be capable of evaluating temperament. To begin, we must hark back to the origin of the breed to understand the basic mental requirements and why they were established.

The German Shepherd dog was originally formed, in the crude state, by the intermingling of the inheritable characters of working sheep-herding breeds. Shepherd dogs of all countries, as a canine class, are bred and selected from individual animals which have intelligence, trainability, and the various mental characteristics that enable them to do their job well. We can assume, then, that the animals from which our breed stems embodied these stable mental qualifications. To establish a standard type, close inbreeding was indulged in, and this brought to light hidden recessives from the intermingled sheep-herding strains. With this selection for type, the basic character and mentality of the breed became less uniform than it had been when only selection for mental factors was involved.

Subsequently, when Germany became industrialized and the need for sheep-herding dogs lessened, Max von Stephanitz, the father of the breed, feared a decline in favor for his beloved Shepherds. To preserve the breed's popularity, he sold it to the politicians and the public as a dog of all-around excellence, with special emphasis on guard and protection work, for use in factories, by the police, and by the armed forces. Selection for these particular traits was then necessary. As time passed, the aptitudes of the Shepherd involved the breed in many other branches of work in his service to mankind. Today, in America, our Shepherds are companions and watchdogs essentially, guard dogs, Seeing Eye, police, war, and general utility dogs particularly. To encompass this wide variety of usefulness, the German Shepherd, as a breed, must possess a fine discriminating mentality, willingness to please, and an incorruptible character.

Temperament is not a simple Mendelian trait. It is the sum total of the animal's mental being, his inherited mind structure and his ability to apply it to experience.

Environment, to a limited extent, can influence eventual temperament, particularly as it is applied to early puppy experience. The dog is a creature of habit and imitation, and a shy bitch can cause shy habit patterns in her young by their imitation of her behavior. But influences of environment are acquired characters, not hereditary patterns, and therefore cannot be transmitted as such. The effect of environment on temperament is negligible, since essentially the greater number of breeders and owners supply proper environment for their dogs. The influence of environment, too, is kept within fairly narrow limits by natural and inherited demarcation. If environment did exert a high percentage of influence, how then explain the shy young dog, raised, fed, handled, and housed exactly the same as his mentally normal run-mate?

Let us first come to terms with the full meaning of this thing called temperament. A dog is not just "shy" or "vicious." An animal which displays these traits is mentally unsound, degenerate, or moronic. He is a constant worry to his owner and a danger to himself, his breed, and anyone with whom he comes in contact. Mental degeneration can and will limit the constantly rising popularity of the breed, as it did once before.

The essence of the German Shepherd dog as an individual breed is based upon type and temperament. Without type, a dog is not fit to be classified as a German Shepherd. Without temperament, a German Shepherd is not fit to be classified as a dog.

We so often hear the phrase, "He is only slightly shy (or overaggressive). I'm taking him to training classes to correct it." If this temperament fault is the rare one of environment it can, in many cases, be corrected. If it is a slight hereditary mental aberration, it can sometimes be covered up or hidden by training to all but the canny observer. But if the taint of mental instability is present as an inherited factor, it will never leave, and to say that a dog is slightly shy or vicious is akin to saying a woman is slightly pregnant; there are degrees in both cases, but the fundamental fact cannot be denied and with the passage of time becomes more evident.

Faults of temperament can be divided into the five basic categories which follow. In each instance the faults discussed are the extremes. There are shadings or degrees from the norm to the extreme and, in some instances, an overlapping of temperament defects. We are, of course, using

Ch. Yola of Longworth
(sire)
Ch. Keno of Longworth
(dam)
Elga v. Saliba
Grand Victrix 1950. Splendid Americanbred bitch type.

Ch. Garry of Benlore
(sire)
Falko of Benlore
(dam)
Ardis of Mergenhaus
A fine Americanbred show
dog and prepotent stud.
Sire of sixty champions.

Ch. Katja v. Blasienberg,
Z.Pr.
(sire)
Samson v. Blasienberg
(dam)
Anni v. Blasienberg
German Siegerin 1928-
1929, Austrian Siegerin
1928, Holland Siegerin
1929, American Grand Victrix and Champion 1930,
Canadian Champion 1931.
A truly great bitch.

extremes to give a completely clear picture of the faults of temperament, since without complete recognition, correction or elimination is impossible.

A *shy* dog is an oversensitive animal, an introvert whose world is too much for him. He lives in a dark mental shell of his own making, peopled by personal dragons and echoing hollowly to frightful sounds. To this dog, most experience is filled with horror and permeated with fear of the unknown. As a living creature he is a pitiful, craven thing whose constant terror of life pleads for release through peaceful death. This is a dog at the extreme limits of shyness. Sometimes we find a degree of timidity in young dogs or puppies, particularly bitches, which must not be confused

Junker z.d. sechs Fidelen, SchH. (sire) Delos v.d. Starrenburg, SchH. II
(dam)
Haja v. Steinanger, SchH. II
A nice young dog owned by Karl Mueller in Tokyo, Japan. This male was SG 2 in the Jugendklasse at the 1965 Sieger Show.

with shyness. It is often due to lack of varied experience with strangeness and new activity.

The *sharp-shy* dog is the epitome of bad temperament. He is easily driven to panic by the unfamiliar. When faced with strange surroundings or the approach of one who is not a familiar, the extreme fear-biter will attempt to escape, bites if he thinks he is cornered, urinates, and permeates the premises with a foul odor which emanates from the anal glands. If you own a dog with these defects, you should have it destroyed no matter how painful it is to you to do so. It may be attached to its own household and the inmates and be sweet and kind with the children, but this is only comparable to the counselor's plea for his criminal client who was "good to his mother." This psychologically unstable animal will, if the occasion arises, bite one of its owners in blind panic without even being aware of having done so.

The *dull* dog is so undersensitive to outside stimuli that he lives in an uncaring world of grayness which has no distinctive contrasts. To some people he is a good dog to have around, since he asks for little other than food and shelter. He is quiet in the house and around the grounds, since there is nothing around him of sufficient interest to arouse him to either curiosity or action. He has no individuality and is as much of a companion as an end table. We do not have many individuals of this character (or lack of character) in the breed.

An *overly sharp*, or *vicious*, dog, unless kept strictly under control or confinement, is as dangerous as a rattlesnake. This is our canine gangster

Landa v.d. Wienerau, SchH. III, FH.
(sire)
Jalk v. Fohlenbrunnen, SchH. III
(dam)
Dixie v.d. Wienerau, SchH. I
Out of a very successful breeding, Landa was German Siegerin 1965.

who obeys no law but the ancient one of club and fang. He is an over-bearing bully who mistrusts everyone and, like his human counterpart, is a menace to society. He is never to be trusted with strangers or other dogs. This animal is generally undersensitive to bodily discomfort or pain. There are much fewer congenitally vicious dogs than shy dogs. An overly aggressive dog can sometimes be made dangerous by environment. He can be trained to attack and bite upon command, and unless he has the intelligence to discriminate, he can become a hair-trigger menace when not under complete control. This same type of animal can be spoiled by over-indulgence and babying until his respect for his owner vanishes, the owner's control is gone, and the dog decides his destiny is his own.

In their invaluable book *Working Dogs*, Humphrey and Warner describe another character trait found in their utility experiments with Shepherds at Fortunate Fields. This trait they label *distrust*. The animals exhibiting

Bill v. Kleistweg

sire: Hein v. Richterbach
dam: Adda v. Reiffeck

1956 Grand Victor. A fine German Import who finished his championship at the Specialty.

this trait are normal and friendly with their own people, but withdraw hastily when approached by strangers. They do not show fear or other symptoms associated with shyness. They are not inclined to bite, are not barkers or overaggressive. They can be taught to attack upon command. Their attitude is one of negative aloofness to strangers. They can be won over only by close association. And even then, the animal itself must be left to make the first actual advances toward friendship.

This trait, distrust, is sometimes found in imported dogs until they become acclimated to their new surroundings. They give their trust, at first, to one person and, though they may appear shy to others they are not, they are distrustful and simply want strangers to leave them alone. Such animals, if trained (and most imports are), will attack fearlessly upon command and exhibit steadiness to sharp sound, noise of every description, and an overwhelmingly foreign atmosphere, evidence that they are exhibiting distrust and not shyness in their actions toward other people. We in America want a cheerful, outgoing dog temperamentally, but the Germans breed for what they label, *"True German Shepherd Aloofness."* The dog from Germany should not carry his heart on his sleeve. This, too, contributes to the temperament characteristic labeled, "distrust." When the import displaying this characteristic becomes at home in his new environment and accepts completely the change thrust upon him, he generally changes in his attitude toward other people, but he will generally always, in some small ways that perhaps only you, the owner, can recognize, be distrustful of any persons who are not included in the immediate family.

In the training of working dogs for specific utilitarian purposes, temperament defects are readily detected, but in the breeding of show dogs, or pets, these faults are many times unnoticed or condoned. It is an undeniable truth that we as frequently make excuses for our dog's mental aberrations, as we do for our children's. Doting owners frequently allow

Cito v.d. Hermanns Schleusse
(sire)
Ajax v. Stieg-Anger
(dam)
Hanna v. Equord

Imported dog who was successfully shown in America.

their congenitally half-witted or gangster dogs to run at large, refusing to admit the menace they represent and condoning their crimes. Such owners are worse than their dogs, causing bad publicity which reflects upon the whole breed. Dogs which are a menace to society should either be destroyed, incarcerated, or rendered incapable of producing their own kind.

The true Shepherd must be an animal fit in body and mentality to do the essential work for which the breed was created. We in America want a German Shepherd which is sweet, kind, and happy in disposition, yet bold and courageous. He must be alert and eager to please and serve. Above all, he must be highly intelligent, for without intelligence, he will not be capable of employing his native temperament and mental ability to the greatest extent. The dog possessing this true Shepherd temperament has no problems. He has trust and confidence in the world, in its seasons, vagaries, and inhabitants and, therefore, he has trust in himself and is at peace with his environment.

In Germany, much more so than in America, great stress is placed upon proper temperament. The German breeders will not tolerate any animal which exhibits mental faults. No animal can be shown in the important classes unless it has acquired a training degree as evidence of its trainability and intelligence. Close checks by area breeding masters aid in eliminating the mentally unfit before they become mature.

The German breeder seldom keeps more than two or three dogs at a time. These dogs have back-yard runs generally, but are not regularly kenneled. They are, instead, an integral part of the family life, living with the family and participating in the family activity. They are taken on buses, shopping, to restaurants, and so forth. Under these conditions, their conduct and temperament must be exemplary and their native intelligence is developed naturally and easily to its fullest extent. We in America, due to our more rapid mode of living, our social commitments, and the myriad other activities, cannot give our dogs the time or the almost perfect environment that the German fanciers can. For this reason our animals should, of necessity, be even more intelligent and of greater mental stability than their relatives abroad to approach our mental ideal.

If the greater percentage of animals in the breed had perfect temperament, it would only be necessary to engage in perfunctory examination of the traits involved as they apply to that part of the standard which speaks of temperament. Unfortunately, this is not the case. Although perhaps 75 per cent of the Shepherds in America today possess temperaments which are adequate to cope with the kind of nonrigid life they lead, Humphrey and Warner, in selecting for working ability, found only a limited number which could be used or bred from. The great majority possessed temperament faults which disqualified them. Admittedly, the utility requirements at Fortunate Fields were rigid; still, we cannot get away from the fact that suitable animals were in the minority. To further accent the value of selective breeding for mental qualities, it must be reported that the Fortunate

Fields experiment, at its beginning, showed a suitability ratio of only 35 per cent and raised that ratio, before the experiment's conclusion, to an estimated 95 per cent of Shepherds capable of working under actual field conditions. W. H. Ebeling, in his invaluable letter to the president of the German Shepherd Dog Club of America, Mr. Burr L. Robbins, which was published in the *Shepherd Dog Review*, reports much the same experience in acquiring and breeding dogs for the Seeing Eye. He writes of the difficulty of finding animals of suitable temperament for this important work. He tells of dogs of beautiful structural quality and seemingly sound temperament which produced 80 per cent mentally useless stock. He proposes this condition came from a piling up or concentration of undesirable mental traits due to line-breeding or inbreeding. Of great interest was Mr. Ebeling's mention of the importation of old-fashioned sheep-herding Shepherds by the late Tobias Ott. These were dogs with no inbreeding, not bred for beauty but only for utility. He speaks of the exciting variations produced by these dogs, and the future plans of breeding them to animals of fine quality to eventually reach a blending of beauty and utility. Mr. Ebeling reports that it took them about twelve years to reach a point where temperament faults were no longer greatly prevalent, and that their stock now shows better than 70 per cent suitability.

This information is important in that it points out that the greater number of our Shepherds, though largely acceptable in temperament for ordinary nonutility environment, are certainly not equipped for specific tasks which should be their heritage. It stresses the fact that, in our search for beauty, we have allowed insidious mental faults to become prevalent to the detriment of the breed. It further reveals that vast improvement can be made in this most important part of the dog's being by recognition of temperament faults and breeding to eliminate them.

The enduring worth and glory of any breed lies in its service to mankind, but that service cannot be realized unless the animals within the breed possess the necessary mental equipment to fulfill their destiny.

Now that we have analyzed that all-embracing word "temperament," it would be wise to go back and quickly check through Chapter Three, The New Era, and review the mental qualities which have come down to our dogs through their forebears. We can readily see that, though selection for homozygosity was attempted in regard to type and body form, here in America mental traits continued to vary greatly from the norm, teetering from one extreme to the other, with a middle ground of normality between the poles. With this genetic background, it is not difficult to see where the inherited mental abnormalities exhibited by some of our animals have come from. Correction for over-all mental breed improvement lies in

Kobeil's Barda

sire: Ch. Ingo Wunschelrute
dam: Evida of Grafmar

1956 Grand Victrix. Personality and class. An American-bred bitch whose winnings denote her worth.

selection in breeding partners and selection of the resultant progeny. The selected mentally sound progeny can then be tested by breeding, eventually fixing the mental type and temperament we want.

Today, with the Shepherd ever gaining in popularity and the subsequent greater activity in breeding, it is essential, above all, to produce and breed from mentally sound stock to preserve this popularity. Relatively few Shepherd owners show or continue to show unless their animals are exceptionally fine specimens. Most of the young stock sold by breeders are destined to become companions, household pets, or natural guards for the home. Most of the purchasers are rank tyros with little knowledge of

221

Ch. Red Rock's Gino, CD.

(sire) Edenvale's Nikki, CD.   (dam) Kay of Ayron

Gino was Grand Victor in 1959. Big, masculine, richly pigmented.

the breed and no great experience in handling or training dogs. It is for these people, for these reasons, that we, in whose hands the destiny of the breed rests, must assume responsibility. We must recognize and perform our duty toward those prospective owners of our breed, and to accomplish this end, we must recognize the paramount importance of sound temperament.

Remember that our Shepherd is different in temperament and structure from other breeds because he has been made so by biological heredity, and this difference has been accentuated by selective breeding for special functions. This is why correct temperament is so important to the breed. Without it, the very purpose of the breed is destroyed, and without purpose, no living thing has worth.

CHAPTER 16

DISEASES AND FIRST AID

The dog is heir to many illnesses and, as with man, it seems that when one dread form has been overcome by some specific medical cure, another quite as lethal takes its place. It is held by some that this cycle will always continue, since it is nature's basic way of controlling species population.

There are, of course, several ways to circumvent Dame Nature's lethal plans. The initial step in this direction is to put the health of your dogs in the hands of one who has the knowledge and equipment, mental and physical, to competently cope with your canine health problems. We mean, of course, a modern veterinarian. Behind this man are years of study and experience and a knowledge of all the vast research, past and present, which has developed the remarkable cures and artificial immunities that have so drastically lowered the canine mortality rate as of today.

Put your trust in the qualified veterinarian and "beware of Greeks bearing gifts." Beware, too, of helpful friends who say, "I know what the trouble is and how to cure it. The same thing happened to my dog." Home doctoring by unskilled individuals acting upon the advice of unqualified "experts" has killed more dogs than distemper.

Your Shepherd is constantly exposed to innumerable diseases through the medium of flying and jumping insects, helminths, bacteria, fungi, and viruses. His body develops defenses and immunities against many of these diseases, but there are many more which we must cure or immunize him against if they are not to prove fatal.

We are not qualified to give advice about treatment for the many menaces to your dog's health that exist and, by the same token, you are not qualified to treat your dog for these illnesses with the skill or knowledge necessary for success. We can only give you a résumé of modern findings on the most prevalent diseases and illnesses so that you can, in some instances, eliminate them or the causative agent yourself. Even more important, this chapter will help you recognize their symptoms in time to seek the aid of your veterinarian.

Though your dog can contract disease at any time or any place, he or she is most greatly exposed to danger when in the company of other dogs at field trials and dog shows or in a boarding kennel. Watch your dog carefully after it has been hospitalized or sent afield to be bred. Many illnesses have an incubation period, during the early stages of which the animal himself may not show the symptoms of the disease, but can readily contaminate other dogs with which he comes in contact. It is easily seen, then, that places where many dogs are gathered together, such as those mentioned above, are particularly dangerous to your dog's health.

Parasitic diseases, which we will first investigate, must not be taken too lightly, though they are the easiest of the diseases to cure. Great suffering and even death can come to your dog through these parasites that prey on him if you neglect to realize the importance of both the cure and the control of reinfestation.

EXTERNAL PARASITES

The lowly flea is one of the most dangerous insects from which you must protect your dog. It carries and spreads tapeworm, heartworm and bubonic plague, causes loss of coat and weight, spreads skin disease, and brings untold misery to its poor host. These pests are particularly difficult to combat because their eggs—of which they lay thousands—can lie dormant for months, hatching when conditions of moisture and warmth are present. Thus you may think you have rid your dog (and your house) of these devils, only to find that they mysteriously reappear as weather conditions change.

When your dog has fleas, use any good commercial flea powder that contains malathion, lindane, or any similar insecticide. Pyrethrins and rotenone flea powders are excellent, but not long lasting. Dust him freely with the powder. It is not necessary to cover the dog completely, since the flea is active and will quickly reach a spot saturated with the powder and die. These compounds are also fatal to lice. DDT in liquid soap is excellent and long-potent, its effects lasting for as long as a week. Your dog's sleeping quarters as well as the animal itself should be treated. Repeat the treatment in ten days to eliminate fleas which have been newly hatched from dormant eggs. Chlorinated hydrocarbons (DDT, chlordane, dieldrin, etc.) are long acting. Organic phosphoriferous substances such as malathion, are quick killers with no lasting effect.

Ch. Hussar of Maur-Ray
(sire)
Ch. Viking v. Hoheluft
(dam)
Ch. Leda of Ireton

A fine Americanbred stud, strong in Pfeffer breeding.

Ch. Eveleys Ailsa of Brinton
English champion. A good moving
dog who exhibits a fine front
assembly.

TICKS

There are many kinds of ticks, all of which go through similar stages in their life process. At some stage in their lives they all find it necessary to feed on blood. Luckily, these vampires are fairly easily controlled. The female of the species is much larger than the male, which will generally be found hiding under the female. Care must be taken in the removal of these pests to guard against the head's remaining embedded in the dog's skin when the body of the tick is removed. Chlorinated hydrocarbons are effective tick removers. Ether or nail-polish remover, touched to the individual tick, will cause it to relax its grip and fall off the host. The heated head of a match from which the flame has been just extinguished, employed in the same fashion, will cause individual ticks to release their hold and fall from the dog. After veterinary tick treatment, no attempt should be made to remove the pests manually, since the treatment will cause them to drop by themselves as they succumb.

MITES

There are three basic species of mites that generally infect dogs, the demodectic mange mite (red mange), the sarcoptic mange mite (white mange), and the ear mite (otodectic mange). Demodectic mange is generally recognized by balding areas on the face, cheeks, and the front parts of the foreleg, which present a moth-eaten appearance. Reddening of the skin and great irritation occurs as a result of the frantic rubbing and scratching of affected parts by the animal. Rawness and thickening of the skin follows. Not too long ago this was a dread disease in dogs, from which few recovered. It is still a persistent and not easily cured condition unless promptly diagnosed and diligently attended to.

Sarcoptic mange mites can infest you as well as your dog. The resulting disease is known as scabies. This disease very much resembles dry derma-

225

titis, or what is commonly called "dry eczema." The coat falls out and the denuded area becomes inflamed and itches constantly.

Ear mites, of course, infest the dog's ear and can be detected by an accumulation of crumbly dark brown or black wax within the ear. Shaking of the head and frequent scratching at the site of the infestation accompanied by squeals and grunting also is symptomatic of the presence of these pests. Canker of the ear is a condition, rather than a specific disease, which covers a wide range of ear infection. Canker can be initiated by ear mite infection.

All three of these conditions should be treated by your veterinarian. By taking skin scrapings or wax particles from the ear for microscopic examination, he can make an exact diagnosis and recommend specific treatment. The irritations caused by these ailments, unless immediately controlled, can result in loss of appetite and weight, and so lower your dog's natural resistance that he is open to the attack of other diseases which his bodily defenses could normally battle successfully.

INTERNAL PARASITES

It seems strange, in the light of new discovery of specific controls for parasitism, that the incidence of parasitic infestation should still be almost as great as it was years ago. This can only be due to lack of realization by the dog owner of the importance of initial prevention and control against reinfestation. Strict hygiene must be adhered to if dogs properly treated are not to be exposed to infestation immediately again. This is particularly true where worms are concerned.

In attempting to rid our dogs of worms, we must not be swayed by amateur opinion. The so-called "symptoms" of worms may be due to many other reasons. We may see the actual culprits in the animal's stool, but even then it is not wise to worm indiscriminately. The safest method to pursue is to take a small sample of your dog's stool to your veterinarian. By a fecal analysis he can advise just what specific types of worms infest your dog and what drugs should be used to eliminate them.

Do not worm your dog because you "think" he should be wormed, or because you are advised to do so by some self-confessed "authority." Drugs employed to expel worms can prove highly dangerous to your dog if used indiscriminately and carelessly, and in many instances the same symptoms that are indicative of the presence of internal parasites can also be the signs of some other affliction.

A word here in regard to that belief that garlic will "cure" worms. Garlic is an excellent flavoring agent, favored by gourmets the world over, but it will not rid your dog of worms. Its only curative power lies in the fact that, should you use it on a housedog who has worms, the first time he pants in your face you will definitely be cured of ever attempting this pseudo-remedy again.

ROUNDWORM

These are the most common worms found in dogs and can have grave effects upon puppies, which they almost invariably infest. Potbellies, general unthriftiness, diarrhea, coughing, lack of appetite, anemia, are the symptoms. They can also cause verminous pneumonia when in the larval stage. Fecal examinations of puppy stools should be made by your veterinarian frequently if control of these parasites is to be constant. Although

1. Flea-host tapeworm. 2. Segment of tapeworm as seen in dog's stool. 3. Common roundworm. 4. Whipworm. 5. Hookworm. 6. Heartworm.

theoretically it is possible for small puppies to be naturally worm free, actually most puppies are born infested (larvae in the bloodstream of the bitch cross the placenta to infect the unborn pups) or contract the eggs at the mother's breast or from the surrounding environment.

The roundworm lives in the intestine and feeds on the dog's partially digested food, growing and laying eggs which are passed out in the dog's stool to be picked up by him in various ways and so cause reinfestation. The life history of all the intestinal worms is a vicious circle, with the dog the beginning and the end host. This worm is yellowish-white in color and is shaped like a common garden worm, pointed at both ends. It is usually curled when found in the stool. There are several different species of this type of worm. Some varieties are more dangerous than others. They discharge toxin within the dog, and the presence of larvae in important organs of the dog's body can cause death.

The drugs most used by kennel owners for the elimination of roundworms are n-butyl-chloride, tetrachlorethylene and the piperazines, but there are a host of other drugs, new and old, that can also do the job efficiently. With most of the worm drugs, give no food to the dog for twenty-four hours, or in the case of puppies, twenty hours, previous to the time he is given the medicine. It is absolutely essential that this starvation limit be adhered to if the drug used is tetrachlorethylene, since the existence of the slightest amount of food in the stomach or intestine can cause death. One tenth c.c. to each pound of the animal's weight up to fifty pounds is the dosage for tetrachlorethylene, followed in one hour with a milk-of-magnesia physic, never an oily physic. Food may be given two hours later. Piperazines are less toxic, and the dog can be fed normally. Large doses of the drug can be given grown dogs without danger.

HOOKWORMS

These tiny worms that live on the blood of your dog, which they get from the intestinal walls, cause severe anemia, groaning, fits, diarrhea, loss of appetite and weight, rapid breathing, and swelling of the legs. Some of the same drugs used to eradicate roundworms will also expel hookworms. Disophenol, in subcutaneous injection, is the newest and most effective hookworm treatment. Tetrachlorethylene, n-butyl-chloride and tolkuene are drugs also used for hookworms.

Good food is essential for quick recovery, with added amounts of liver and raw meat and iron tonics incorporated in the diet. Blood transfusions are often necessary if the infestation has been heavy. If one infestation follows another, a certain degree of immunity to the effects of the parasite seems to be built up by the dog. A second treatment should be given two weeks following the initial treatment.

WHIPWORMS

These small, thin whiplike worms are found in the intestines and the ceacum. Those found in the intestines are reached and killed by the same drugs used in the eradication of roundworms and hookworms. Most worm medicines will kill these helminths if they reach them, but those which live in the ceacum are very difficult to reach. They exude toxins which cause debilitation, anemia, and allied ills, and are probably a contributing factor in lowering the resistance to the onslaught of other infections. The usual symptoms of worm infestation are present, especially vomiting, diarrhea, and loss of weight. Phthalofyne is an effective whipworm eradicator. It can be administered by either intravenous injection or by oral tablets.

TAPEWORMS

Tapeworms are not easily diagnosed by fecal test, but are easily identified when visible in the dog's stool. The worm is composed of two distinct parts, the head and the segmented body. It is pieces of the segmented body that we see in the stools of the dog. They are usually pink or white in color and flat. The common tapeworm, which is most prevalent in our dogs, is about eighteen inches long, and the larvae are carried by the flea. The head of the worm is smaller than a pinhead and attaches itself to the intestinal wall. Contrary to general belief, the dog infested with tapeworms does not possess an enormous appetite, rather it fluctuates from good to poor. The animal shows the general signs of worm infestation. Often he squats and drags his hindquarters on the ground. This is due to tapeworm segments moving and wriggling in the lower bowels. One must be careful in diagnosing this symptom, as it may also mean that the dog is suffering from distended anal glands.

Arecolene is one of the most efficient expellers of tapeworms. Dosage is approximately one-tenth grain for every fifteen pounds of the dog's weight, administered after twenty hours of fasting. No worm medicine can be considered 100 percent effective in all cases. If one drug does not expel the worms satisfactorily, then another must be tried.*

HEARTWORM

This villain inhabits the heart and is the most difficult to treat. The worm is about a foot long and literally stuffs the heart of the affected animal. It is prevalent in the southern states and has long been the curse of sporting-dog breeds. This does not signify that other dogs cannot become infected, since the worm is transmitted principally through the bite of an infected mosquito, which can fly from an infected southern canine visitor directly to another dog and do its dire deed.

The symptoms are: fatigue, gasping, coughing, nervousness, and sometimes dropsy and swelling of the extremities. Treatment for heartworms definitely must be left in the hands of your veterinarian. A wide variety of drugs are used in treatment, the most commonly employed are the arsenicals, antimony compounds, and caracide. Danger exists during cure when dying worms move to the lungs, causing suffocation, or when dead worms, in a heavily infested dog, block the small blood vessels in the heart muscles. The invading microfilariae are not discernible in the blood until nine months following introduction of the disease by the bite of the carrier mosquito.

In an article on this subject in *Field and Stream* magazine, Joe Stetson describes a controlled experiment in which caracide was employed in periodic treatments as a preventive of heartworm. The experiment was carried out over a period of eighteen months, during which time the untreated dogs became positive for heartworm and eventually died. A post mortem proved the presence of the worm. The dogs that underwent scheduled prophylaxis have been found, by blood test, to be free of circulating microfilariae and are thriving.

COCCIDIOSIS

This disease is caused by a tiny protozoan. It affects dogs of all ages,

* New formula VERMIPLEX, manufactured by Pitman-Moore Co. for the removal of round, hook and tape worms in dogs, is easy to use and very efficient.

but is not dangerous to mature animals. When puppies become infected by a severe case of coccidiosis, it very often proves fatal, since it produces such general weakness and emaciation that the puppy has no defense against other invading harmful organisms. Loose and bloody stools are indicative of the presence of this disease, as is loss of appetite, weakness, emaciation, discharge from the eyes, and a fever of approximately 103 degrees. The disease is contracted directly or through flies that have come from infected quarters. Infection seems to occur over and over again, limiting the puppy's chance of recovery with each succeeding infection. The duration of the disease is about three weeks, but new infestations can stretch this period of illness on until your puppy has little chance to recover. Strict sanitation and supportive treatment of good nutrition—utilizing milk, fat, kaopectate, and bone ash (a tablespoonful a day for Shepherd puppies), with added dextrose and calcium—seem to be all that can be done in the way of treatment. Force feed the puppy if necessary. The more food that you can get into him to give him strength until the disease has run its course, the better will be his chances of recovery. Specific cures have been developed in other animals and poultry, but not as yet in dogs. Fragmentary clinical evidence would seem to indicate that sulfamethazine may give some control in canine coccidiosis.

SKIN DISEASES

Diseases of the skin in dogs are many, varied, and easily confused by the kennel owner as to category. All skin afflictions should be immediately diagnosed by your veterinarian so that treatment can begin with dispatch. Whatever drug is prescribed must be employed diligently and in quantity and generally long after surface indications of the disease have ceased to exist. A surface cure may be attained, but the infection remains buried deep in the hair follicles or skin glands, to erupt again if treatment is suspended too soon. Contrary to popular belief, diet, if well balanced and complete, is seldom the cause of skin disease.

Eczema

The word "eczema" is a much-abused word, as is the word "dermatitis." Both are used with extravagance in the identification of various forms of skin disorders. We will concern ourselves with the two most prevalent forms of so-called eczema, namely wet eczema and dry eczema. In the wet form, the skin exudes moisture and then scabs over, due to constant scratching and biting by the dog at the site of infection. The dry form manifests itself in dry patches which irritate and itch, causing great discomfort to the dog. In both instances the hair falls out and the spread of the disease is rapid. The cause of these diseases is not yet known, though many are thought to be originated by various fungi and bacteria and

THE SHEPHERD SERVES

SENTRY DUTY

Alert and ready, guarding America's coastline.

GERMAN SHEPHERD CLUB OF LONG ISLAND DRILL TEAM

One of the greatest pleasures in owning a dog is having the opportunity to work with him.

aggravated by flea allergic conditions and self trauma. The quickest means of bringing these diseases under control is through the application of a good skin remedy often combined with a fungicide, which your veterinarian will prescribe. An over-all dip, employing specific liquid medication, is beneficial in many cases and has a continuing curative effect over a period of days. Injectable or oral anti-inflammatory drugs are often employed as supplementary treatment.

Ringworm

This infection is caused by a fungus and is highly contagious to humans. In the dog it generally appears on the face as a round or oval spot from which the hair has fallen. It is not as often seen in long-coated dogs as it is in shorter-coated dogs. Ringworm is easily controlled by the application of iodine glycerine (50 per cent of each ingredient) or a fungicide such as girseofulvin, a definite cure for ringworm.

Acne

Your puppy will frequently display small eruptions on his belly or eyelids, paws and muzzle. The rash is caused by a bacterial infection of the skin glands and hair follicles and is not serious if treated early. Wash the affected areas with alcohol or witch hazel and apply a healing lotion or powder. Hormonal imbalances can cause specific skin conditions that are best left to the administrations of your veterinarian.

Hookworm Larvae Infection

The skin of your dog can become infected from the larvae of the hookworm acquired from muddy hookworm-infested runs. The larvae become stuck to his coat with mud and burrow into the skin, leaving ugly raw red patches. One or two baths in warm water to which an antiseptic has been added usually cures the condition quickly.

DEFICIENCY DISEASES

These diseases, or conditions, are caused by dietary deficiencies or some condition which robs the diet of necessary ingredients. Anemia, a deficiency condition, is a shortage of hemoglobin. Hookworms, lice, and any disease that depletes the system of red blood cells, are contributory causes. A shortage or lack of specific minerals or vitamins in the diet can also cause anemia. Not so long ago, rickets was the most common of the deficiency diseases, caused by a lack of one or more of the dietary elements: vitamin D, calcium, and phosphorus. There are other types of deficiency diseases originating in dietary inadequacy and characterized by unthriftiness in one or more phases. The cure exists in supplying the missing food factors to the diet. Sometimes, even though all the necessary dietary elements are present in the food, some are destroyed by improper feeding procedure. For example, a substance in raw eggs, avertin, destroys biotin, one of the

B-complex group of vitamins. Cooking will destroy the avertin in the egg white and prevent a biotin deficiency in the diet.

BACTERIAL DISEASES

In this group we find leptospirosis, tetanus, pneumonia, and many other dangerous diseases. The mortality rate is generally high in all of the bacterial diseases, and treatment should be left to your veterinarian.

Leptospirosis

Leptospirosis is spread most frequently by the urine of infected dogs, which can infect for six months or more after the animal has recovered from the disease. Rats are the carriers of the bacterial agent that produces this disease. A dog will find a bone upon which an infected rat has urinated, chew the bone, and become infected with the disease in turn. Leptospirosis is primarily dangerous in the damage it does to the kidneys. Complete isolation of affected individuals to keep the disease from spreading and rat control of kennel areas are the chief means of control. Vaccines are employed by your veterinarian as a preventive measure. Initial diagnosis is difficult, and the disease generally makes drastic inroads before a cure is effected. It has been estimated that fully 50 per cent of all dogs throughout the world have been stricken with leptospirosis at one time or another, and that in many instances the disease was not recognized for what it was. The disease produced by *Leptospira* in the blood of humans is known as Weil's disease.

Tetanus

Lockjaw bacteria produce an exceedingly deadly poison. The germs grow in the depths of a sealed-over wound where oxygen cannot penetrate. To prevent this disease, every deep wound acquired by your dog should be thoroughly cleansed and disinfected, and an antitoxin given the animal. Treatment follows the same general pattern as prevention. If the jaw locks, intravenous feeding must be given.

Tonsillitis

Inflammation of the tonsils can be either of bacterial or virus origin. It is not a serious disease in itself, but is often a symptom of other diseases. The symptoms of tonsillitis are enlarged and reddened tonsils, poor appetite, vomiting, and optic discharge. The condition usually runs its course in from five to seven days. Penicillin, aureomycin, terramycin, chloromycetin, etc., have been used with success in treatment.

Pneumonia

Pneumonia is a bacterial disease of the lungs of which the symptoms are poor appetite, optic discharge, shallow and rapid respiration. Affected animals become immune to the particular type of pneumonia from which they have recovered. Oral treatment utilizing antibiotic or sulfa drugs, combined with a pneumonia jacket of cloth or cotton padding wrapped around the chest area, seems to be standard treatment. Pneumonia is quite often associated with distemper.

VIRAL DISEASES

The dread viral diseases are caused by the smallest organisms known to man. They live in the cells and often attack the nerve tissue. The tissue thus weakened is easily invaded by many types of bacteria. Complications then set in, and it is these accompanying ills which usually prove fatal. The secondary infections can be treated with several of the "wonder" drugs, and excellent care and nursing is necessary if the stricken animal is to survive. Your veterinarian is the only person qualified to aid your dog when a virus disease strikes. The diseases in this category include distemper, infectious hepatitis, rabies, kennel cough, and primary encephalitis —the latter actually inflammation of the brain, a condition characterizing several illnesses, particularly those of viral origin.

Distemper

Until recently a great many separate diseases had been lumped under the general heading of distemper. In the last few years modern science has isolated a number of separate diseases of the distemper complex. Thus, with more accurate diagnosis, great strides have been made in conquering, not only distemper, but these other, allied diseases. Distemper (Carre) is no longer prevalent due to successful methods of immunization, but any signs of illness in an animal not immunized may be the beginning of the disease. The symptoms are so similar to those of various other diseases that only a trained observer can diagnose correctly. Treatment consists of the use of drugs to counteract complications arising from the invasion of secondary diseases and in keeping the stricken animal warm, well fed, comfortable and free from dehydration until the disease has run its course. In many instances, even if the dog gets well, he will be left with some dreadful souvenir of the disease which will mar him for life.

The tremendous value of immunization against this viral disease cannot be exaggerated. Except for the natural resistance your animal carries against disease, it is the one means of protection you have against this killer. There have been various methods of immunization developed in the last several years, combining several vaccines in one. Injections can be given at any age, even as early as six or eight weeks, with a booster shot when recommended by your veterinarian. They do not affect the tissues, nor do they cause any ill effects to other dogs in a kennel who come in contact with the vaccinated animal.

At the canine research laboratories of Cornell University veterinarians have developed a new heterotypic vaccine (an original concept in immunology) for new-born puppies that gives them immediate and effective protection against distemper. Colostrum in the mother's milk protects the young from distemper and, in so doing, also makes negative the ordinary homotypic distemper vaccine which has been in general use. The result of this natural protection is that one never knows if the puppies have defense against this dread disease during their most vulnerable period. The heterotypic vaccine is not effected by the bitch's colostrum because it (the vaccine) does not contain canine virus, it is a human measles vaccine.

Infectious Hepatitis

This disease attacks dogs of all ages, but is particularly deadly to puppies. We see young puppies in the nest, healthy, bright and sturdy; suddenly they begin to vomit, and the next day they are dead of infectious hepatitis; it strikes that quickly. The disease is difficult to diagnose correctly, and there is no specific treatment that will cure it. Astute authorities claim that if an afflicted dog survives three days after the onslaught of the disease he will, in all probability, completely recover. Treatment is symptomatic and directed at supporting the functions of the ailing liver. Prevention is through vaccination. Veterinarian vaccine programs usually combine distemper, hepatitis, and often leptospirosis vaccines.

It has been found that the effective coverage period of all vaccines is less than former expectation. Distemper vaccine, or the combination vaccine (distemper, hepatitis, leptospirosis) should be renewed every six months to a year (especially if the animal is being exposed through showing, obedience trials, etc.), if absolute immunity is to be expected.

Rabies

This is the most terrible of diseases, since it knows no bounds. It is transmissible to all kinds of animals and birds, including the superior animal, man. To contract this dread disease, the dog must be bitten by a rabid animal or the rabies virus must enter the body through a broken skin surface. The disease incubation period is governed by the distance of the virus' point of entry to the brain. The closer the point of entry is to the brain, the quicker the disease manifests itself. We can be thankful that rabies is not nearly as prevalent as is supposed by the uninformed. Restlessness, excitability, perverted appetite, character reversal, wildness, drowsiness, loss of acuteness of senses, and of feeling in some instances, foaming at the mouth, and many other lesser symptoms come with the onslaught of this disease. Diagnosis by trained persons of a portion of the brain is conceded to be the only way of determining whether an animal died of rabies or of one of the distemper complex diseases. Very little has been done in introducing drugs or specifics that can give satisfaction in combatting this disease, perhaps evaluation of the efficacy of such products is almost impossible with a disease so rare and difficult to diagnose.

Holde v. Frickenhausl, SchH. III, AD.

(sire) Condor vom Sixtberg, SchH. II, AD.

(dam) Tanka v. Zollgrenzschutz-Haus, SchH. III

A fine, young daughter of the Volker son, Condor v. Sixtberg. A top "V" bitch in Germany, Holde is living proof of the quality of her genetic heritage. Owner and breeder, Nikolaus Seemann.

Cyrus v. Baltikum, SchH. III, FH.

(sire) Cherry v.d. sieben Pappeln, SchH. II, FH.

(dam) Dina v. Schloss Isenburg, SchH. I

A fine animal with a particularly excellent front assembly, Cyrus was a low S.G. at the '64 Sieger Show, but in 1965 almost made Sieger when given the coveted VA2 rating.

Quarantine, such as that pursued in England, even of six-months' duration, is still not the answer to the rabies question, though it is undeniably effective. It is, however, not proof positive. Recently a dog on arriving in England was held in quarantine for the usual six months. The day before he was to be released to his owners, the attendant noticed that he was acting strangely. He died the next day. Under examination his brain showed typical inclusion bodies, establishing the fact that he had died of rabies. This is a truly dangerous disease that can bring frightful death to animal or man. It should be the duty of every dog owner to protect his dog, himself, his family, and neighbors from even the slight risk that exists of contracting rabies by having his dog immunized. In many states immunization is compulsory.

FITS

Fits in dogs are symptoms of diseases rather than illness itself. They can be caused by the onslaught of any number of diseases, including worms, distemper, epilepsy, primary encephalitis, poisoning, etc. Running fits can also be traced to dietary deficiencies. The underlying reason for the fits, or convulsions, must be diagnosed by your veterinarian and the cause treated.

DIARRHEA

Diarrhea, a loose, watery movement, is often a symptom of one of many other diseases. But if, on taking your dog's temperature, you find there is no fever, it is quite possible the condition has been caused by either a change of diet, of climate or water, or even by a simple intestinal disturbance. A tightening agent such as Kaopectate should be given. Water should be withheld and corn syrup, dissolved in boiled milk, substituted to prevent dehydration in the patient. Feed hard-boiled eggs, boiled milk, beef, boiled white rice, cracker, kibbles, or dog biscuits. Add a tablespoonful of bone ash (not bone meal) to the diet. If the condition is not corrected within two or three days, if there is an excess of blood passed in the stool, or if signs of other illness become manifest, don't delay a trip to your veterinarian.

CONSTIPATION

If the dog's stool is so hard that it is difficult for him to pass it and he strains and grunts during the process, then he is obviously constipated. The cause of constipation is generally one of diet. Bones and dog biscuits, given abundantly, can cause this condition, as can any of the items of diet mentioned above as treatment for diarrhea. Chronic constipation can result in hemorrhoids which, if persistent, must be removed by surgery. The cure for constipation and its accompanying ills is the introduction of laxative food elements into the diet. Stewed tomatoes, buttermilk, skim milk, whey, bran, alfalfa meal, and various fruits can be fed and a bland physic given. Enemas can bring quick relief. Once the condition is alleviated, the dog should be given a good balanced diet, avoiding all types of foods that will produce constipation.

EYE AILMENTS

The eyes are not only the mirror of the soul, they are also the mirror of many kinds of disease. Discharge from the eyes is one of the many symptoms warning of most internal viral, helminthic, and bacterial diseases. Of the ailments affecting the eye itself, the most usual are: glaucoma, which seems to be a hereditary disease; pink eye, a strep infection; cataracts, opacity of the lens in older dogs; corneal opacity, such as follows some cases of infectious hepatitis; and teratoma or tumors. Mange, fungus, inturned lids, and growths on the lid are other eye ailments. The wise procedure is to consult your veterinarian for specific treatment.

When the eyes show a discharge from reasons other than those that can be labeled "ailment," such as irritation from dust, wind, or sand, they should be washed with warm water on cotton or a soft cloth. After gently washing the eyes, an ophthalmic ointment combining a mild anesthetic and antiseptic can be utilized. Butyn sulphate, 1 per cent yellow oxide of mercury, and 5 per cent sulphathiazole ointment are all good. Boric acid seems to be falling out of favor as an ophthalmic antiseptic. The liquid discharged by the dog's tear ducts is a better antiseptic, and much cheaper.

ANAL GLANDS

If your dog consistently drags his rear parts on the ground or bites this area, the cause is probably impacted anal glands. These glands, which are located on each side of the anus, should be periodically cleared by squeezing. The job is not a nice one, and can be much more effectively done by your veterinarian. Unless these glands are kept reasonably clean, infection can become housed in this site, resulting in the formation of an abscess which will need surgical care. Dogs that get an abundance of exercise seldom need the anal glands attended to.

The many other ailments which your dog is heir to, such as cancer, rupture, heart disease, fractures, and the results of accidents, etc., must all be diagnosed and tended to by your veterinarian. When you go to your veterinarian with a sick dog, always remember to bring along a sample of his stool for analysis. Many times samples of his urine are needed too. Your veterinarian is the only one qualified to treat your dog for disease, but protection against disease is, to a great extent, in the hands of the dog's owner. If those hands are capable, a great deal of pain and misery for both dog and owner can be eliminated. Death can be cheated, investment saved, and veterinary bills kept to a minimum. A periodic health check by your veterinarian is a wise investment.

We come now to a very controversial subject which is prominent in the minds of many dog fanciers at this time and so must be discussed here. The subject we mean is . . .

SUBLUXATION (HIP DYSPLASIA)

First let us define the word. *Subluxation* means partial dislocation, or incomplete dislocation. As this partial dislocation refers to no specific section of the skeletal structure, subluxation means an incomplete dislocation of *any* joint. In common usage, however, this term has come to mean the partial dislocation of the femur and pelvis. It is in this more specific sense that it is used here. In this condition, the hip socket is shallow, allowing the femoral head, or ball part of the femur, to slip out of the socket partially or entirely. In the process of slipping, the femoral head becomes injured or flattened out, wearing to a flattened surface to compensate for the shallowness of the hip socket. The condition called coxa plana (coxa meaning hip joint and plana meaning flat) would seem to fit more closely the picture of what we call subluxation. Dorland's American Illustrated Dictionary defines coxa plana as "osteochondritis deformans juvenilis, a disease characterized by atrophy and rarefaction of the head of the femur during the age of growth, resulting in a shortened and thickened femoral neck and a broad, flat femoral head. Called also Perthes' disease, Calve-Perthes' disease, Legg's disease, pseudo-coxalgia." Osteochondritis is an inflammation of both bone and cartilage. Coxa valga is defined as a deformity of the neck of the femur, producing in the limb marked external rotation, increased abduction, and decreased adduction.

To eliminate confusion, we will continue to call this condition subluxation, though as we progress it becomes clearer that it fits the definitions above more closely than it does the vague, all embracing definition of the word we use.

When the femoral head, flattened, begins to move from the shallow hip socket, the gristlelike capsule that surrounds this area thickens to hold the femur in place. The femoral head moves farther from the hip socket, becoming more deformed. Calcium deposits appear, filling in the gap. The area becomes inflamed, and an arthritic condition appears. Eventually the thickening of the capsule reaches a peak, as do the calcium deposits. When this occurs, the capsule breaks under stress, and the condition reaches a point where the afflicted animal must be destroyed.

The condition generally becomes apparent between the ages of three to twelve months and is thought to be congenital. There are a wide range of theories as to the basic cause of this ailment, ranging from individual intolerance of excess vitamin intake to undue stress upon the pelvic area due to excessive angulation. The latter theory can be almost ruled out entirely, since the incidence of subluxation is as prevalent in breeds not noted for acute angulation. In fact, Konde (1947) describes a subluxation of the coxo-femoral joint in German Shepherd dogs, which he reports is congenital and probably due to abnormal hip joints developed by breeding for long, low, extremely angulated rear quarters. Yet Moltzen-Nielson (1937) had formerly called what seems to be the same hip condition, in terriers, Calve-Perthes' disease, indicating that the condition is hereditary, but that the exact mode of inheritance is not known. Terriers, of course, are not noted for acute hindquarter angulation.

The theory most widely subscribed to at this time is that subluxation is both congenital and hereditary. In man the parallel ailment is considered to be the result of a recessive factor, and it is considered by many to be of the same origin in dogs. In litters which have come to our attention in which one or more puppies have shown the symptoms ascribed to the ailment, the ratios involved have not presented a clear genetic picture. This could be due to absorption of some of the fetuses before birth, early death of some of the young, or artificial culling of the litter. Whatever the cause, the percentage of affected individuals does not disclose the expected genetic ratio.

No real studies have been made of the mode of inheritance of the condition as it exists in dogs, assuming that it is an inheritable disease. If it is inheritable, it is still too early to come to any conclusion as to whether it is caused by recessive genes, masked dominants, or any other inheritable cause.

Hip dysplasia is graded as to intensity and the gravity of the defect

Basko v.d. Kahler Heide, SchH. II (sire)
Zibu v. Haus Schutting, SchH.III (dam)
Nixe a.d. Eremitenklause, SchH. I

This good moving male was VA I at the 1966 Sieger Show.

designated numerically. Thus a grade 1 is much less pronounced on the X-ray picture than a grade 4, which is the most aggravated indication of the disease.

But this numerical grading system means nothing in terms of future disability, the clinical picture, or genetic transmission (if this last exists in connection with subluxation). It is probably merely the difference in penetration of the defect.

Often imported German dogs who are subluxed (though, due to lack of X-rays, they are not recognized as such in Germany), do not exhibit any of the outward signs of hip dysplasia and, in this country, show a faultless and floating gait. But, after being here a while, they begin to break down in the hindquarters and an X-ray shows definite dysplasia of the hip. The reason for this is that these dogs, in their native country, Germany, are trained like athletes and kept in constant hard and vigorous shape. But, after some time on our shores, where this type of regimented training is not indulged in, the animals become soft and the ligaments and muscles of the hindquarters lose their taut strength. When this happens the defect of subluxation becomes evident.

This observation could fit nicely into the theory advanced by Dr. Wayne H. Riser, which has to do with the failure of good contact between the femoral head and the acetabulum due to a lack of muscle pull and ligament tautness in that area. It is a moot question as to whether softness, or lack of muscular strength in that specific area causes the defect, or whether the dysplastic condition causes deterioration of the muscles and ligaments that are pertinent to the area.

The condition can also be caused by an accident, a possibility which must not be overlooked. X-ray seems to be the only means of complete recognition of the condition. Yet the pliability of a puppy's bones and the position assumed by the puppy under X-ray can sometimes result in a picture that would seem to be the beginning of subluxation when it is not. A Shepherd bitch brought to a veterinary clinic recently had a history of subluxation. She showed all the outward signs: the square hips, typical movement, and evidenced pain in the hind parts when she jumped or moved quickly. For reasons other than the manifestation of this ailment, she was subsequently destroyed. In the post mortem, the rear end of the animal was freed and the muscles cut away. But before muscles and ligaments were completely severed from the pelvic and upper femoral area, the movement of the femoral head in the hip socket was tested and seemed normal. When the femur and pelvis were bared, it was found that the hip socket was normally deep and the femoral head round, normal, and fitted snugly within the socket; there was no sign of subluxation. The bitch was then a year old. Undoubtedly there was something drastically wrong with this bitch which affected her hindquarters and her mode of locomotion, but it was not subluxation. Possibly the symptoms were due to a degeneration of certain nerves in the spinal column, and this could have been caused by injury or disease. The cause of her affliction could have been congenital or hereditary, or both. But we can only guess, with no real foundation of substantiating fact. Perhaps this was an isolated case, but if it wasn't, it gives us cause to wonder how many other dogs said to be subluxed, as was this bitch, fall into the same category as she does.

The picture of subluxation must take much more time and study before it comes into complete focus and absolute clarity is established. Until that time arrives, it would be best to keep our minds clear and receptive to new ideas and theories.*

Some authorities think that subjecting a pup to X-ray to determine whether or not it has dysplasia could possibly effect later sexual potency. Yet this is the only sure way we have to recognize the disease.

ADMINISTERING MEDICATION

Some people seem to have ten thumbs on each hand when they attempt to give medicine to their dog. They become agitated and approach the task with so little sureness that their mood is communicated to the patient, increasing the difficulties presented. Invite calmness and quietness in the patient by emanating these qualities yourself. Speak to the animal in low, easy tones, petting him slowly, quieting him down in preparation. The administration of medicine should be made without fuss and as though it is some quiet and private new game between you and your dog.

At the corner of your dog's mouth there is a lip pocket perfect for the administering of liquid medicine if used correctly. Have the animal sit, then raise his muzzle so that his head is slanted upward looking toward the sky. Slide two fingers in the corner of his mouth where the upper and lower lip edges join, pull gently outward, and you have a pocket between the cheek flesh and the gums. Into this pocket pour the liquid medicine at the rate of approximately two tablespoonfuls at a time for a full-grown Shepherd. Keep his head up, and the liquid will run from the pocket into his throat and he will swallow it. Continue this procedure until the complete dose has been given. This will be easier to accomplish if the medicine

---

* In a controlled experiment utilizing over 250 dogs and taking several years (Fidelco Breeders Foundation, Inc., of which Ernest H. Hart is an officer), it was found that dysplastic parents produced over 90% affected offspring. When one parent is dysplastic and the mate normal, almost 50% of the progeny are free of dysplasia. When both parents and grandparents have normal hips, and there are a number of long working, HGH animals behind them, which we can assume had good hips (pedigree depth), more than 90% of the progeny have acceptable hips.

has been spooned into a small bottle. The bottle neck, inserted into the lip pocket, is tipped, and the contents drained at the ratio mentioned above.

To give pills or capsules, the head of the patient must again be raised with muzzle pointing upward. With one hand, grasp the cheeks of the dog just behind the lip edges where the teeth come together on the inside of the mouth. With the thumb on one side and the fingers on the other, press inward as though squeezing. The lips are pushed against the teeth, and the pressure of your fingers forces the mouth open. The dog will not completely close his mouth, since doing so would cause him to bite his lips. With your other hand, insert the pill in the patient's mouth as far back on the base of the tongue as you can, pushing it back with your second finger. Withdraw your hand quickly, allow the dog to close his mouth, and hold it closed with your hand, but not too tightly. Massage the dog's throat and watch for the tip of his tongue to show between his front teeth, signifying the fact that the capsule or pill has been swallowed.

In taking your dog's temperature, an ordinary rectal thermometer is adequate. It must be first shaken down, then dipped in vaseline, and inserted into the rectum for approximately three-quarters of its length. Allow it to remain there for no less than a full minute, restraining the dog from sitting completely during that time. When withdrawn, it should be wiped with a piece of cotton, read, then washed in alcohol—never hot water. The arrow on most thermometers at 98.6 degrees indicates normal human temperature and should be disregarded. Normal temperature for your grown dog is approximately 101 degrees; normal puppy temperature

Nixe a.d. Eremitenklause, SchH. I
(sire)
Arras v. Adam-Riesezwinger,
 SchH. III, FH.
(dam)
Halla a.d. Eremitenklause, SchH. I
A top German show bitch and the product of a successful breeding that has been repeated many times, Nixe is the dam of Basko v.d. Heide, as well as other quality progeny. She was V5 at the '65 Sieger Show.

varies between $101\frac{1}{2}$ to 102 degrees. Excitement can raise the temperature, so it is best to take a reading only after the dog is calm.

In applying an ophthalmic ointment to the eye, simply pull the lower lid out, squeeze a small amount of ointment into the pocket thus produced, and release the lid. The dog will blink, and the ointment will spread over the eye.

Should you find it necessary to give your dog an enema, employ an ordinary human-size bag and rubber hose. For a Shepherd a catheter is not necessary. Simply grease the rubber hose tip with vaseline and insert the hose well into the rectum. The bag should be held high for a constant flow of water. A quart of warm soapy water or plain water with a tablespoonful of salt makes an efficient enema.

FIRST AID

Emergencies quite frequently occur which make it necessary for you to care for the dog yourself until veterinary aid is available. Quite often emergency help by the owner can save the dog's life or lessen the chance of permanent injury. A badly injured animal, blinded to all else but abysmal pain, often reverts to the primitive wanting only to be left alone with his misery. Injured, panic-stricken, not recognizing you, he might attempt to bite when you wish to help him. Under the stress of fright and pain, this reaction is normal in animals. A muzzle can easily be slipped over his foreface, or a piece of bandage or strip of cloth can be fashioned into a muzzle by looping it around the dog's muzzle, crossing it under the jaws, and bringing the two ends around in back of the dog's head and tying them. Snap a leash on to his collar as quickly as possible to prevent him from running away and hiding. If it is necessary to lift him, grasp him by the neck, getting as large a handful of skin as you can, as high up on the neck as possible. Hold tight and he won't be able to turn his head far enough around to bite. Lift him by the hold you have on his neck until he is far enough off the ground to enable you to encircle his body with your other arm and support him or carry him.

Every dog owner should have handy a first-aid kit specifically for the use of his dog. It should contain a thermometer, surgical scissors, rolls of three-inch and six-inch bandage, a roll of one-inch adhesive tape, a package of surgical cotton, a jar of vaseline, enema equipment, bulb syringe, ten c.c. hypodermic syringe, flea powder, skin remedy, tweezers, ophthalmic ointment, paregoric, kaopectate, peroxide of hydrogen, merthiolate, a good antiseptic powder, alcohol, ear remedy, aspirin, milk of magnesia, castor oil, mineral oil, dressing salve.

We have prepared two charts for your reference, one covering general first-aid measures and the other a chart of poisons and antidotes. Remember that, in most instances, these are emergency measures, not specific treatments, and are designed to help you in aiding your dog until you can reach your veterinarian.

FIRST-AID CHART

EMERGENCY	TREATMENT	REMARKS
Accidents	Automobile, treat for shock. If gums are white, indicates probable internal injury. Wrap bandage tightly around body until it forms a sheath. Keep very quiet until veterinarian comes.	Call veterinarian immediately.
Bee stings	Give paregoric, 2 teaspoonfuls for grown Shepherd, or aspirin to ease pain. If in state of shock, treat for same.	Call veterinarian (Antihistamine tablets are also effective.)
Bites (animal)	Tooth wounds: area should be shaved and antiseptic solution flowed into punctures with eye dropper. Iodine, merthiolate, etc., can be used. If badly bitten or ripped, take dog to your veterinarian for treatment.	If superficial wounds become infected after first aid, consult veterinarian.
Burns	Apply strong, strained tea to burned area, followed by covering of vaseline, local anesthetic ointment, antibiotic, antiseptic ointment, etc.	Unless burn is very minor, consult veterinarian immediately.
Broken bones	If break involves a limb, fashion splint to keep immobile. If ribs, pelvis, shoulder, or back involved, keep dog from moving until professional help comes.	Call veterinarian immediately.
Choking	If bone, wood, or any foreign object can be seen at back of mouth or throat, remove with fingers. If object can't be removed or is too deeply imbedded or too far back in throat, rush to veterinarian immediately.	
Cuts	Minor cuts: allow dog to lick and cleanse. If not within his reach, clean out with peroxide, then apply merthiolate. Severe cuts: apply pressure bandage to stop bleeding—a wad of bandage over wound and bandage wrapped tightly over it. Take to veterinarian.	If cut becomes infected or needs suturing, consult veterinarian.
Dislocations	Keep dog quiet and take to veterinarian at once.	

245

Drowning	Artificial respiration. Lay dog on his side, push with hand on his ribs, release quickly. Repeat every 2 seconds. Treat for shock.	
Electric shock	Artificial respiration. Treat for shock.	Call veterinarian immediately.
Heat stroke	Quickly immerse the dog in cold water until relief is given. Give cold water enema. Or lay dog flat and pour cold water over him, turn electric fan on him, and continue pouring cold water as it evaporates.	Cold towels pressed against abdomen and back of head aid in reducing temp. quickly if quantity of water not available.
Porcupine quills	Tie dog up, hold him between knees, and pull all quills out with pliers. Don't forget tongue and inside of mouth.	See veterinarian to remove quills too deeply imbedded.
Shock	Cover dog with blanket. Allow him to rest and soothe with voice and hand.	Alcoholic beverages are NOT a stimulant. Bring to veterinarian.
Poisonous snake bite	Cut deep X over fang marks. Drop potassium permanganate into cut. Apply tourniquet above bite if on foot or leg.	Apply first aid only if a veterinarian or a doctor can't be reached.
Wasp stings	Plain vinegar dabbed on sting area. If in state of shock treat for same.	

TREATMENT FOR POISON

The important thing to remember when your dog is poisoned is that prompt action is imperative. Administer an emetic immediately. Mix hydrogen peroxide and water in equal parts. Force eight to ten tablespoonfuls of this mixture down your dog, or up to twelve tablespoonfuls (this dosage for a fully grown Shepherd). In a few minutes he will regurgitate his stomach contents. Once this has been accomplished, call your veterinarian. If you know the source of the poison and the container which it came from is handy, you will find the antidote on the label. Your veterinarian will prescribe specific drugs and advise on their use.

The symptoms of poisoning include trembling, panting, intestinal pain, vomiting, slimy secretion from mouth, convulsions, coma. All these symptoms are also prevalent in other illnesses, but if they appear and investigation leads you to believe that they are the result of poisoning, act with dispatch as described above.

POISON	HOUSEHOLD ANTIDOTE
ACIDS	Bicarbonate of soda
ALKALIES	Vinegar or lemon juice
(cleansing agents)	
ARSENIC	Epsom salts
HYDROCYANIC ACID	Dextrose or corn syrup
(wild cherry; laurel leaves)	
LEAD	Epsom salts
(paint pigments)	
PHOSPHORUS	Peroxide of hydrogen
(rat poison)	
MERCURY	Eggs and milk
THEOBROMINE	Phenobarbital
(cooking chocolate)	
THALLIUM	Table salt in water
(bug poisons)	
FOOD POISONING	Peroxide of hydrogen, followed by enema
(garbage, etc.)	
STRYCHNINE	Sedatives, Phenobarbital, Nembutal.
DDT	Peroxide and enema

CHAPTER 17

THE STANDARD OF THE GERMAN SHEPHERD DOG

GENERAL APPEARANCE

The first impression of a good German Shepherd dog is that of a strong, agile, well-muscled animal, alert and full of life. It should both be and appear to be well balanced, with harmonious development of the forequarter and hindquarter. The dog should appear to the eye, and actually be, longer than tall, deep-bodied, and presenting an outline of smooth curves rather than corners. It should look substantial and not spindly, giving the impression, both at rest and in motion, of muscular fitness and nimbleness without any look of clumsiness or soft living.

The ideal height for dogs is 25 inches, and for bitches, 23 inches at the shoulder. This height is established by taking a perpendicular line from the top of the shoulder blade to the ground with the coat parted or so pushed down that this measurement will show only the actual height of the frame or structure of the dog. The working value of dogs above or below the indicated heights is proportionately lessened, although variations of an inch above or below the ideal heights are acceptable, while greater variations must be considered as faults. Weights of dogs of desirable size in proper flesh and condition average between 75 and 85 lbs., and of bitches, between 60 and 70 lbs.

The Shepherd should be stamped with a look of quality and nobility—difficult to define but unmistakable when present. The good Shepherd dog never looks common.

The breed has a distinct personality marked by a direct and fearless, but not hostile, expression, self-confidence and a certain aloofness which does not lend itself to immediate and indiscriminate friendships.

Secondary sex characteristics should be strongly marked, and every animal should give a definite impression of masculinity or femininity, according to its sex. Dogs should be definitely masculine in appearance and deportment; bitches unmistakably feminine without weakness of structure or apparent softness of temperament.

Male dogs having one or both testicles undescended (monorchids or cryptorchids) are to be disqualified.

The condition of the dog should be that of an athlete in good condition, the muscles and flesh firm and the coat lustrous.

The Shepherd is normally a dog with a double coat, the amount of undercoat varying with the season of the year and the proportion of the

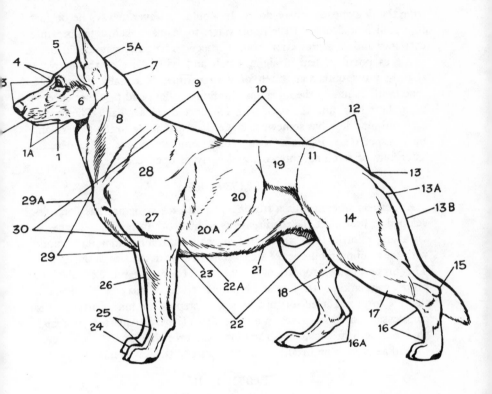

PARTS OF THE SHEPHERD LABELLED

1. Lip corner (flew). 1a. Jaw (lower). 2. Muzzle. 3. Foreface. 4. Stop. 5. Skull. 5a. Occiput. 6. Cheek. 7. Crest (of neck). 8. Neck. 9. Withers. 10. Back. 11. Hip. 12. Croup. 13. Tail set. 13a. Point of haunch or buttocks. 13b. Tail or stern. 14. Thigh (quarter, haunch). 15. Point of hock. 16. Metatarsus. 16a. Hock. 17. Lower thigh. 18. Point of stifle (knee). 19. Loin. 20. Ribs. 20a. Chest. 21. Abdomen. 22. Bottom line. 23. Elbow. 24. Feet (paws). 25. Pastern. 26. Forearm. 27. Upper arm. 28. Shoulder blade. 29. Forechest. 29a. Prosternum (breastbone). 30. Shoulder.

time the dog spends out-of-doors. It should, however, always be present to a sufficient degree to keep out water, to insulate against temperature extremes and as a protection against insects. The outercoat should be as dense as possible, hair straight, harsh and lying close to the body. A slightly wavy outercoat, often of wiry texture, is equally permissible. The head, including the inner ear, foreface and legs and paws are covered with short hair, and the neck with longer and thicker hair. The rear of fore and hind legs has somewhat longer hair extending to the pastern and hock respectively. Faults in coat include complete lack of any undercoat, soft, silky or too long outercoat and curly or open coat.

STRUCTURE

A German Shepherd is a trotting dog and his structure has been developed to best meet the requirements of his work in herding. That is to say a long, effortless trot which shall cover the maximum amount of ground with the minimum number of steps, consistent with the size of the animal. The proper body proportion, firmness of back and muscles and the proper angulation of the fore and hindquarters serve this end. They enable the dog to propel itself forward by a long step of the hindquarter and to compensate for this stride by a long step of the forequarter. The high withers, the firm back, the strong loin, the properly formed croup, even the tail as balance and rudder, all contribute to this same end.

PROPORTION

The German Shepherd dog is properly longer than tall with the most desirable proportion as 10 is to 8½. We have seen how the height is ascertained; the length is established by a dog standing naturally and four-square, measured on a horizontal line from the points of the prosternum, or breast bone, to the rear edge of the pelvis, the ischium tuberosity, commonly called the sitting bone.

ANGULATION

(a) Forequarter—the shoulder blade should be long, laid on flat against the body, with its rounded upper end in a vertical line above the elbow, and sloping well forward to the point where it joins the upper arm. The wither should be high with shoulder blades meeting closely at the top, and the upper arm set on at an angle approaching as nearly as possible a right angle. Such an angulation permits the maximum forward extension of the foreleg without binding or effort. Shoulder faults include too steep or straight a position of either blade or upper arm, too short a blade or upper arm, lack of sufficient angle between these two members, looseness through lack of firm ligamentation, and loaded shoulders with prominent

250

pads of flesh or muscles on the outer side. Construction in which the whole shoulder assembly is pushed too far forward also restricts the stride and is faulty.

(b) Hindquarter—the angulation of the hindquarter also consists ideally of a series of sharp angles as far as the relation of the bones to each other is concerned, and the thighbones should parallel the shoulder blade while the stiflebone parallels the upper arm. The whole assembly of the thigh, viewed from the side, should be broad, with both thigh and stifle well muscled and of proportionate length, forming as nearly as possible a right angle. The metatarsus (the unit between the hock joint and the foot commonly and erroneously called the hock) is strong, clean and short, the hock joint clean-cut and sharply defined.

HEAD

Clean-cut and strong, the head of the Shepherd is characterized by nobility. It should seem in proportion to the body and should not be clumsy, although a degree of coarseness of head, especially in dogs, is less of a fault than overrefinement. A round or domey skull is a fault. The muzzle is long and strong with the lips firmly fitted, and its top line is usually parallel with an imaginary elongation of the line of the forehead. Seen from the front, the forehead is only moderately arched and the skull slopes into the long wedge-shaped muzzle without abrupt stop. Jaws are strongly developed. Weak and too narrow underjaws, snipey muzzles and no stop are faults.

(a) Ears—the ears should be moderately pointed, open toward the front, and are carried erect when at attention, the ideal carriage being one in which the center lines of the ears, viewed from the front, are parallel to each other and perpendicular to the ground. Puppies usually do not permanently raise their ears until the fourth or sixth month, and sometimes not until later. Cropped and hanging ears are to be discarded. The well-placed and well-carried ear of a size in proportion to the skull materially adds to the general appearance of the Shepherd. Neither too large nor too small ears are desirable. Too much stress, however, should not be laid on perfection of carriage if the ears are fully erect.

(b) Eyes—of medium size, almond shaped, set a little obliquely and not protruding. The color as dark as possible. Eyes of lighter color are sometimes found and are not a serious fault if they harmonize with the general coloration, but a dark brown eye is always to be preferred. The expression should be keen, intelligent and composed.

(c) Teeth—the strong teeth, 42 in number—20 upper and 22 lower—are strongly developed and meet in a scissor grip in which part of the inner surface of the upper teeth meets and engages part of the outer surface of the lower teeth. This type of bite gives a more powerful grip than one in which the edges of the teeth meet directly, and is subjected to less wear. The dog is overshot when the lower teeth fail to engage the inner surfaces of the upper teeth. This is a serious fault. The reverse condition—an undershot jaw—is a very serious fault. While missing premolars are frequently observed, complete dentition is decidedly to be preferred. So-called distemper teeth and discolored teeth are faults whose seriousness varies with the degree of departure from the desired white, sound coloring. Teeth broken by accident should not be severely penalized but worn teeth, especially the incisors, are often indicative of the lack of a proper scissor bite, although some allowance should be made for age.

NECK

The neck is strong and muscular, clean-cut and relatively long, proportionate in size to the head and without loose folds of skin. When the dog is at attention or excited, the head is raised and the neck carried high, otherwise typical carriage of the head is forward rather than up and but little higher than the top of the shoulder, particularly in motion.

TOP LINE

(a) Withers—the withers should be higher than and sloping into the level back to enable a proper attachment of the shoulder blades.

(b) Back—the back should be straight and very strongly developed without sag or roach, the section from the wither to the croup being relatively short. (The desirable long proportion of the Shepherd dog is not derived from a long back but from over-all length with relation to height, which is achieved by breadth of forequarter and hindquarter viewed from the side.)

(c) Loin—viewed from the top, broad and strong, blending smoothly into the back without undue length between the last rib and the thigh, when viewed from the side.

(d) Croup—should be long and gradually sloping. Too level or flat a croup prevents proper functioning of the hindquarter, which must be able to reach well under the body. A steep croup also limits the action of the hindquarter.

(e) Tail—bushy, with the last vertebra extended at least to the hock joint, and usually below. Set smoothly into the croup and low rather than high. At rest the tail hangs in a slight curve like a sabre. A slight hook— sometimes carried to one side—is faulty only to the extent that it mars, generally, appearance. When the dog is excited or in motion, the curve is accentuated and the tail raised, but it should never be lifted beyond a line at right angles with the line of the back. Docked tails, or those which have been operated upon to prevent curling, disqualify. Tails too short, or with clumpy ends due to the ankylosis or growing together of the vertebrae, are serious faults.

BODY

The whole structure of the body gives an impression of depth and solidity without bulkiness.

(a) Forechest—commencing at this prosternum, should be well-filled and carried well down between the legs with no sense of hollowness.

(b) Chest—deep and capacious with ample room for lungs and heart. Well carried forward, with the prosternum, or process of the breast bone, showing ahead of the shoulder when the dog is viewed from the side.

(c) Ribs—should be well-sprung and long, neither barrel shaped nor too flat, and carried down to a breast bone which reaches to the elbow. Correct ribbing allows the elbow to move back freely when the dog is at a trot, while too round a rib causes interference and throws the elbow out. Ribbing should be carried well back so that loin and flank are relatively short.

(d) Abdomen—firmly held and not paunchy. The bottom line of the Shepherd is only moderately tucked up in flank, never like that of a greyhound.

LEGS

(a) The bone of the legs should be straight, oval rather than round or flat and free from sponginess. Its development should be in proportion to the size of the dog and contribute to the over-all impression of substance without grossness. Crooked leg bones and any malformation such as, for example, that caused by rickets, should be penalized.

(b) Pastern—should be of medium length, strong and springy. Much more spring of pastern is desirable in the Shepherd dog than in many other breeds as it contributes to the ease and elasticity of the trotting gait. The upright terrier pastern is definitely undesirable.

(c) Metatarsus—the so-called "hock"—short, clean, sharply defined and of great strength. This is the fulcrum upon which much of the forward movement of the dog depends. Cow hocks are a decided fault but before penalizing for cow hocks, it should be definitely determined, with the animal in motion, that the dog has this fault, since many dogs with exceptionally good hindquarter angulation occasionally stand so as to give the appearance of cow hockedness which is not actually present.

(d) Feet—rather short, compact with toes well-arched, pads thick and hard, nails short and strong. The feet are important to the working qualities of the dog. The ideal foot is extremely strong with good gripping power and plenty of depth of pad. The so-called cat-foot, or terrier foot, is not desirable. The thin, spread or hare-foot is however, still more undesirable.

PIGMENT

The German Shepherd dog differs widely in color and all colors are permissible. Generally speaking, strong rich colors are to be preferred, with definite pigmentation and without the appearance of a washed-out color. White dogs are not desirable, and are to be disqualified if showing albino characteristics.

GAIT

(a) General Impression—the gait of the German Shepherd dog is out-reaching, elastic, seemingly without effort, smooth and rhythmic. At a walk it covers a great deal of ground, with long step of both hind and fore-leg. At a trot, the dog covers still more ground and moves powerfully but easily with a beautiful co-ordination of back and limbs so that, in the best examples, the gait appears to be the steady motion of a well-lubricated machine. The feet travel close to the ground, and neither fore nor hind feet should lift high on either forward reach or backward push.

(b) The hindquarter delivers, through the back, a powerful forward thrust which slightly lifts the whole animal and drives the body forward. Reaching far under, and passing the imprint left by the front foot, the strong arched hind foot takes hold of the ground; then hock, stifle and upper thigh come into play and sweep back, the stroke of the hind leg finishing with the foot still close to the ground in a smooth follow-through. The over-reach of the hindquarter usually necessitates one hind foot passing outside and the other hind foot passing inside the track of the fore-feet and such action is not faulty unless the locomotion is crabwise, with the dog's body sideways out of the normal straight line.

(c) In order to achieve ideal movement of this kind, there must be full muscular co-ordination throughout the structure with the action of muscles and ligaments positive, regular and accurate.

(d) Back transmission—the typical smooth, flowing gait of the Shepherd dog cannot be maintained without great strength and firmness (which does not mean stiffness) of back. The whole effort of the hindquarter is transmitted to the forequarter through the muscular and bony structure of the loin, back and withers. At full trot, the back must remain firm and level without sway, roll, whip or roach.

(e) To compensate for the forward motion imparted by the hindquarter, the shoulder should open to its full extent—the desirability of good shoulder angulation now becomes apparent—and the forelegs should reach out in a stride balancing that of the hindquarter. A steep shoulder will cause the dog either to stumble or to raise the forelegs very high in an effort to co-ordinate with the hindquarter, which is impossible when shoulder structure is faulty. A serious fault results when a dog moves too low in front, presenting an unlevel top-line with the wither lower than the hips.

(*f*) The Shepherd dog does not track on widely separated parallel lines as does the terrier but brings the feet inward toward the middle line of the body when at trot in order to maintain balance. For this reason a dog viewed from the front or rear when in motion will often seem to travel close. This is not a fault if the feet do not strike or cross, or if the knees or shoulders are not thrown out, but the feet and hocks should be parallel even if close together.

(*g*) The excellence of gait must also be evaluated by viewing from the side the effortless, properly co-ordinated covering of ground.

CHARACTER

As has been noted before, the Shepherd dog is not one that fawns upon every new acquaintance. At the same time, it should be approachable, quietly standing its ground and showing confidence and a willingness to meet overtures without itself making them. It should be poised, but when the occasion demands, eager and alert; both fit and willing to serve in any capacity as companion, watchdog, blind leader, herding dog or guardian, whichever the circumstances may demand.

The Shepherd dog must not be timid, shrinking behind its master or handler; nervous, looking about or upward with anxious expression or showing nervous reactions to strange sounds or sights, nor lackadaisical, sluggish or manifestly disinterested in what goes on about him. Lack of confidence under any surroundings is not typical of good character; cases of extreme timidity and nervous unbalance sometimes give the dog an apparent, but totally unreal, courage, and it becomes a "fear biter," snapping not for any justifiable reason but because it is apprehensive of the approach of a stranger. This is a serious fault subject to heavy penalty.

In summary: It should never be forgotten that the ideal Shepherd is a working animal, which must have an incorruptible character combined with body and gait suitable for the arduous work which constitutes its primary purpose. All its qualities should be weighed in respect to their contribution to such work, and while no compromise should be permitted with regard to its working potentiality, the dog must nevertheless possess a high degree of beauty and nobility.

Evaluation of Faults—Note: Faults are important in the order of their group, as per group headings, irrespective of their position in each group.

Disqualifying Faults—Albino characteristics; cropped ears; hanging ears (as in a hound); docked tails. *Very Serious Faults*—Major faults of tem-

Gisa v. Rugeried, SchH. III
This lovely imported bitch is shown going Best of Breed at the Long Island Specialty.
She had been a VA bitch in Germany prior to her importation. Owned by Robert and
Rose-Marie Brandenburg.

perament; undershot lower jaw. *Serious Faults*—Faults of balance and proportion; poor gait, viewed either from front, rear or side; marked deficiency of substance (bone or body); bitchy male dogs; faulty backs; too level or too short croup; long and weak loin; very bad feet; ring tails; tails much too short; rickety condition; more than four missing premolars or any other missing teeth, unless due to accident; lack of nobility; badly washed-out color; badly overshot bite. *Faults*—Doggy bitches; poorly carried ears; too fine heads; weak muzzles; improper muscular condition; faulty coat, other than temporary condition; badly affected teeth. *Minor Faults*—Too coarse heads; hooked tails; too light, round or protruding eyes; discolored teeth; condition of coat, due to season or keeping.

Author's Note: Orchidism is a disqualifying fault in all breeds.

CHAPTER 18

LET'S DISCUSS THE STANDARD

A *standard* is a written analysis of a breed. The essence of its combined perfections present to the reader a word picture of a mythical superdog toward which the fanciers must strive. In its entirety, the standard disciplines in selection and rejection toward an ethical center or objective, which is the betterment of the breed.

There have been many who have complained that our German Shepherd standard, as it exists today, is too wordy and unwieldy. Others have suggested that a condensed version be printed for the use of judges, to be used by them in the nature of a freshener prior to judging assignments. Perhaps a better choice of words, in some few instances, would aid in shortening the standard as written, but not to any appreciable extent. It was evidently the purpose of those who were instrumental in fashioning the standard to make it so clear and concise that the reader could, as closely as the written word permits, visualize the ideal. In this design they were eminently successful to the degree that such a document can be successful. Any failure of the reader to know our breed in all its detail does not reflect upon the standard. Rather, it can be blamed upon lack of visual imagination, or faulty interpretation of the written word by the reader. Standards can be too short or too vague, omitting succinct details that, in essence, differentiate the particular breed from all other breeds. A standard is never too long if it is concise and functionally complete as is the standard of the German Shepherd dog.

To print a condensed form for the edification of judges is to defeat entirely one of the major purposes of the written standard. If a judge, asked to pass upon our breed in the show ring, feels it necessary to refresh his memory before facing his classes, surely the exhibitor at that particular show would feel greatly relieved if the judge studied the standard in its entirety rather than in condensed form. Judging being what it is, in many instances it might even be on the better side of safety to print the standard in large letters on huge cards with interpretive illustrations, to be erected around the ring for the edification of some of our judges.

The standard, as it exists, is a worth-while word picture of our breed. Interpretation of many of the passages is necessarily vague as to degree and can only be determined by comparison. In these instances, visual support is needed to fortify the script. In this chapter you will find illustrations which, when accompanying the text, certainly lead to clarification. To the novice particularly, such illustrations should aid greatly in forming a true mental picture of the breed ideal.

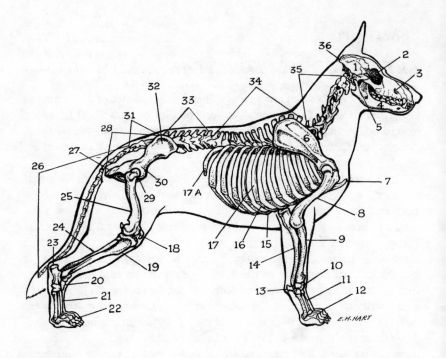

SKELETON OF A GERMAN SHEPHERD DOG

1. Cranium (skull). 2. Orbital cavity. 3. Nasal bone. 4. Mandible (jaw bone). 5 Condyle.
6. Scapula (shoulder blade, including spine and acromion process of scapula). 7. Prosternum. 8. Humerus (upper arm). 9. Radius (front forearm bone—see Ulna). 10. Carpus
(pastern joint. Comprising seven bones). 11. Metacarpus (pastern. Comprising five bones).
12. Phalanges (digits or toes). 13. Pisiform (accessory carpal bone). 14. Ulna. 15. Sternum. 16. Costal cartilage (lower, cartilaginous section of ribs). 17. Rib bones. 17a.
Floating rib (not connected by costal cartilage to sternum). 18. Patella (knee joint). 19.
Tibia (with fibula comprises shank bone). 20. Tarsus (comprising seven bones. 21. Metatarsus (comprising five bones). 22. Phalanges (toes or digits of hind foot). 23. Os calcis
(point of hock). 24. Fibula. 25. Femur (thigh bone). 26. Coccygeal vertebra (bones of tail.
Number varies—18 to 23 normal). 27. Pubis. 28. Pelvic bone entire (pubis, ilium, ischium).
29. Head of femur. 30. Ischium. 31. Sacral vertebra (comprising five fused vertebra). 32.
Ilium. 33. Lumbar vertebra. 34. Thoracic vertebra (dorsal, with spinal process or withers).
35. Cervical vertebra (bones of the neck). 36. Occipit.

A standard should not be considered rigid and unchangeable. Time brings faults and virtues to a breed which must be recognized and the standard changed in certain particulars to accommodate new values. Since the standard is a yardstick for the show ring and the breeder, evaluation of new trends should be qualified not only by cosmetic application, but by genetic implication as well. Thus, faults which are of an inheritable nature should be penalized far more severely than those which are transient.

In the initial paragraphs of the standard, under "General Appearance,' we find reference to nobility—"difficult to define but unmistakable when present." To clarify this statement, we must recognize nobility in our Shepherd as an integral part of strength, not delicacy. Incorrect interpretation can lead to overrefinement. Delicacy no doubt can reflect an essence of beauty, but inevitably leads to well-bred decadence, loss of vigor, and a slowing of race rate. In 1930, von Stephanitz, as an introductory theme for the *Koerbook* of that year, wrote an article entitled, "What is Nobility?" In that article he stressed the fact that " 'Nobility' has nothing in common with the worthless shell of surface beauty." It lies rather "in the complete suitability of structure for the purposes demanded of it; this includes firm nerves, willingness to accomplish, even if it be only to accomplish the reproduction of its kind." He speaks of mother dogs which are "too noble." Undoubtedly he is referring to bitches of overrefinement, a reference which complements an earlier definition of the subject made by him in which he classifies "nobility of appearance" as a combination of "robust health, strong constitution and typical expression." Nobility is indeed a word "difficult to define." The closest we can come to a true definition is that beauty, strength, and fearlessness combined result in an aura of "breediness" which is the essence of nobility.

Under the heading of "Proportion" we find that the standard advocates a proportion of length to height as 10 is to $8\frac{1}{2}$. Here we must take issue with the standard. In the experiments undertaken at Fortunate Fields it was proven that for structural excellence permitting the highest percentage of breed utility, the Shepherd should be only slightly longer than he is high, proportionately as 10 is to 9 and no more than 10 is to 8.8. It was on these proportions that they based their own standard of perfection in the development of a strain of German Shepherds combining working ability and beauty of conformation. It is significant, too, that in Germany, where utility is of paramount importance, the relationship between length and height should be set at 10 to 9. One suspects that these proportions in our standard were taken more from "what we had" than from "what we should achieve." Though our Shepherd *should* be longer than he is high, he should nevertheless be compact enough so that his center of balance in motion is not too far from his extremities. The dog which stands over too much ground finds it hard to recover from each motion of propulsion, and therefore lacks endurance in motion.

"Angulation," in the standard, mentions a construction fault of the shoulder assembly in which the involved skeletal structure is assembled too far forward, limiting reach. It makes no mention, however, of "false fronts," in which this structural fault, or lack of shoulder angulation, is present but hidden by an exaggeration of the prosternum. When this area of the forechest is well filled, a "false front" results, which gives the appearance of a well-laid back shoulder assembly when such condition does not truly exist. No mention is made, either, of the relation of the wither to the position of the elbow. The wither should be long and, with the proper shoulder angulation, a plumb line dropped from the middle of the wither to the ground should touch the back edge of the elbow and fall against and parallel with the back edge of the front leg, as seen in profile. The illustrations which accompany this text will further clarify the need for a ninety-degree angulation of the shoulder. The dotted lines which run upward from the bottom, forming a triangle, indicate the possibility of extension of the front legs, when the dog gaits, with correct and with incorrect shoulder angulation.

For correct reach and a workable shoulder assembly a long upper arm (humerus) suspended at the correct angle is absolutely necessary. This is the important section of the shoulder assembly, the part that, to a greater extent, moves, and it must have length and the proper angulation

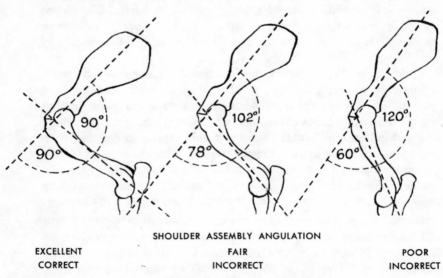

SHOULDER ASSEMBLY ANGULATION

| EXCELLENT | FAIR | POOR |
| CORRECT | INCORRECT | INCORRECT |

extension of reach is indicated by broken lines

Correct proportion
of leg length and body
depth to total height at withers.

to pivot to full extension. The flat shoulder blade (scapula), to which it attaches, can be less than perfect if the humerus is long and well laid-back.

In the discussion of hindquarter angulation, no mention is made of the second thigh, which should be well developed and strong, giving a smooth and powerful sweep to the quarters.

In America, we favor stronger angulation behind than is called for in Germany. It is interesting to note the relation of the German ideal, in this respect, to the standard as proposed at Fortunate Fields. Again we would remind you that the Fortunate Fields standard was based on extensive scientific study by Humphrey and Warner, with the emphasis on the relative value of structural beauty as it affects utility. This section of the Fortunate Fields' standard specifically states: "Standing naturally, a line dropped from the point of the buttocks should cut the fibula just in front of the hock and continue down, slightly in front of the hind leg. There should be a variation of not more than one inch between the dropped line and the front of the hind leg (hock). Extreme length of fibula places the hocks inches behind the dropped line and is considered a serious fault (overangulated)."

In the section devoted to "Body" in our standard, no relative proportions are mentioned. The body, or middle-piece, from the withers to the elbow of the front leg, should be 45 per cent of the total measurement from the withers to the ground. The remaining 55 per cent is accredited to the length of the leg (front) from the elbow to the ground. This gives us the necessary long-running gear. An animal which is short in leg length makes negative correct angulation in shoulder and hindquarter, since the shortness of his legs prohibits an easy, ground-covering reach when at trot. Over-all length of body is also exaggerated when sufficient length of leg is not present.

Under "Pigment" it would be better to disqualify all white dogs, whether they be albinos or the recessive white with dark eyes and nose. Mention should also be made of the desirability of uniform density of color. If the tan color on the legs fades to a much lighter color on the inside of the legs and feet, particularly if accompanied by white toenails, it is an indication of fading pigmentation.

When we come to the evaluation of faults, we would certainly put major faults of temperament at the top of the list of "Disqualifying Faults," and change albino characteristics to read, "All pure-white dogs."

Improper muscular condition is generally a temporary fault and should be listed under "Minor Faults." But protruding eyes, which are listed under "Minor Faults," should be segregated from the other minor fault of "too-light eyes," and moved up into the "Fault" grouping, since it is an inherited fault which can change the true and typical expression of the Shepherd head.

Typical male Shepherd head   Poor head

We have left "Movement or Gait" to the last. We do not find fault with the interpretation of this important phase of the standard except in that portion which begins, "The over-reach of the hindquarter usually necessitates . . . " In a later paragraph the standard refutes this assumption by

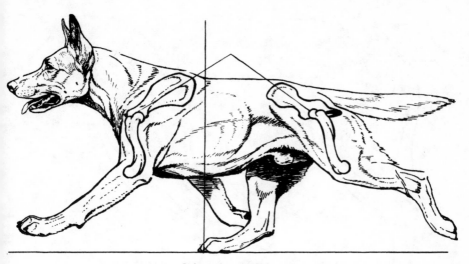

Balanced, extended trot

stating: "The German Shepherd does not track on widely parallel lines
. . . but brings the feet inward toward the middle line of the body when
at trot in order to maintain balance." The center of balance when gaiting in
a well-proportioned Shepherd would be approximately in a vertical line
with the joining point of the long wither and the back. The animal, in a
full, strong trot, reaches forward with each hind leg to this point and
inward toward the center of the body. The front legs, co-ordinating the
balance, can then move backward on the outside of the hind legs without
striking. This gives us a balanced, straightforward trot, eliminating the
necessity for "one hind foot passing outside and the other hind foot
passing inside the track of the forefeet . . ." When a dog trots on lead,
however, this usually does occur. Incidently, dogs of normal structure of
all breeds track on parallel lines when at a walk or very slow trot. The late
Lloyd C. Brackett, in his excellent articles in the *Shepherd Dog Review*
(January, February, 1953), under the heading "Information Please,"
makes the important point that the German Shepherd should travel close
behind. The reason for this is obvious when we know that the dog in full
trot must reach inward toward his center of balance with each hind foot,
then propel forward by thrust. If he did not move fairly close behind, this
thrust would lose forward propulsion by pushing the body at a slight angle
toward the opposite side instead of straight forward.

In the mass of specifications in the standard relating to gait, not enough
is said of evaluating gait in profile. It is in the side view that we can determine so many important characteristics of true Shepherd movement.
Here we can evaluate strength of back, reach, balance, topline, and trans-

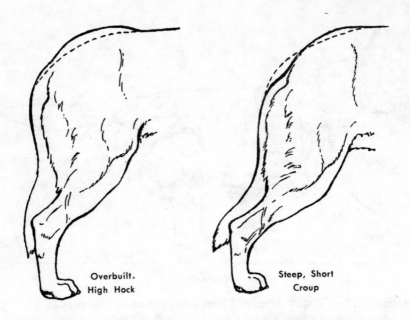

Overbuilt.
High Hock

Steep, Short
Croup

mission of power through croup, loin, back, and withers. Here, too, we can view that element of floating suspension which gives the Shepherd in motion an activated beauty which is unsurpassed by any other breed.

The true Shepherd dog movement is one of complete economy, a ground-eating, gliding trot which is the result of a harmonious application of the sum total of the animal's correct structure. The skeletal framework must be correct as to circumference and quality of bone. The bones must be correctly proportioned in length and engage to form the required angles. The muscles that overlay the skeleton must be strong, elastic, and work in unison. The tendons must be strong and flexible. Feet should be well padded and knuckled up. And of prime importance is complete balance of the over-all structure when in motion.

The Shepherd gait is a four-beat trot, made effortless when proper body proportion and angulation of shoulder and hindquarter enable the animal to reach long forward, both front and rear, while moving the feet close to the ground. Propulsion comes from the hindquarters, while the front assembly takes the thrust, balancing and co-ordinating. The croup should be long and sloped enough to enable the hindquarters to reach separately far under the dog to the center of balance. Sufficiently long bones and correct angulation behind are also necessary to this same objective. The hindquarters need great power and unrestricted musculature to propel smoothly. Both loin and back must be short and strong to transmit the power of movement to the forequarters, from propulsion to balance. The desired ninety-degree angle of the shoulder assembly enables the skeletal structure to open fully and extend the leg far forward to balance the forward weight and thrust of the head and neck, which is characteristic of the Shepherd in motion. The front feet should be larger and more compact than the rear feet, to support and co-ordinate the extra structure of chest, head, and neck.

A very real and definite quality of gait is not mentioned in the standard at all and, as a matter of fact, is not even known or recognized by many judges, here or abroad. I refer to the difference in movement between the sexes. Just as a male human walks, trots, runs, and in general handles the physical manifestation of his masculinity in a manner that differentiates him from the opposite sex, so does a male dog move in a way different from the female. A bitch who moves well is all feminine grace and floating, ballet lightness, while a male exhibits a stallion-like forward surge denoting strength and power. This essence of potent male vigor is particularly noted when the dog moves toward the observer.

Males that do not obviously exhibit the necessary secondary sex characteristics, in other words, bitchy males, move like females, lacking the dynamic, forceful, forward thrust of movement that, though smooth and adding to the floating fleetness of the gait, endows the good, strongly masculine male with all the elements of a kind of suggestive, aggressive swagger.

Shy animals, both dogs and bitches, gait as though trotting on eggs which they are afraid to break, giving the observer an impression of excellent movement. But the floating lightness of their gait as they spurn the ground is merely a manifestation of their fear.

For true economy and long-lasting power of movement, study the gait of that wild canine, the timber, or gray, wolf. (*Canis occidentalis.*) The gait of the wolf is similar to the gait of the Shepherd. Notice how closely he moves behind to reach under and propel with the least effort. Notice, too, the large size, heavy padding, and symmetrical formation of the wolf's feet, which seem to sponge and absorb all shock from movement. Strangely

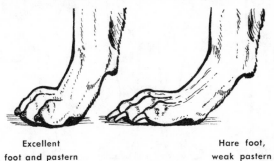

Excellent
foot and pastern

Hare foot,
weak pastern

enough, unlike his relative the dog, the wolf paces when walking (both front and rear legs on one side of body moving in same direction at same time, backward or forward). The big jungle cats, bears, and many other species of wild animal all pace. Go to your local zoo and spend some time watching and absorbing the structure of the wolf. Though generally lacking in depth and in bone, remember that these specimens have not had the benefit of selection by man, only nature, and she selects specifically for utility. Note the strength of head and muzzle of the wolf, the lack of extreme angulation of the hindquarters which, nevertheless, exhibit beauty in turn and power. Notice the length of leg for reach and propulsion, the back, withers, and croup. Our Shepherd, of all breeds, is closest in conformation to the basic family *Canidae* and, from an analysis of the natural structural beauty of the wolf, we return to an appreciation of the basic functional values which are so often lost, or forgotten, in the maze of fads and fancies that plague any breed.

Again referring to Mr. Brackett's articles, we read with conviction his opinion regarding the so-called "French" fronts. That such a condition does exist as a fault of bone structure we know he would agree. But, as he points out, the majority of Shepherds will stand naturally and easily, with front feet slightly turned out, in an "east and west" position rather than directly in line with the forearm when there is no structural fault present. He also states that many judges penalize this stance heavily, without realizing that it is not necessarily associated with faulty structure. If the dog moves correctly when trotting toward the observer, this position of the

Excellent front	East and west, pinched elbows, too narrow	Barrel legged, loaded shoulders, poor feet

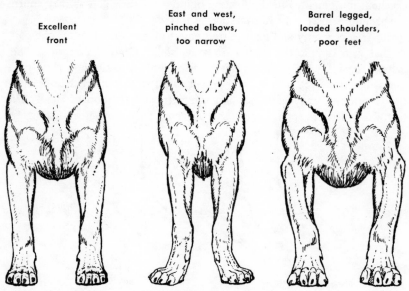

feet when standing, if not exaggerated, should not be condemned. A slight turning out of the front feet when at ease can be attributed to the angulation of the pastern, a necessary structural idiosyncrasy of the Shepherd which is needed to achieve "spring." Many young dogs exhibit this "east and west" position of the feet in a more extreme form due to lack of mature bulk and puppy looseness of ligaments. This passes with maturity.

Standards for our breed differ in many essentials in various countries, conforming to the needs and qualifying values of the breeders of those countries. German authorities brought to our shores for judiciary assignments inevitably elevate imports to the highest honors. This is to be expected, since the imports they put up are generally top German dogs which conform to the German standard of today. Missing teeth in Germany are strongly penalized, but our standard (and rightly so) does not dictatorially demand full dentition, though it is definitely desired. Should missing teeth become greater in number and prevalency, so that the fault becomes a very definite trend, then it is time to penalize this fault severely and check its growing incidence.

German judges stress the relative depth of body to the length of the front legs, desiring a 45 per cent to 55 per cent comparative ratio. This ratio gives us the long running gear which is essential to proper Shepherd movement, but it also gives us a shallow body which will, unless checked, result in a return to the high, square dogs which were anathema to von Stephanitz and his cohorts in the early 'twenties. We have advocated these same proportions of 45 per cent depth of body to elbow and 55 per cent

Excellent rear	Cowhocked, dewclaws

distance from elbow to ground, since this ratio lends itself best to utility. We have, however, established this important difference: the brisket should drop well below the elbow line, so that we have, relatively, only 45 per cent of daylight under the dog, as opposed to the German ideal of 55 per cent. Approximately 5 per cent of our 55 per cent total depth of body can be attributed to coat, thus leaving us a true 50 per cent depth of body to complete height from ground to withers. These percentages give us the necessary length of running gear coupled with greater depth of body and proportionate roominess throughout the body which can be utilized by the internal organs, as well as giving aesthetic value to physcial harmony.

We have advocated that the relationship between height and length should be as 9 is to 10 rather than as $8\frac{1}{2}$ is to 10, not because these are the proportions called for in the mother country of the breed, but because it has been found by test that there is a strong correlation between these proportions and basic efficiency (Humphrey and Warner). Remember, too, that all definite measurements are guides which depend upon other physical values to give balance, and balance, coupled with breed type, is the most necessary essential to physical worth. We do not arm ourselves with a tape measure when establishing the surface value of an individual, but we must have some yardstick of comparison.

We so often hear the argument that missing teeth do not stop the dog from eating, incorrect angulation does not keep him from moving, nor poor ear carriage prevent him from hearing–and these arguments are valid, to a certain point. Yet if we do not breed toward a standard ideal, uniformity becomes completely lost, and we might just as well breed mongrels whose sole value lies in physical and mental equipment sufficient to sustain life.

Care must be taken to avoid any great exaggeration of particular sections of the Shepherd's anatomy (overangulation of the hindquarter assembly is a prime example). When exaggeration occurs, true balance and function is destroyed, and the people dealing with the breed, in time, lose touch with natural essentials. This sad state of affairs has occurred in numerous other breeds, and we don't want it to happen to our Shepherds.

In Germany much stress is put upon over-all balance, nobility, secondary sex characteristics, and working qualities. They give more than lip service to the maxim we've repeated before, "Shepherd dog breeding is working dog breeding." This attitude is stressed repeatedly in their very real absorption in working trials and competition of all kinds, and in their critical interest in temperament and the scores their animals make in their Schutzhund and other training degrees. In America obedience work is fairly well divorced from the conformation ring, but not so in Germany. There working and showing walk hand in hand, for a mature dog cannot be shown in the regular classes of any show without at least one Schutzhund degree.

It is often said of Shepherds in Germany, by importers, that a specific dog is not of "American type." This means that the animal is of that working type that the Germans value so highly and so indicate with high placements and awards at their shows. Not slick and perfect in outline as we judge Shepherds here, not animals modeled for a beauty show such as our exhibitions are in the U.S., these working type show Shepherds have faults, but they are strong, rugged, balanced animals, definitely expressing their sex, and from whom emanate an aura of nobility, character, and the will to perform any task. Occasionally one of these dogs who has garnered high honors in the fatherland is brought to our shores and exhibited, and is so consistently ignored by our judges that the owner quits showing the animal in disgust. Bitch owners fail to use the dog because the word is spread by so-called "authorities" that the animal is, to use their own elegant phraseology, a "bum" (this same connotation is often attached to dogs that do a great deal of winning under many different judges, proving that it is evidently untrue), and so a rich source of valuable genetic material is lost to the breed.

In Germany, a dog possessing some very few visible, but not exaggerated, faults that would defeat him in competition in this country, is often the victor under a German judge, over a more perfect animal if the former dog exhibits the valuable attributes of balance, nobility, strength, good and tireless gait, and working ability (and comes from a good "family"), to a greater extent than the more perfectly formed animal. Especially would this be true if the dog was also possessed of a quality that defies description, an essence of noble greatness, found only occasionally, but recognized by the truly knowledgeable Shepherdist for its precious distinction. The ability to weigh these nebulous but so important qualities of the German Shepherd dog, and to be able to balance them correctly on the judicial scale against other, more obviously interpreted elements of conformation, is alien to too many American judges.

Rittmeister von Stephanitz summed up the German attitude in these few but succinct words: "I have often urged that judging should not confine itself to mere details, and in particular not allow itself to be misled by false interpretations of beauty. Our Shepherd dog happens to be a working dog, and shall continue as such."

It is a pity that when a breed standard is devised, extensive scientific study is not readily available to determine the correlation of genetic values to physical appearance. Humphrey and Warner (as have other scientists working with other breeds), in extensive investigation into the inheritance of German Shepherd dogs, found a correlation between light eyes and

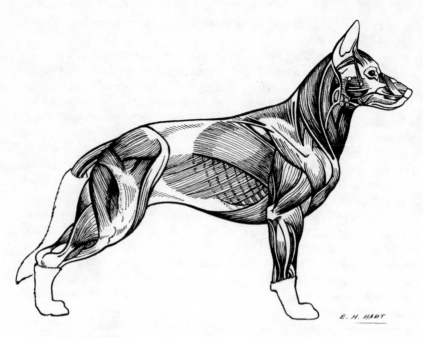

 is placed above.

E. H. HART

MUSCULATURE OF THE GERMAN SHEPHERD DOG

high intelligence. Though dark-eyed dogs certainly exhibit greater cosmetic attributes, it may be that we are lowering our standard of breed intelligence by attempting to breed out the light eye. Relationship between other genetic and physical manifestations have been found which should be studied before set standards are drawn up. It is difficult to eliminate one gene in a linked series without eliminating, or affecting, the other genes in the same chromosome. It is entirely feasible that the gene for light eyes is inexorably linked with one or more genes that possess direct relationship to high intelligence and, in selecting for dark eyes, we are also, unknowingly, selecting for lower mental ability as well.

Someday sufficient and conclusive enough proof will be established by exhaustive scientific research to enable us to chart correlations between linked genetic and physical manifestations. We can then rewrite our standard to incorporate these associated characteristics and, by canny breeding, produce Shepherds so far superior to any other known canine group that the breed will stand alone and above all the rest of its species.

CHAPTER 19

THE FUTURE

What does the future hold for our breed? We are not seers so we cannot predict the future. We can only review what has gone before and refrain from repeating the mistakes of the past or present and so find advancement in the time to come.

Since the days of von Stephanitz and the breed's beginning we have seen it rise to the heights of popularity and fall to the depths of disfavor. We have seen changes in type toward definite ideals and have seen those ideals discarded when the end result was not wholly satisfactory. We have seen the successful results of intelligent breeding programs nullified or demolished by greed or the careless practices of unthinking amateurs. We have seen "kennel blindness" and the worship of titles or "tags" result in the production of worthless animals. We have seen valuable breeding stock overlooked and lost to the future in favor of more glamorous contemporaries whose value may or may not have been as great. We have seen judging and exhibiting practices which discourage the tyro and disgust the ringsider. We have seen worthy animals criticized into oblivion by unfounded and malicious gossip, and deadly disease or ill-advised husbandry take their toll of valuable stock. We have seen the Shepherd survive two world wars and numerous periods of adverse publicity and uninformed criticism. Yet, through it all, we have seen a relatively steady climb toward greater beauty and utility and the survival of a breed whose innate qualities have such undeniable value that it continues to flourish in all parts of the world even in the face of periodic adversity.

In the final analysis the future of the German Shepherd dog is up to you, the owners and breeders. You must carry the responsibility for molding the future of the breed. New theories, new techniques, new discoveries are constantly being made in the many fields of scientific endeavor. Never-ending research uncovers new concepts in canine medicine, nutrition, physiology, psychology and genetics. Immunities and cures are in the process of development which will destroy diseases that today take a terrible toll. Under the microscope and in the testing kennel old problems are being met and defeated. Geneticists probe ever deeper into the why of being, giving us, if we will look for them, new answers to our breeding problems. We must face this future with open minds and with tolerance. We must learn to understand new concepts and avoid harking back blindly to the incomplete knowledge of the past. It is, then, our job to take the new tools we have been given to work with and use them well.

THE SHEPHERD SERVES

A "SEEING EYE" SHEPHERD

While many German Shepherds are used in guide work, only those trained at Morristown, N.J., can rightly be called "Seeing Eye Dogs." No greater service can the breed perform than to bring new independence and freedom to the blind.

HERDING SHEEP

The ancient heritage of the breed. Gottfried v. Kleinsteffin, C.D.X., son of Nox of Ruthland, and Asta v. Terryville, German bred. Two working shepherds owned and trained by Clifford Hendricks.

In you, the breeder, is vested the power to fashion heredity, to mold life, in this Shepherd breed. Yes, you can use this power that creates life and change, that brings special life-forms into being. You can design this pattern of heredity. To do so you must be aware of the power you have, and have the intelligence to use it well. If the future is to give us those things which we want for our breed, then we must clear our minds of inaccuracy and absorb truth instead. This is the future; a time when yesterday's miracles become today's facts.

So we come to the last page of our book, the last sentence, the last word. Yet, we do not feel that this should be labeled "The End," for beyond the last word that we write lie the many new words the future will write, continuing and improving on what you have read here. No, we will not call this "The End." Let us instead, borrow the title of our first chapter, and anticipating that which lies before us in the future, name this just . . .

THE BEGINNING

APPENDICES

List of American Grand Victors and Victrixes

	Grand Victor	Grand Victrix
1918	Komet v. Hoheluft	Lotte v. Edelweiss
1919	Appollo v. Huenenstein	Vanhall's Herta
1920	Rex Buckel	Boda v.d. Fuerstenburg
1921	Grimm v.d. Mainkur, PH	Dora v. Rheinwald
1922	Erich v. Grafenwerth, PH	Debora v. Weimar
1923	Dolf v. Duesternbrook, PH	Boda v.d. Fuerstenburg
1924	Cito Bergerlust, SchH	Irma v. Doernerhof, SchH
1925	Cito Bergerlust, SchH	Irma v. Doernerhof, SchH
1926	Donar v. Overstolzen, SchH	Asta v.d. Kaltenweide, SchH
1927	Arko v. Sadowaberg, SchH	Inky of Willowgate
1928	Arko v. Sadowaberg, SchH	Erich's Merceda of Shereston
1929	Arko v. Sadowaberg, SchH	Katja v. Blaisenberg, ZPr
1930	Bimbo v. Stolzenfels	Christel v. Stimmberg, PH
1931	Arko v. Sadowaberg, SchH	Gisa v. Koenigsbruch
1932	Not awarded	Not awarded
1933	Golf v. Hooptal	Dora of Shereston
1934	Erikind of Shereston	Dora of Shereston
1935	Nox of Glenmar	Nanka v. Schwyn
1936	Not awarded	Frigga v. Kannenbaeckerland
1937	Pfeffer von Bern, ZPrMH	Perchta v. Bern
1938	Pfeffer von Bern, ZPrMH	Giralda's Geisha
1939	Hugo of Cosalta, C.D.	Thora von Bern of Giralda
1940	Cotswold of Cosalta, C.D.	Lady of Ruthland
1941	Nox of Ruthland	Hexe of Rotundina
1942	Noble of Ruthland	Bella von Haus Hagen
1943	Major of Northmere	Bella von Haus Hagen
1944	Nox of Ruthland	Frigga von Hoheluft
1945	Adam of Veralda	Olga of Ruthland
1946	Dex of Talladega, C.D.	Leda vom Leibestraum
1947	Dorian v. Beckgold	Jola v. Leibestraum
1948	Valiant of Draham, C.D.	Duchess of Browvale
1949	Kirk of San Miguel	Doris v. Vogtlandshof
1950	Kirk of San Miguel	Yola of Long-Worth
1951	Jory of Edgetowne, C.D.	Tawnee v. Leibestraum
1952	Ingo Wunschelrute	Afra v. Heilholtkamp
1953	Alert of Mi-Noah's	Ulla of San Miguel
1954	Brando v. Aichtal	Jem of Penllyn
1955	Rasant v. Holzheimer Eichwald	Solo Nina of Rushagen
1956	Bill v. Kleistweg	Kobeil's Barda
1957	Troll v. Richterbach, SchH. III	Jeff-Lynnes Bella
1958	Yasko v. Zenntal, SchH. III	Tan-Zar Desiree
1959	Red Rocks Gino, CD.	Alice v.d. Guten Fee, SchH. I
1960	Axel v.d. Poldihaus	Robin of Kingscroft
1961	Lido v. Mellerland	Nanhall's Donna

1962	Yorkdom's Pak	Bonnie Bergere of Ken-Rose
1963	Condor v. Stoerstrudel	Hessian's Vogue
1964	No competition	
1965	Brix v. Grafenkrone, SchH. III	Marsa's Velvet of Malabar
1966	Ch. Yoncalla's Mike	Ch. Hanarob's Touche

The Grand Victor and Grand Victrix were known as Grand Champions from 1920 to 1925.

List of German Siegers and Siegerins

Sieger	Sire and Dam
1899 Joerg v.d. Krone, 163	Sparwasser Strain Nelly
1900 & Hektor v. Schwaben, 13 1901	Horand v. Grafrath I Mores v. Plieningen, 159 H.G.H.
1902 Peter v. Pritschen, 148 Kr. H.	Horand v. Grafrath I Lotte v. Klosterfeld
1903 Roland v. Park, 245	Sieger Hektor v. Schwaben, 13 Flora I v. Karlsruhe
1904 Aribert v. Grafrath, 517	Audifax v. Grafrath, 368 H.G.H. Sigrun v. Grafrath, 252
1905 Beowulf v. Nahegau, 733	Beowulf, 10 Walpurga v. Nahegau, 899
1906 & Roland v. Starkenburg, 1537 1907	Heinz v. Starkenburg Bella v. Starkenburg
1908 Luchs v. Kalsmunt Wetzlar, 3371	Graf Eberhardt v. Hohen Esp, 1135 Minka Barbarossa, 1034
1909 Hettel Uckermark, 3897	Sieger Roland v. Starkenburg, 1537 Gretel Uskermark, 849
1910 Tell v.d. Kriminalpolizei, 8770	Sieger Luchs v. Kalsunt Wetlar, 337 Herta v.d. Kriminalpolizei, 3951
1911 & Norbert v. Kohlwald, 9264 1912	Beowulf v. Kohlwald Siegerin Hella v. Memmingen
1913 Arno v.d. Eichenburg, 24876	Sieger Tell v.d. Kriminalpolizei, 8770 Diana v.d. Blosenburg, 8273
1919 Dolf v. Duesternbrook, 67486 P.H.	Luchs Uskermark, 35361 P.H. Dorte v. Riedekenburg
1920 Erich v. Grafenwerth, 71141 P.H.	Alex v. Westfalenheim, 59298 Bianka v. Riedekenburg, 46053
1921 Harras v.d. Juech, 67926 P.H.	Nores v.d. Kriminalpolizei, 60933 Lora Hildenia, 54241
1922 & Cito Bergerslust, 105327 1923 Sch.H.	Geri v. Oberklamm, 65867 P.H. Goda v. Mundtsdorf, 68249
1924 Donar v. Overstolzen, 220839 Sch.H.	Orpal v. Grünen Eck, 92981 Sch.H. Blanka v.d. Urftalsperre, 116149
1925 Klodo v. Boxberg, 135239 Sch.H.	Sieger Erich v. Grafenwerth, 71141 P.H. Elfe v. Boxberg, 135239 Sch.H.

1926 & Erich v. Glockenbrink,	Gundo Isentrud, 196077
1928 275752 Sch.H.	Dolli v. Glockenbrink, 176906
1927 Arko v. Sadowaberg, 253490	Cuno v. Wohwinkel, 115807
Sch.H.	Afra v. Jahnplatz, 158069
1929 Utz v. Haus Schütting,	Sieger Klodo v. Boxberg, 135239 Sch.H.
331999 Z.Pr.	Donna Z. Reurer, 255893 Sch.H.
1930 & Herold a.d. Niederlausitz,	Otlan v. Blasienberg, 309762 H.G.H.
1931 355573 Sch.H.	Burga v.d. Laemmerherde, 212551 H.G.H., Sch.H.
1932 Hussan v. Haus Schütting,	Sieger Utz v. Haus Schütting, 331999 Z.Pr.
375476 Z.Pr.	Cora v.d. Sennhütte, 121283 Sch.H.
1933 Odin v. Stolzenfels, 406023	Curt v. Herzog Hedan, 348365 Sch.H.
Z.Pr.	Bella v.d. Jagdschloss Platte, 377856 Z.Pr.
1934 Cuno v. Georgentor, 416055	Bero v.d. Deutschen Werken, 382840 Sch.H.
Z.Pr.	Afra v. Georgentor, 336385 Z.Pr.
1935 Jalk v. Pagensgrüb, 443657	Erich v. Pagensgrüb, 395058 Z.Pr.
Z.Pr.	Gudrun v. Pagensgrüb, 411631 P.H.
1936 Arras a.d. Stadt Velbert,	Luchs of Ceara, 421211
462958 Z.Pr.	Siegerin Stella v. Haus Schütting, 428493 Sch.H.
1937 Pfeffer v. Bern, 466407 Z.Pr.	Dachs v. Bern, 429017 Z.Pr.
	Clara v. Bern, 430250 Z.Pr.

Siegerin	*Sire and Dam*
1899 Lisie v. Schwenningen, 30	Basko Wachsmuth
	Schäfermadchen v. Hanau, 154
1900 Canna	Parents unknown
1901 Elsa v. Schwaben, 34	Carex Plieningen, 158 H.G.H.
	Fides v. Neckarursprung, 19 H.G.H.
1902 & Hella v. Memmingen, 329	Beowulf, 10
1903	Nelly Eislingen, 11
1904 Regina v. Schwaben, 411	Beowulf, 10
	Siegerin Elsa v. Schwaben, 34
1905 Vefi v. Niedersachsen, 339	Beowulf, 10
	Nelly v. Eislingen, 11
1906 Gretel Uckermark	Beowulf, 10
	Hexe v. Hohen Esp, 357 H.G.H.
1907 Hulda v. Siegestor, 2581	Sieger Roland v. Starkenburg, 15, 37
	Adelheid v. Siegestor, 1476
1908 Flora v.d. Warthe, 4831	Sieger Roland v. Starkenburg
	Julie v. Brenztal
1909 Ella v. Erlenbrunnen, 4540	Dewett Barbarossa, 630
	Siegerin Hella v. Memmingen, 329
1910 Flora v.d. Kriminalpolizei,	Sieger Luchs v. Kalsmunt Wetzlar, 3371
12965	Herta v.d. Kriminalpolizei, 3951
1911 & Hella v.d. Kriminalpolizei,	Sieger Tell v.d. Kriminalpolizei, 8770
1912 13748	Fanny v.d. Kriminalpolizei, 3950
1913 Frigga v. Scharenstetten,	Horst v. Boll, 8306 P.H.
18742	Adelheid v. Scharenstetten, 10263

1919 & Anni v. Humboldtpark,	{ Alex v. Westfalenheim, 59298
1920 66522	{ Helga v. Riedekenburg, 42309
1921 Nanthild v. Riedekenburg,	{ Jung Tell v.d. Kriminalpolizei, 24511 P.H.
75116 P.H.	{ Bella v. Riedekenburg, 46051
1922, Asta v.d. Kaltenweide, 106899	{ Sieger Erich v. Grafgenwerth, 71141 P.H.
1923 and 1924 Sch.H.	{ Flora v. Oeringen, 70381 P.H.
1925 Seffe v. Blasienberg, 182066	{ Caro v. Blasienberg, 97750 (of Welham)
Sch.H.	{ Wanda v. Blasienberg, 85876 H.G.H.
1926 Arna a.d. Ehrenzelle, 150526	{ Claus v.d. Fuerstenburg, 71177
Sch.H.	{ Hidda v. Flandersbach, 84455
1927 Elli v. Fuerstensteg, 299846	{ Baron v. Borkhofen, 138456 P.H.
Z.Pr.	{ Annerl v. Morteltal, 235051 Sch.H.
1928 & Katja v. Blasienberg, 336693	{ Samson v. Blasienberg, 182663 P.H.
1929 Z.Pr.	{ Anni v. Blasienberg, 97749 H.G.H.
1930 Bella v. Klosterbrunn,	{ Erich v. Geisenhof, 310732 P.H.
364404 Z.Pr.	{ Boda v. Westfalenplatz, 199233 Sch.H.
1931 Illa v. Helmholtz, 394384	{ Alf v.d. Webbelsmannslust, 299684 Sch.H.
Z.Pr.	{ Dea v. Helmholtz, 337485
1932 Birke v. Blasienberg, 413611	{ Baron v.d. Deutschen Werken, 382838 Z.Pr.
Z.Pr.	{ Eiche v. Blasienberg, 355340 Z.Pr.
1933 Jamba v. Haus Schütting,	{ Sieger Hussan v. Haus Schütting, 375476 Z.Pr.
424469 Z.Pr.	{ Sonja v. Haus Schütting, 387563 Z.Pr.
1934 Grete v.d. Raumannskaule,	{ Dux v. Haus Schütting, 395091 P.H.
433216 Sch.H.	{ Gisa v. Godorf, 343754 P.H.
1935 & Stella v. Haus Schütting,	{ Sieger Hussan v. Haus Schütting, 375476 Z.Pr.
1936 428493 Sch.H.	{ Flora v. Hils, 375744
1937 Traute v. Bern, 477694 Z.Pr.	{ Bodo v.d. Brahmenau, 434957 H.G.H., Z.Pr.
	{ Vicki v. Bern, 388637 Z.Pr.

The Sieger title was continued again in 1955 with the crowning of Alf v. Nordfelsen as Sieger and Muschka v. Tempelblick, Siegerin. Add, then, to the list of Siegers and Siegerins the following names:

1955 Sieger, Alf v. Nordfelsen	{ Axel v. Deininghauserheide
	{ Carin v. Bombergschen Park
1955 Siegerin, Muschka v. Tempelblick	{ Arno v.d. Pfaffenau
	{ Nandl v.d. Stuveschacht
1956 Sieger, Hardt v. Stuveschacht	{ Rolf v. Osnabruckerland
	{ Amala v. Stuveschacht
1956 Siegerin, Lore v. Tempelblick	{ Berusko v. Tempelblick
	{ Elfi v. Tempelblick
1957 Sieger, Arno v. Haus Gersie	{ Edo v. Gehrdener Berg
	{ Delia v. Walburgitor
1957 Siegerin, Wilma v. Richterbach	{ Axel v. Deininghauserheide
	{ Hexe v. Richterbach
1958 Sieger, Condor v. Hohenstamm	{ Arko v.d. Delog
	{ Asta v.d. Jakobsleiter
1958 Siegerin, Mascha v. Stuhri-Gau	{ Brando v. Tappenort
	{ Werra z.d. Sieben-Faulen

1959	Sieger, Volker v. Zollgrenzschutz-Haus	{ Harry v. Donaukai Perle v. Zollgrenzschutz-Haus
1959	Siegerin, Assja v. Geigerklause	{ Cäsar v.d. Malmannsheide Blanka v. Sandbachdamm
1960	Sieger, Volker v. Zollgrenzschutz-Haus	{ Harry v. Donaukai Perle v. Zollgrenzschutz-Haus
1960	Siegerin, Mascha v. Stuhri-Gau	{ Brando v. Tappenort Werra z.d. Sieben-Faulen
1961	Sieger, Veus v.d. Starrenburg	{ Alf v. Nordfelsen Ilsa v.d. Starrenburg
1961	Siegerin, Assie v. Hexenkalk	{ Fero v. Emsschleuse Cora v.d. Malmannsheide
1962	Sieger, Mutz a.d. Kuckstrasse	{ Condor v. Hohenstamm Mori v. Gieser Waldchen
1962	Siegerin, Rike v. Colonia Agrippina	{ Unfried v. Colonia Agrippina Forma v. Colonia Agrippina
1963	Sieger, Ajax v. Haus Dexel	{ Bodo v. Tannenbuch Amsel v. Haus List
1963	Siegerin, Maja v. Stolperland	{ Marko v. Boxhochburg Werra v. Osnabruckerland
1964	Sieger, Zibu v. Haus Schutting	{ Donar v.d. Firnskruppe Niobe v. Haus Schutting
1964	Siegerin, Blanka v. Kisskamp	{ Mutz a.d. Kuckstrasse Iris v. Walienhof
1965	Sieger, Hanko v. Hetschmuhle	{ Witz v. Haus Schutting Eva v.d. Hetschmuhle
1965	Siegerin, Landa v.d. Wienerau	{ Jalk v. Fohlenbrunnen Dixie v.d. Wienerau
1966	Sieger, Basko v.d. Kahler Heide	{ Zibu v. Haus Schutting Nixe a.d. Eremitenklause
1966	Siegerin, Cita v. Gruchental	{ Cello a.d. Forsthausstrasse Mira v.d. Balinger Bergen

Glossary

of Pertinent German Words, Terms, and Abbreviations

Translations from German Pedigrees

Rude	male	*W.T.-Wurf Tag* ..	date whelped
Hundin	female	*Z.-Zuchter*	breeder
Wurf	litter	*B.-Besitzer*	owner
Welpe	young puppy	*A.-Amme*	foster mother
Eltern	parents	*V.-Vater*	sire (father)
Gross Elthern	grandparents	*M.-Mutter*	dam (mother)
Ur-Gross Eltern...	great-grandparents	*S.Z.*	stud book
Gedeckt.........	date of mating	*Angekoert*	recommended for breeding

German Show Ratings

V.A.	Select Class	*A.-Ausreishend* ..	Sufficient
V.-Vorzuglich	Excellent	*M-Mangelhaft* ...	Faulty
S.G.-Sehr Gut ...	Very Good	*O.-Zero*	Failed, N.G.
G.-Gut	Good	*Auslese Klass*	Selection Class (*See V.A.*)

Sr.-Sieger................ German Grand Victor
Sgrn.-Siegerin .... German Grand Victrix

NOTE: The Sieger and Siegerin titles were discontinued in 1938 and replaced by the Select Class (*V.A.*) and were continued again in 1955 combined with the *V.A.* class.

German Working Dog Ratings

P.H.-Polizei Hund .... police dog
H.G.H.-Herden Gebrauchshund .... herding dog
Bl.H.-Blinden Hund .... blind guide dog
S.H.-Such Hund .... tracking dog
F.H.-Fahrten Hund .... trailing dog
D.H.-Dienst Hund .... service dog
S.H.-Sanitats Hund .... Red Cross dog
Gr.H.-Grenzen Hund .... border patrol dog
M.H.-Militar Hund .... army dog
Law.H.-Lawinen Hund............... avalanche dog
Sch.H.-Schutz Hund .... protection dog
Kr.H.-Kriegshund .... war dog
Z.Pr.-Zucht prufung .... has pass Breed Survey and is recommended for breeding.
Leistungssieger and *Leistungssiegerin* .... all around working dog champions of the year in their sex.
Preishuten Sieger and *Siegerin* .... sheepherding champions of the year in their respective sexes.

German Show Classes and Clubs

J.Kl.-Jugend Klasse	youth class, 12 to 18 months
J.H.Kl.-Junghund Klasse	young dog class, 18 to 24 months
G.H.Kl.-Gebrauchshund Klasse	dogs with Sch. 1, 2, or 3 training degrees over 2 years of age.
A.Kl.-Alters Klasse	dogs of over 2 years of age with no training degrees.
S.V.-Verein für Deutsche Shäferhunde	German Shepherd Dog Club (National)
O.G.-Ortsgruppe	regional clubs
H.G.H. Sonderklasse	dogs who have a sheepherding degree and work as herders. Over 2 years of age.
Zuchtgruppen	breeding groups (kennel)
Nachkommengruppen	sire and progeny groups

German Training Commands

Bei Fuss	Heel!		*Bleib*	Stay!
Setz	Sit!		*Gib laut*	Speak!
Platz	Down!		*Pass auf*	On the alert!
Komm	Come!		*Fass*	Attack!
Such	Go find! (Search! Seek!)		*Pfui*	Shame! No!
Bringen	Bring! (Fetch!)		*Hopp*	Hop! (Jump!)
Nein	No!		*Steh*	Keep standing!
Geh Weiter	Go on!		*Voraus*	In front! (Move ahead!)
Aus	Out! Let go!		*Halten*	Halt!

Bibliography

Arenas, N., and Sammartino, R., *"Le Cycle Sexuel de la Chienne." Etude Histol. Bull. Histol. Appl. Physiol. et Path.*, 16:299 (1939).

Ash, E. C., *Dogs: Their History and Development*, 2 vols., London, 1927.

Anrep, G. V., "Pitch Discrimination in the Dog." *J. Physiol.*, 53:376–85 (1920).

Barrows, W. M., *Science of Animal Life*. New York, World Book Co., 1927.

Brackett, Lloyd C., "Information Please." *Shep. Dog Rev.* (Jan., Feb., 1953).

Burns, Marca, 1952. The Genetics of the Dog, Comm. Agri. Bur., Eng. 122 pp.

Castle, W. E., *Genetics and Eugenics*, 4th ed., Cambridge, Mass., Harvard University Press, 1930.

Darwin, C., *The Variation of Animals and Plants Under Domestication*, New York, D. Appleton Co., 1890.

Davenport, C. B., *Heredity in Relation to Eugenics*. New York, Henry Holt & Co., Inc., 1911.

Dorland, W. A. N., A.M., M.D., F.A.C.S., *The American Illustrated Medical Dictionary*. Philadelphia, W. B. Saunders Co., 1938.

Duncan, W. C., *Dog Training Made Easy*. Boston, Little, Brown & Co., 1940.

Dunn, L. C., and Dobzhansky, T., *Heredity, Race and Society*. New York, New American Library of World Literature, 1946.

Ebeling, W. H., "Twenty-five Years of the Seeing Eye." *Shep. Dog Rev.* (Jan., 1954).

Elliot, David D., *Training Gun Dogs to Retrieve*. New York, Henry Holt & Co., 1952.

Evans, H. M., and Cole, H. H., "An Introduction to the Study of the Oestrus Cycle of the Dog." *Mem. Univ. Cal.*, Vol. 9, No. 2.

Goldbecker, W., "Sires of Yesterday and Today." *Shep. Dog Rev.* (Dec., 1952).

———— and Hart, E. H., "Hints on Showing the Shepherd." *Shep. Dog Rev.* (June, May, 1952).

Hart, E. H., "Artificial Insemination." *Your Dog* (March, 1948).

———— "The Judging Situation." *Your Dog* (March, 1948).

———— 1950. Doggy Hints. Men Mg. Zenith Pub. Co.

———— "Judgment Day." *Shep. Dog Rev.* (Jan., 1953).

———— *This Is The Puppy*. T.F.H. Publications, Inc., New Jersey, 1962.

———— *Encyclopedia of Dog Breeds*. T.F.H. Publications, Inc., 1966.

———— *How To Train Your Dog*. T.F.H. Publications, Inc., New Jersey, 1966.

———— *Dog Breeders Handbook*. T.F.H. Publications, Inc., New Jersey, 1966.

———— *Your Shepherd Puppy*. T.F.H. Publications, Inc., New Jersey, 1966.

———— *This Is The Weimaraner*. T.F.H. Publications, Inc., New Jersey, 1965.

Hermansson, K. A., "Artificial Impregnation of the Dog." *Svensk. Vet. Tidshr.*, 39:382 (1934).

Humphrey, E. S., Articles on "The German Shepherd Dog." *The Bulletin Shep. Dog Cl. of Amer.* (1923–1927).

———— "Mental Tests for Shepherd Dogs." *J. of Hered.*, 25:129 (1934).

————, and Warner, Lucien, *Working Dogs*. Baltimore, Johns Hopkins Press, 1934.

Keeler, C. E., and Trimble, H. C., "Inheritance of Dewclaws." *J. of Hered.*, 29:145 (1938).

Kelly, G. L., and Whitney, L. F., Prevention of Conception in Bitches by Injections of Estrone. *J. Ga. Med. Assoc.*, 29:7 (1940).

Kraus, C., *"Beitrag zum Prostatakrebs und Kryptorchismus des Hundes."* *Frankfurter Zeitsch. Path.*, 41:405 (1931).

Krushinsky, L. A., "A Study of the Phenogenetics of Behaviour Characters in Dogs." *Biol. Journ. T.*, VII, No. 4, Inst. Zool., Moscow State Univ. (1938).

Laughlin, H. H., "Racing Capacity of Horses." Dept. of Genetics 37–73. Yearbook, Carn. Inst., No. 30, *The Blood Horse*, 1931.

MacDowell, E. C., "Heredity of Behaviour in Dogs." Dept. of Genetics, *Yearbook*, Carn. Inst., No. 20, 1921, 101–56.

Müller, Friedrich, *Geschichte des Verein für Deutsche Schäferhunde.* 1899–1949. S.V., Augsburg, 1949.

Nagel, W. A., *Der Farbensinn des Hundes. Zbl. Physiol.*, 21 (1907).

Otto, Ernst, *Breed Survey*, Vol. I and Vol. II. New York, Shep. Dog Club of Amer. Inc., 1926–1928.

Pearson, K., and Usher, C. H., "Albinism in Dogs." *Biometrica*, 21:144–163 (1929).

Razran, H. S., and Warden, C. J., "The Sensory Capacities of the Dog (Russian Schools)." *Psychol. Bulletin* 26, 1929.

Roesbeck, Dr., *40 Jahre Arbeit für den Deutschen Schäferhunde.* S. V., Augsburg, 1939.

Schwabacher, J., *The Popular Alsatian*, rev. ed., Popular Dogs Publishing Co., Ltd., 1950.

Stephanitz, Max von, *The Shepherd Dog in Word and Picture.* Jena, Anton Kampfe, 1923.

———— "What is Nobility?" *Koerbook.* S. V., Augsburg, 1930.

Stetson, J., "Heartworm Can Be Controlled." *Field and Stream* (June, 1954).

Telever, J., 1934. When Is the Heat Period of the Dog?

Whitney, L. F., *The Basis of Breeding.* N. H. Fowler, 1928.

———— *How To Breed Dogs.* New York, Orange Judd Pub. Co., 1947.

———— *Feeding Our Dogs.* New York, D. van Nostrand Co., Inc., 1949.

———— *Complete Book of Dog Care.* Garden City, L.I., Doubleday & Co., Inc., 1953.

———— and Whitney, G. D., *The Distemper Complex.* Orange, Conn., Practical Science Pub. Co., 1953.

Index